First Published in Great Britain 1989
by Silent Books, Swavesey, Cambridge CB4 5RA

© copyright Charles Caruana 1989

ISBN 1 85183 015 4

Typeset by 🖅 Tek Art Ltd, Croydon, Surrey

Printed in Great Britain by
St Edmundsbury Press, Bury St Edmunds, Suffolk

ACKNOWLEDGEMENTS

The author is deeply indebted to Brother C.D. Taylor,
Brother Ignatius Chincotta, Mrs Lilian Serra for typing the
manuscript so many times over, to the British Museum,
to the Public Records, to the Sacred Congregation of
Propaganda Fide Archives, to the Diocesan Archives of
Cadiz, the Gibraltar Government Archives, the Garrison
Library, the Curator of the Gibraltar Museum, Mr George
Palo, Mr John Fernandez, Mr Anselmo Torres, The El
Calpense, The Gibraltar Chronicle.

CONTENTS

INTRODUCTION

Many authors have written about the Rock from the viewpoint of its flora and fauna, its fortifications and sieges, its military role. Some have made an occasional reference to its civilian population, though for at least one author Gibraltarian society consisted solely of British army officers and their families. Writers in more recent times have indeed recognized the existence of civilians upon the Rock, some being inclined to look upon them as hybrids, bastards, smugglers, "panzistas", people with no identity or culture of their own, people without a history.

The present work, however, focusses attention on the leaders (priests, bishops and religious) of a particular group – The Roman Catholics, a majority group on the Rock. It sketches the development, over a period of 280 years, into a fully-fledged local or "particular" Church – to use Vatican II terminology – of what was at first a handful of disparate families who chose to remain behind at the time of the Great Exodus from the Peñon in 1704, and others who sought the Pax Britannica. The reader may ultimately be led to wonder about a possible connection between the motives behind their choice and the characteristics of the people who today constitute the Roman Catholic Church of Gibraltar.

Before 1704, church life on the Rock was subject to Spanish influence and control; today the Roman Catholic diocese of Gibraltar is co-terminous with the limits of the Garrison and City of the British-held peninsula, cared for by an active indigenous clergy, and totally independent of outside jurisdiction, except for the brotherly relationship between its bishop and the Bishop of Rome, and its fraternal, cultural and practical links with the hierarchy of Great Britain.

Events marking the emergence of this Church are not without interest. Not every local Church has seen its bishop put in prison, or forced to enter his diocese by the back door in order to avoid violence at the hands of certain members of his flock, or dashing up Main Street in a cab for safety's sake, or taking refuge with his family because laymen blocked the entrance to the episcopal residence. It is not altogether usual for a monsignor to have the stole torn from his shoulders when standing at the altar, or to be cat-called and chased into the presbytery by the faithful. Not every diocese has seen its schools closed without warning, and its religious teachers locked out of their rty by laymen or told to clear out of town. Not every town has seen ırts march four abreast through its streets, after the manner of a Roman ıphal procession, in celebration of victorious proselytism. Not every local rch has been evacuated almost totally from its home base and scattered to the four winds, to return once again to the old haunts, all the stronger in its faith for the experience. What smaller diocese than that of Gibraltar has developed in recent centuries in the whole of the Catholic Church? What town of comparable size can boast two cathedrals and two bishops, who live in peaceful accord despite the Reformation? This tiny Roman Catholic diocese has, in its short life-span, seen its bishops attend two General Councils of the Universal Church – Vatican I and Vatican II. Gibraltar may claim to be unique on these grounds alone, quite apart from the fact that very little conflict comes to the surface despite the presence of all the elements – especially religious and racial – that elsewhere lead to anything but peace and harmony.

Gibraltar is no bigger than the towns in which St. Paul established his "young Churches", described in his letters and in the Acts of the Apostles. Like many of those Churches, Gibraltar's was subject to many and varied influences and dangers, but, through good times and bad, went on developing.

The families who remained under British rule after 1704 were soon living in ethnic groups in different districts: The Spanish, the Portuguese, the Jewish and the Genoese. These racial and/or religious groups might have constituted explosive material in so small an area. It was, of course, understandable that in the quite new circumstances ensuing from the victory of 1704, people of the same origin, customs and language should seek and find mutual and moral support through living close to one another under a "conqueror". The pattern of their existence changed, however, as economic life developed.

Not only had they to work with one another but also with people outside their particular circle; they had to acquire some knowledge of another language in order to deal with employers or employees, or to assist at church services and so on. The many attacks that came from the enemy without served to emphasise the common interests of those within the fortress. A sense of unity was likewise fostered among the civilians by the threat of expulsion, should any disorder arise through their fault, to disturb the life of the garrison. Trouble between Jews and Christians as well as trading disputes had to be brought to the notice of the Governor's secretary. Non-acceptance of the solution he might propose would result in expulsion from the Rock. An eighteenth-century Spanish historian (Ayala) expressed his wonder at the peace and harmony reigning among the inhabitants, despite their racial and religious differences.

This harmonious development was due in no small measure to the role played by the various British Governors. Like the centurion in another seaport, described by St. Luke, they had the interests of the local population at heart even though they differed from the population by blood and religion. They tried to be fair to all sides. They fully accepted the presence of the Jews who had settled on the Rock since 1704 and stayed behind. When the British crown, under diplomatic pressure from Spain, agreed, by the Treaty of Utrecht (1713), not to allow Jews to settle on the Rock, the Governors showed themselves unwilling to take action against anyone who had come there since 1704. The Jews had, in any case, come from Morocco, with whose king Britain had concluded a treaty of friendship: the Governors did not want to offend him by acting against his subjects. They procrastinated in the face of various orders coming from the Court of St. James. A short respite was essential, they maintained, before those persons could be expelled, as they were too involved in the business affairs of the fortress. The British forces had been well fed through the good offices of the Jews. The latter's debts and other matters should first be settled. In their hearts of hearts, the Governors on the spot knew what local feeling was, what the needs and priorities of Gibraltar were, and respected them. They were convinced that the persons under attack were part and parcel of the new British Gibraltar, and acted accordingly.

The Governors were likewise respectful of the freedom to exercise one's religion granted by the Treaty of Utrecht. It was a just and prudent step on the part of the Protestant Governor to appoint a Roman Catholic priest to look after the Roman Catholic community. From the very beginning the Governors provided every assistance to the Catholics, while being resolved to exclude from British territory, as delineated by the Treaty, any type of Spanish ecclesiastical jurisdiction. They adhered closely to protocol and law – perhaps too closely sometimes. At all events, no obstacles were placed in the way of full ecclesial development, so that as speedily as in any other part of the world, and despite greater difficulties than those experienced in many other places, a native clergy and a highly aware, educated laity emerged, with an ecumenical outlook second to none.

There is no intention, when names are mentioned in the record that follows, of maligning those who made our history or of offending their descendants. It is in the interest of profiting from history that this story is told.

PART ONE

Gibraltar cut off
from Cadiz

CHAPTER ONE

Fr. Romero de Figueroa and Transition

Three months after Louis XIV, King of France, had accepted the Spanish throne for his Bourbon grandson, the duc Philip D'Anjou, he invaded the Spanish Netherlands. By appropriating to himself the Dutch Barrier Forts on February 1701, he alerted the concern of the other European Countries. These interpreted Louis' action as an abuse of the newly acquired union with Spain. The imbalance of power favouring the French monarchy had to be corrected. Britain, Holland, and later on Portugal, united with Austria to form the Grand Alliance. The War of the Spanish Succession commenced in 1702.[1]

The Grand Alliance was intent on dethroning the Bourbon Philip and raising to the Spanish throne the Hapsburg Prince Charles of Austria. This feat was to be carried out with the support of the Spanish people who were more inclined to the Hapsburg dynasty and would physically rise against the Bourbons once the Grand Alliance entered the scene. The British Fleet was to transport the invading troops to the Mediterranean Sea. For complete success of this campaign it was essential that the Grand Alliance should take possession of a sea-port in the South. Three names were mentioned: Cadiz, Barcelona and Port Mahon.

It was thought opportune to aim at the capture of Cadiz. A few attempts to force the city to surrender failed. While other methods that would not involve the destruction of the city were being considered – for the invading forces would, in the event of success, have to live alongside the local popultion – the generals felt that their men would benefit from some rest on shore, at a remove from the city of Cadiz.

Once ashore, however, the troops got out of hand. Merry-making in Puerto Santa Maria led to wild drunkenness, resulting in violence, house-breaking, the ransacking of wine cellars, the pillaging of churches and the destruction of convents. This was the fourth occasion on which British troops had gone on the rampage in the neighbourhood of Cadiz in the south of Spain. The effect was as disastrous and terrifying as the previous ones, and took place contrary to the explicit command of the authorities. A marine had already been publicly executed before the incidents took place. After the event General O'Hara and others were court-martialled for their naiveté in allowing the forces to go ashore to rest.[2] After this example of barbarous behaviour on the part of the troops, the fleet sailed away.

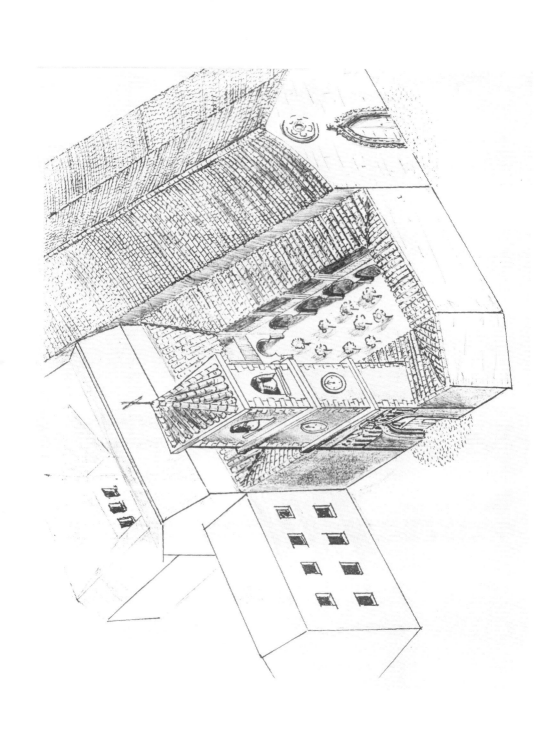

The Bishop of Cadiz, Don Juan Alonzo De Talavera, was well aware of the dangers implicit in the presence of the Grand Alliance forces in the vicinity of the Straits of Gibraltar.[3] He was all too conscious of the possible harm its troops could bring to Gibraltar which was part of his diocese. He knew that the Rock was the envy of many nations for its strategic position in the Mediterranean Sea. He felt very strongly that the failure to capture Cadiz would tempt them to try their chances on Gibraltar. So he wrote a letter to Father Juan Romero de Figueroa who was parish priest of Gibraltar and its surrounding area. In the letter the Bishop gave Father Romero the necessary powers to grant to the religious-order priests stationed on the Rock whatever spiritual "faculties" they might require, should the people be cut off from the ordinary communication with their bishop. There were approximately 40 priests in the fortress-city which, small though it was, was endowed with four monasteries with their adjacent churches and twelve other churches, oratories and shrines.[4]

The horrifying news of what had transpired in the Port of Cadiz had reached the ears of the Gibraltarians and Father Romero. He was very grateful to the bishop for the communication and for the powers granted to him. Nevertheless he did not see any need for implementing the terms of the letter since there were no signs of the enemy in the vicinity.

Father Romero was a cultured and artistic character who had received his priestly formation in Cadiz and had distinguished himself in the study of the classics. He was born in Gibraltar on 1 September 1646, and so was 56 years of age when he received that letter from Bishop Talavera. Just as Gladstone was a passionate patriot and lover of his religion, so was Father Romero a champion of his birthplace and its deeply rooted religion. He lost no opportunity to record in the church registers whatever he considered to be important for the benefit of the future people of the Rock. He was fanatically fond of the Church of St. Mary the Crowned and St. Bernard of which he was parish priest. He was actually baptised in it and he hoped to be buried there. The church was built as a mosque in the year 1333 by Prince Abdul Malik.[5] Historians record that this mosque was a princely one with a beauty and delicate décor comparable to that of Cordoba. Later on, early in the 16th century, the Catholic Kings of Spain ordered it to be stripped of its Moorish craftsmanship and reconstructed in the Gothic style. A tower was raised and the monarchs donated bells, a clock and a royal coat of arms which was placed above the entrance to the courtyard, the Patio de los Naranjos. Father Romero loved watering the orange trees from the yard's own centre well. This church boasted five benefices. It was therefore assumed that whoever obtained the appointment of Cura of this parish was assured of a comfortable and affluent existence.

A treasured tradition connected with this church but of an earlier origin, and one which Father Romero cherished dearly, was the devotion to Nuestra Señora de Europa. What Our Lady of Walsingham is to the English, Czestochowa to the Polish, Guadalupe to Mexicans and Lourdes to the French, was Nuestra Señora de Europa to Father Romero and the people of

Gibraltar. A shrine dedicated to the Mother of Christ under that same title had been set up at the southern tip of the Rock in 1462. When the principal mosque in town was transformed into a Gothic-style church in the early 16th century it was named St. Mary the Crowned after Our Lady of Europe which devotion was approved by Rome and accepted universally. To the title was added the name of St. Bernard because Gibraltar was captured from the moslems on his feast day.

There were approximately 6,000 residents in Gibraltar with a handsome garrison to protect them and defend the fortress. So untroubled had the town been for the first couple of years since the War of Succession started that the Marquis of Villadarias considered it safe enough to march his troops out of the fortress to inspect the territories adjacent to the Rock and thus exercise his men. Little did he imagine that thirty miles away between Ceuta and Melilla along the North African coast the Grand Alliance generals and admirals were holding a Council of War. It was decided there that the French fleet in the Atlantic would be stopped from entering the Mediterranean Sea to join its sister fleet. It meant taking control of the Straits of Gibraltar.

Father Romero received notice of the impending danger. The battleships were sailing into the harbour. He immediately empowered the priests with the necessary spiritual faculties and sent his family post-haste to Ronda, high up in the mountains. He wrote his impressions of the attack into the church registers. After some laconic introductory remarks he notes:

"Fatality. . . . On the 1st August. . . . the English Fleet arrived".[6]

"Confusion and terror. . . . On Saturday 2nd August. . . . they discharged bombshells at midnight. . . . Unspeakable weeping and lamentation, anguish and grief".

"On Sunday, 3rd August. . . . a bombardment took place from 5 o'clock in the morning until one o'clock in the afternoon".

"28,000 shots as well as bombshells were fired, and on this day the fortress capitulated and surrendered".

"On the morning of the 4th August, the terms of surrender having been accepted, and the New Mole having been occupied, the English went to Nuestra Señora de Europa and plundered her sanctuary. They carried off 12 silver lamps, candelabra, lecterns, crowns, jewels and consecrated vessels, all the clothing of many of the families that had fled there, and when there was nothing else to loot, they removed the head of the image and the Infant Jesus and threw them on the ground among the rocks. "

This rough treatment of a popular statue loomed large in the minds of the Gibraltarians and the Spanish nation in general. When the story of the british attack was noised abroad in Spain, a public procession was held in the capital to make reparation for the insult offered by the heretics to the person represented by the statue. "O my native city! I will not forsake thee and my ashes will be mingled with thine." From a diary of the Chaplain of the Fleet it emerges that the residents who had taken refuge at the Shrine of Our Lady of Europa at the South to escape the hazards of the bombardment, on hearing that the marines had landed at the New Mole and by so doing would most probably cut them off from their husbands, panicked and started to return to the city. As they did so they were ambushed and used as instruments for the surrender. While loyal to the crowned King Philip V, the authorities were compelled to surrender in order to recover their families.

"On the 6th August 1704, once this poor city was in the hands of the English army, and according to the agreed terms of capitulation, permission was granted to the inhabitants who wished to remain in the city with their possessions; and whoever wanted to leave, could take with him his possessions; but the bombshells and shots caused so much terror, that out of the one thousand families in the city there remained a mere twelve persons. They left their native land, their homes, possessions and produce. That day was a painful spectacle of laments and tears of the women and children who saw themselves leaving this place and getting lost in the open fields at the height of the summer season."

Once they were gone, the British pillaged whatever business premises and dwellings they found unoccupied, including the house of the parish priest and his assistant, Don Juan Ascencio Roman, who were busy protecting their church.

"In this parish church and in its baptismal font I received the Holy Sacrament of Baptism on 1 September 1646. . . . For this reason, and seeing that the forty priests here did not want to remain, I decided to stay in my parish, thus severing myself from the loving company of my sisters and nephews whom I sent to Ronda. Don Juan Asencio Roman, the assistant vicar, followed my example and with me continued to carefully guard against this church being profaned or pillaged by keeping continuous watch for many days and nights."

This building thus escaped damage, as also did the church of La Merced (Whitefriars) and that of the True Cross. During the several days and nights that Fr. Romero spent in the church he tidied up the marriage registers "for the sake of my successors in centuries to come". Many may well feel that he had a remarkable sense of history for one who was born and bred and worked on what is, after all, just a rocky peninsula at the tip of the continent of Europe.

The terms of the evacuation were more generous than Fr. Romero's account might suggest. The officers and soldiers of the former garrison were allowed to take baggage and horses with them; they were offered boats for the conveyance of extra baggage; they were permitted to take out three brass cannon of different calibre with twelve corresponding rounds of powder and shot, together with supplies of bread, meat and wine enough for a six days' journey. Carts could be used for the heavy road baggage. The belongings of the regidores, officers and other gentlemen were not to be searched. Everything was done in the best of gentlemanly traditions. For those who decided to remain behind on the Rock – some thirty families or so –

> *"religion and all tribunals will remain intact and without disturbance, on condition that the oath of fidelity be taken to the majesty of Charles III, the lawful king and master".*

The whereabouts of all stores of arms and ammunition and food had to be made known.

That the 6,000 residents of the city should decide to abandon the Rock must arouse amazement. A few reasons based on historical facts are called for. The priests and religious can be covered by a single explanation. Besides being foreigners, most of them must have been motivated by the mere recollection of the fact that the British were famous for invading Cadiz and Vigo, ransacking churches, convents, houses, and raping women. The terrible abuses at Cadiz only eighteen months earlier were still vivid in their memory. They would not remain behind to witness horrors being committed by barbarous Protestants. They were unaware that the invading troops were, besides the British marines, made up of Portuguese, Catalans, Dutch and Austrians, most of whom were Catholics. Then there were the other residents who were owners of vast industries in the hinterland and The Campo area. Extensive farming, cattle-breeding, tunny-fishing, vineyards and forests were successfully managed from the Rock to Tarifa in the West, to Guadiaro in the East and to Jimena in the North. The owners of these fruitful industries lived in Gibraltar with their families and servants. Ever since Henry IV annexed the Campo area to the Rock, people who settled in Gibraltar would be granted a plot of land in the hinterland as a reward. Those who had come had made a success of their lands. Surely these proprietors, uncertain of what the future would hold for them under the British, would not remain on the Rock. Some of these landowners showed their patriotism by placing the wood of their forests at the disposal of the Marquis of Villadarias to enable him recapture the Rock. Others left simply and solely out of loyalty to the Bourbon King. No doubt in quitting they were moved by a blend of all these reasons.

A twofold authority was set up on the Rock: Prince George Hesse D'Armstad looked after the interests of the Hapsburg King's civilian subjects, while Commander Henry Nugent was in charge of the fortifications and the defence and care of the Garrison.[7] A certain Col. Joseph Bennet was given the task of making an assessment of the situation of the civilian population. He finally calculated that about 1,500 families had left and that roughly thirty family groups had stayed.[8] The latter were listed as living on their own property, receiving provisions of fresh food and being exempt from paying taxes. The nucleus of the future population of Gibraltar consisted of a number of persons without families (Maria Baratone, Francisco Galbes, Pedro de

Mendoza, Francisco de Tapia, Pedro de Meza, Jacome de Pluma, Joseph Spinosa, Francisco Verda, Mariana de Mendoza, Dr. Fernandez Truxillo and the bell-ringer Bartolo, a hermit (Brother Juan); some friars (Gabriel de Miranda, Juan Nuñez and Diego Ramos), and two priests (Fr. Romero and Fr. Jose de Pania); Madalena de Guzman and her daughter; Michael Perez and his brother. Besides these there were the families of Francisco Abegero; Joseph de Anquita; Andres de Arenas) Jaime Barleta; Juan Bastistaga; Juan Biera; Juan Guerrero; Diego Jimenez; Nicholas de la Rosa, Diego Lorenzo, Maria Machado, Palomina, Pedro Machado, Marco Perez, Pedro de Robles, Bernardo Rodriguez, Gonzalo Romero, Andres de Sosa, Juan de Tanger, Esteban de Uniate and Francisco Ximenez.

Within seven weeks of capturing the Rock, the British, in preparation for a counter-attack, had turned the marshy lands between Spain and the fortress into an artificial sea and obtained supplies of fresh food from Jewish traders in North Africa.

The counter-attack came from 9,000 Spaniards and 3,000 French.[9]

> *"On October the fourth, a fleet of as many as twenty French ships anchored. . . . they landed guns, bombshells and shots. . . . constructed approaches between Windmills and the gullet, setting in them twenty-eight battering cannons and four mortars. On 26 October, the battery began to fire. . . . it dismantled the whole artillery of the flank and curtain at Landport, and some cannons fell into the moat. . . . we had bombs day and night."*

Romero records his being in the courtyard of the church when a shell hit the wall above the Capilla de Hierro, bounced on the roof and dropped in front of him. On another occasion, while he was saying Mass, a shell came in through the north window, struck the reredos and stuck there in the heavy carvings, where it was left "so that posterity would realize the sufferings we have gone through". Commander Nugent was killed during this day-and-night bombardment, but relief came on 9 November with the arrival of the English fleet under Sir John Leake.

Fr. Romero himself witnessed a further unexpected attack by the Spaniards on 11 November:

> *"There appeared on the shoulder of the mountain over two hundred men, who could be seen by any observer in town. They reached the saddle, from where they dislodged six Englishmen who were keeping guard. The people from the town came to their assistance from different directions and they were stopped, although they fought for over an hour. Those who could, fled along the saddle and others fell over the rock. Both sides lost many in the battle held on the hill."*

On 15 November, while the priest was in church, one of the three windmills in which gunpowder was stored blew up, and doors and windows all over the town were shattered. "The whole place shook", he recorded: someone had been smoking carelessly; and some 200 persons died, a like number being wounded.

Though the siege was lifted after six months, the cordon built across the sandy isthmus between the Rock and the mainland prevented any communication with Cadiz until November 1707. During all that time Fr. Romero had heard nothing from his mother and sister in Ronda. There had, however, been some questioning of his authority: were the powers delegated to him by the Bishop valid only for the time of the original emergency, but not continuously thereafter? As soon as he was able to get a message through to the bishop of Cadiz he put his difficulty to him. The bishop answered in the affirmative, gave him his total support, and raised him to the position of Vicar General.

Fr. Romero had critics outside the Rock among his former clerical colleagues who accused him of imprudence, arguing that he had put himself in needless danger, was moreover a traitor to his nation, and had acted out of self interest.[10] He appears to have thought out his position quite well: if the conquerors had been the Turks or the Moors, he would have acted in the same fashion, he said. Anyway, he maintained, the Bishop of Cadiz approved of his actions as holy and heroic. He denied that greed was his motive: his purpose had been to protect the church and its treasures, and to maintain continuity of divine worship. He had indeed been in great danger over and over again – even when saying Mass – and had felt deeply the absence of his relations and friends. But he had protected the church, and he had never been forced to sell anything belonging to it in order to live. He pointed out that when the British took over the place by force, the outcome was much less disastrous than similar events in other places and times and circumstances. The authorities had respected the terms of capitulation, and had fed those who stayed behind from August 1704 to that very day. It was in April 1717 that he wrote this defence.

Among the various moves to end the war was an offer by Philip V to cede Gibraltar to Britain if the latter would recognize his right to the throne of Spain.[11] In signing the Treaty of Peace and Friendship of 13 July 1713, Britain made it clear that it looked upon the "cession" by Spain as a mere acknowledgement of British sovereignty over what was already a British possession by right of conquest. Article X of the Treaty of Utrecht stated that the Catholic King for himself and for all his successors "yields the full and whole propriety of the city of Gibraltar together with its port and defences and fortifications. . . . to be held and enjoyed absolutely with all manner of rights and for ever without exception or any impediment" but "without any territorial jurisdiction and without any open communication by land with the country round about" (this was to avoid fraudulent importing of goods). In special circumstances it provided for "lawful purchases, for ready money, in the neighbouring territories of Spain, of provisions and other things necessary for the use of the Garrison, the inhabitants and the ships in the harbour". . . . . "No leave shall be given under any pretence whatsoever. . . . either to Jews or to Moors to reside or have their dwellings in the said town and no shelter be allowed to any Moorish ships of war in the harbour". Free exercise of their religion shall be granted to the inhabitants of the town". It was also agreed that, should Britain ever wish to grant, sell or alienate the fortress, the preference of having it should be given to the Spanish crown.

Not long afterwards, King Philip claimed back Gibraltar on the grounds that its cession had been forced from him. For his part, the Bishop of Cadiz claimed that the good of the Roman Catholic religion could only be ensured if he himself had the power to appoint priests to care for the faithful and could visit them whenever necessary.[12] Quite apart from questions of sovereignty, the Bishop felt bound by ecclesiastical law to carry out these pastoral duties, and he wrote to the Governor along these lines. The Governor's reply stretched a point: the Bishop would only be allowed to visit the Rock as a bona fide visitor, and the Governor, as the representative of the British monarch, would politely and gladly receive him and his entourage in Government House.

In October 1717, the Bishop arrived with his companions. The latter stayed in the Governor's house but the Bishop preferred to lodge with his Vicar General, alleging that the peace and quiet of the priests' house fitted in better with the Bishop's needs. The Bishop had special meetings with Government officials, and was escorted all over the town by specially appointed officers who fulfilled their task courteously and correctly: he was hardly ever left alone.

It must have been at night-time that he examined the registers of St. Mary the Crowned. By doing this he felt he was fulfilling his canonical duties and wrote in the registers directions about the future. He found the records in excellent order. He warned against leaving vacant spaces in them in order to avoid later fraudulent insertions. He discovered that the Catholics under the new regime were in no respect deprived of the practice of their religion. The priest was free to baptise, marry or bury the people provided the authorities were informed beforehand. Matrimonial cases had to go before a marriage tribunal, and in cases of mixed religions when dispensations would likely be needed he established the necessary provisions: he gave the Vicar General powers to set up such a tribunal whenever necessary. Programmes were drawn up for the religious instruction of people who would possibly want to learn about the Catholic Faith. Arrangements were made for the formation of a simple school to cater for about thirty boys. This was to be done in the parish church. Jewels and church treasures were to be sent to the mainland.

All this subterfuge activity was discovered a long time afterwards. But the Bishop of Cadiz was most unhappy that his episcopal jurisdiction over the people of the parish, which was canonically under him, was not accepted by the British authorities in Gibraltar. He corresponded with the Spanish Cortes in Madrid in an endeavour to circumvent opposition to his carrying out his duties openly in Gibraltar. He was preoccupied with the appointment of a successor to Father Juan Romero de Figueroa who had grown very weak. It was when he was pressing Madrid for some solution to this apparent deadlock that Father Romero died. The news was deeply felt not only by the residents of Gibraltar but by the Bishop of Cadiz himself.

Father Lopez Peña conducted the funeral service with great dignity and solemnity in the presence of the Governor, other officials and the majority of the Catholic community. Father Romero's remains were buried right in front of the High Altar of the church he was so attached to, such was the regard the people had for him. A short time before he had written these lines in the Baptismal Register:

"I beg and appeal to all my brothers and successors in charge of this Church, through the generosity of God's mercy towards us, to remember me in their sacrifices and prayers to God, if only for having preserved and protected this Church and its relics and treasure at the cost of so many frights, dangers and labours. And for having looked after the baptism and matrimonial books from which they may obtain certain material recompense. So I expect from their charity, and may God preserve them in His grace. Amen."

By the time Father Romero died, the number of settlers on the Rock had increased enormously. It was something that Col. Joseph Bennet could not understand considering there were so many precautions taken to control the entry of foreigners to the place. It emerged that these settlers concentrated in particular districts, grouping themselves according to the places of origin. Hence, in the course of the eighteenth century, districts known as Portuguese Town, Jewish Town, Hardy Town, Black Town, Irish Town, developed.[13] There is no mention of Genoese Town, but there was a large concentration of Genoese from the outset at Catalan Bay. There were far more Genoese in town, but they were not located in such a concentrated fashion as the other nationalities.

In 1720, all these people were keen to identify themselves with the Garrison. In town, orders were given for civilians to take up arms. In Catalan Bay, the Genoese would take over guard duties to relieve the Catalan Battalion in charge of guarding the east side of the Rock. It was also about this time that King George I decreed that the law to be used in Gibraltar was to be the Spanish law, whereas until then, unruly people had been charged according to military law or disciplined through the instrumentality of their respective Consuls.

CHAPTER TWO

The Junta of Elders

When Father Romero de Figueroa died on 7 June 1720, the Catholic population was not left orphaned and unattended. There, looking after the immediate needs of the Catholics, was Father Joseph Lopez Peña who, while ageing, was nevertheless as active and conscientious as Romero had been. Bishop Armengual, anticipating the need to send a successor to Fr. Romero, had ordered his Curia in Cadiz to select and send someone to the Rock. The one chosen was Father Francisco Roman Trujillo, but he was not to the Bishop's liking. By the time he did get to the Rock Father Romero was already dead. Father Francisco Roman Trujillo in fact entered Gibraltar as a visitor, in September 1720, four months after Father Romero was buried. He claimed to be the rightful successor to the late parish priest, but the people, and worse still, the Governor would not accept him. Regardless of the attitude of those who surrounded him Father Trujillo continued on the Rock and signed himself in the registers as "Parish Priest". He was ostracised by all.

Father Lopez Peña would not tolerate such an impossible situation. He set off for Cadiz to thrash out the whole affair with the Bishop. The Governor and people wanted Father Lopez and not Trujillo as the successor. Since the Bishop had not totally approved of his Curia's original choice anyhow, he hesitated no further and gave Father Lopez Peña all the faculties necessary to look after the people of the Rock. Father Trujillo raised no problem when Father Lopez returned with the faculties. He yielded and worked happily with Lopez for a year.

Father Lopez attended the multiple needs of the fast-growing population of Gibraltar. From time to time he would be visited by priests, experts in Christian doctrine, who came to teach would-be converts to the Catholic religion. Among these priests were Fathers Gregorio Antonio Sabanda, Isidoro del Olmo y Paxares, Ventura de Pardo, Rodrigo Quinones, Jose del Castillo, and Rojas. Some of these would even stay for long spells and assist Father Lopez who had only Father Bernardo de Molina with him. These priests would recruit enough men to keep alive certain confraternities that had formerly been active – the Confraternity of the Holy Eucharist, for example, that of Jesus del Gran Poder and the Guild of Our Lady of Europa. The latter group devoted itself to the practical task of caring for the poor and seeing to the proper burial of the penniless. Its spiritual aim was to encourage devotion to the Blessed Virgin, and to this end it organized regular excursions and pilgrimages to the Shrine of Our Lady of Europa at the south end of the Rock. It was on her feast day each year that the members paid a contribution to the fund of the poor. The confraternity was run by a committee and a chairman in the presence of the priest.

In 1726, Father Lopez Peña, the successor to Father Romero, asked for a contribution of two duros, or dollars, instead of the customary one. A certain Genoese, Francisco Feroci, a wealthy member of the committee, refused to pay, arguing that the chairman was wealthier than he and yet paid only when and what he felt like.[1] For persisting in this point of view and not contributing like other members, Feroci was threatened with excommunication – a serious penalty, it would seem, for a slight fault. On 25 August 1726, an official document of excommunication was read out during High Mass and a copy nailed on the church door to the effect that Feroci was publicly excommunicated for disobedience to the commands of the vicar, and that no Catholic might "treat and correspond with him. . . . under pain of excommunication". Some Protestant friends of his wife suggested to Feroci that he might as well join their Church now; and he wrote to the Governor about his decision to voluntarily leave the Catholic Church; "I Francisco Feroci, by the grace of God, having been excommunicated by Joseph Lopez Peña and Bernardo Molina, declare myself. . . . on this day, 25 August 1726, of the English Apostolic Church, because of the ill treatment of the said Padre Peña who excommunicated me for one dollar". Governor Kane published his reaction the following day, stating that anyone who did not "traffic or correspond with Feroci and his family in the same freedom and manner as they were wont before the excommunication would be expelled from this town along with their families".

Six days later, an official statement by Feroci of his renunciation of the Romish Church and his adherence to the "Protestant religion as professed in ye Church of England" was, with the Governor's permission, pinned up in the English church. Fr. Lopez sent his sacristan to tear down the notice. The Governor was immediately informed, and he took legal steps against the priests that same day. All concerned in the affair were brought before Mr. J.G. Morrice, the Judge Advocate of the garrison and City of Gibraltar. Frs. Lopez and Bernardo de Molina were found guilty of breaking the King's Laws and express General Orders, made the very previous year, applying to all troops and inhabitants of Gibraltar:

> *"The clergy of the Romish Church are not to act in anything tending to the Inquisition. . . . "*[2]

Before the end of the month, the two priests found themselves being escorted at bayonet point to the frontier.[3]

The parish priest's act of defiance turned out to be the tip of an iceberg. It was discovered that both Father Romero and then Father Lopez had been transferring all kinds of precious articles belonging to the different churches in Gibraltar.[4] It came to light that through the medium of Spanish visitors or traders these treasures were being transferred secretly to assigned churches in Spain. Bishop Armengual himself also revealed that, when he visited Gibraltar in 1717, he actually performed his canonical duties. He brought this to light in his attempt to obtain a rightful entrance into Gibraltar. Such revelations of smuggling and breach of trust made the British authorities suspicious of Spanish clergymen. In future such situations were not to happen. The priests responsible were not to be allowed to remain on the Rock. The two who were allowed to be on the Rock at the time were Father Rojas and Father Sabanda. Both were well known by the people but, of the two, the Bishop of Cadiz preferred Father Sabanda. When the Governor, acting in accordance with the wishes of the people, appointed Father Sabanda to succeed as parish priest, the Bishop was pleased.

Aware that he had no faculties to operate as parish priest, Father Sabanda went to Cadiz for them. He also went in order to obtain the Holy Oils required for Baptisms. By this time the Siege, begun by the Conde de la Torre in 1727, was well consolidated and all communications to and from the Rock were cut off. Father Sabanda was shut out of the city and Father Rojas was left to look after the spiritual needs of the Catholics without express spiritual faculties normally granted by a Bishop. Hard though this must have been for the priest, he was also impeded from ever being appointed parish priest: the Governor did not want any more Spanish priests with authority over or governing the Catholics and the property of the Church on the Rock. As in Menorca later on, the Church in Gibraltar was no longer to be associated with the church system in Spain.[5] So General Clayton planned a new organization to assist him in carrying this out. At the Governor's request Father Rojas called together the heads of the three existing confraternities for the purpose of selecting a committee which was to be approved by the Governor. This committee of laymen would assist the priest-in-charge on matters concerning the maintenance of the church and its contents. It was to ensure that the emoluments for services rendered were received and the priests duly rewarded. The committee was to be re-elected each year for the Governor to approve. It was to be the first lay institution to be created on the Rock. It was to be known as the Junta of Elders and it was to have a remarkable influence on the growth of the Church in Gibraltar, as will become clear in the course of this story.

A kind of Presbyterian element was thus unwittingly introduced to the small Christian community which was barely twenty-five years old and yet was marked with an air of individualism; for it remained Spanish-speaking but grew into an Italo-Iberian body which claimed more and more to be British, and was canonically linked to a diocese in a foreign country while forming part of the Universal Church. The attitude of mind which was to develop as a result of the introduction of this new structure was to prove at times to be somewhat alien to what the reader might expect of people with a Catholic upbringing.

This structure was not peculiar to Gibraltar. What in Gibraltar people knew as the Junta of Elders, the people in New Orleans knew as the "Marguillers". Was it a mere coincidence that the "Marguillers" should become so prominent soon after Bishop Francisco Porro, born in Gibraltar, left his mission around the Mississippi valley? Did he introduce the "Marguillers" there after seeing the practical use made of such a structure on the Rock?[6]

In Gibraltar, even a century and more after the invention of the Junta, one and the same generation of Gibraltarians could give support to the Pope, when he was attacked by nationalistic forces in Italy and deprived of the Papal States, yet claim for itself in Gibraltar, not only church property, but powers that had always been a papal prerogative and were intimately linked to the spiritual sphere. Fortunately, in recent times the Second Vatican Council has abundantly provided every possibility for the assimilation and the channelling along right lines of whatever remains of those exaggerated lay aspirations, by defining much more clearly and theologically, and positively encouraging, the role of the laity, so necessary for the growth of the Church.

Pastoral difficulties continued during the siege that began in 1727. The principal church was transformed into a hospital. Services were held in a reduced section of it. In the war years, the priest was able to baptise new-born children but there was inevitably a long delay before they could be anointed with the Holy Oils. All four acting-Governors – Kane, Hargrave, Clayton and Sabine – tried to find a satisfactory solution to the religious problem.[7]

Meanwhile Bishop Armengual de la Mota indomitably continued to press for recognition of his canonical authority over the parish of British Gibraltar. Seeing that his efforts to move the Court of St. James through the normal channels went for nothing, he pleaded with the Papal Nuncio in Spain to intervene and bring about a settlement on this matter. In a letter to the Papal Nuncio the Bishop expressed his thanks for passing the message and then revealed to him that the people of Gibraltar were having recourse to Menorca for priests to help out.

It was in November 1733 that Dr. Francisco Ignacio Ximenez arrived from Port Mahon. He worked with Father Rojas, but it took a short time for the Elders to notice that, with his theological and spiritual formation, Dr. Ximenez was the suitable priest to take charge of the parish. The Governor was duly informed of his suitability, and after swearing allegiance to His Britannic Majesty, arrangements were made for Dr. Ximenez's formal installation by the Governor himself.

This ceremony took place with great solemnity in the beautiful Moorish Patio de los Naranjos adjoining the Church of St. Mary the Crowned. There His Excellency the Governor physically handed over to the new incumbent priest, the keys of the church accompanied by a mandate to work closely with the Junta of Elders. This ritual became the prototype for future successive installations.

Dr. Ximenez knew that his appointment by the protestant Governor carried no authority in the eyes of the Catholic Church. In order to obtain the necessary jurisdiction and hence perform validly his new charge over the people, he appealed to the Bishop of Cadiz for authority. Don Thomas del Valle, who was as displeased as his predecessor with the isolated and independent attitude of Fr. Rojas, welcomed the arrival of the new priest.[8] The spiritual welfare of the people, the Bishop thought, could not but improve. Dr. Ximenez was made a Vicar General and granted the necessary ecclesiastical powers or faculties.

Dr. Ximenez, unlike Fr. Rojas, corresponded with the Bishop regularly. It appears that Fr. Rojas in his old age, would not release his hold on the activities of the church and the faithful. In fact the baptisms, weddings and funerals were mostly administered by Fr. Rojas. Dr. Ximenez was allowed to perform one Christening in May 1731, when the child of the Dutch Consul in Gibraltar was baptised. It was really in 1737 that Dr. Ximenez actually assumed full command of the church's affairs without Fr. Rojas's intervention.

The Bishop of Cadiz was pleased with the manner in which Dr. Ximenez was conducting himself. Visitors to the Rock came back reporting the spiritual progress of the people there. Furthermore, Dr. Ximenez had expressly manifested his disappointment at missing the opportunity of meeting the Archbishop of Seville on the latter's visit to Cadiz. This was a most unexpected openness on the part of Dr. Ximenez.

Suddenly the Bishop changed his attitude towards Dr. Ximenez. On 12 December 1738, Count Marsillac informed the Bishop that the Marquis of Tabuérniga had fled and taken refuge in Gibraltar. The assumption was that the Marquis had fled to the Rock to marry Miss Petronilla Bracamonte. The Bishop ordered the priest to report on his whereabouts and the pretended marriage.[9]

Dr. Ximenez did not reply to the infuriated Bishop's missives. Perhaps there was nothing to write back on the subject since the marriage records do not show anyone named Tabuérniga. The Bishop concluded that Dr. Ximenez had acted unfavourably because he had something to hide. When he sought the support of the French Consul to depose Dr. Ximenez the Bishop did not hesitate to accuse him of abandoning his duties and of being over-fond of the bottle. The Bishop wanted another young Genoese priest, the assistant, to take over.

The French Consul in Gibraltar in June 1742 refused to accept the unfounded accusations against Dr. Ximenez. No heed was taken of the Bishop's machinations and Dr. Ximenez continued with his obligations with the assistance of a young Genoese priest, Fr. Domingo Finocchio, from Mahon.

Dr. Francisco Ximenez died on 12 August 1743. The Governor with the approval of the Junta of Elders named Father Finocchio, the only other priest on the Rock, as the "padre vicario de la parroquia", and he was duly installed. Like his predecessor the Genoese priest appealed to Don Thomas del Valle, Bishop of Cadiz, for the appropriate ecclesiastical powers.[10]

Always solicitious for the spiritual welfare of the Gibraltarians and having approved this candidate for the Office even before Dr. Ximenez died, the Bishop named him Vicar General with the powers required. It appears, however, that Fr. Finocchio was dissatisfied with the ecclesiastical powers he had received. In the ensuing month Fr. Finocchio informed the bishop that a petition had been sent to Rome for the granting of the title of Notary Apostolic. Such a title would ameliorate the situation of the pastor of souls in Gibraltar. This petition was granted by Rome on 27 February 1744.[11]

The priest was aware that he was unable to exercise his newly-acquired powers of a Notary Apostolic unless he made an act of faith and took the oath, if not before the Bishop, at least before an authorised person or persons. Fr. Finocchio nevertheless considered that, in the absence of both, even a private fulfilment of those two requirements was sufficient. Two years later, on 28 September 1746, Finocchio wrote to the Bishop about the state of affairs of Catholics in Gibraltar and made a profession of faith and an oath of fidelity in writing, finding it impossible to do it in person.

As the months elapsed, news came to the Bishop of Fr. Finocchio's strange behaviour. The spiritual development of the people appeared to be suffering seriously and so the Bishop found it necessary to reprimand him. Fr. Finocchio, in turn, attributed all occurrences to his lack of proper jurisdiction. He insisted that the many difficulties and problems encountered could only be met with Ordinary Jurisdiction. Fr. Finocchio put it to the Bishop that if he did not obtain this Ordinary Jurisdiction from the Inquisitorial Tribunal of Madrid, he would appeal to Rome for it himself. He needed all the jurisdiction the Missionaries in Africa possessed.[12]

For eight months he endeavoured to defend himself against the many accusations brought against him to the Bishop. Eventually he asked the Bishop for permission to resign from his Office and retire to his home because of sickness. Word had got around that he had a weakness for the fair sex. Whether true or false, the scandal had become impossible to bear.

Fr. Finocchio assured the Bishop he would remain looking after the church until his successor had arrived from Port Mahon. He sailed to Liorna in Genoa some days after the new priest, Fr. Antonio Foncubierta, had set foot on the Rock. The Governor, interested in seeing that succession of priests flowed smoothly, had not only granted him permission of residence even before he arrived, but promptly appointed him priest-in-charge with the customary ceremonials.

The Junta of Elders informed Don Thomas del Valle who the new priest was; that he was in possession of high qualifications in Philosophy, Theology, and Canon Law. They had found Fr. Foncubierta most suitable for the office of Vicar and the Governor had already made the necessary appointment. The Elders now requested the Bishop to grant Fr. Foncubierta the spiritual authority to fulfil his duties properly.[13]

Perhaps to impress the Bishop a little more, Fr. Foncubierta wrote to him on 20 December 1747. He pointed out that he was alone in charge of the spiritual welfare of the people. On 5 January 1748 the Elders petitioned the Bishop to grant him permission to celebrate more than one Mass on Sundays and Holy Days. They claimed that the Catholic population had increased substantially lately, hence the need for the extra Masses.[14]

On 17 January 1748 Don Thomas del Valle made Fr. Foncubierta the new Vicar General of Gibraltar. His conduct and general attitude pleased everyone. In fact, when six months had elapsed, the Junta of Elders took it on itself to express to the Bishop its satisfaction at the Menorcan priest's behaviour and powerful preaching.

It was because of his outspokenness "in season and out of season", that he found an unsurmountable opposition. In his sermons on Confession and Holy Communion Fr. Foncubierta was direct, persuasive and expected the faithful to react and avail themselves of the Sacraments. It appears that a gentleman, Mr. Andrew Gavino and family would not make use of the Sacraments. Fr. Foncubierta's ensuing pressing sermons were taken to allude to Mr. Gavino and so the latter took it on himself to teach this priest a lesson.[15]

Fr. Foncubierta described to the Bishop that Andrew Gavino was known to direct a guild of Freemasons and was very friendly with the Governor's Secretary. He had on many occasions threatened other devoted persons with expulsion. On this occasion he was making certain he expelled Fr. Foncubierta from the fortress. The Governor, however, would do nothing until the two priests requisitioned from Port Mahon had arrived.

It was on 26 December 1749 that the new priest arrived from Menorca. He was Fr. John Febrer. The Junta of Elders, led by Don Bartolome Danino, approached the Governor and asked him to refrain from expelling Fr. Foncubierta and appointing the newcomer. Simultaneously the Junta wrote to the Bishop to ask him to hesitate granting the new priest all the faculties. But it was in vain. The Governor, influenced by his Secretary, expelled Fr. Foncubierta who sailed to Port Mahon in a battleship on 8 January 1749, and placed Fr. Febrer in charge of the people.

The Bishop would not blind himself to the needs of the faithful. The recommendations to withold any authority could only aggravate the spiritual disorder already found in Gibraltar. He therefore granted Fr. Febrer the powers to administer the Sacraments. To all intents and purposes the Vicar was still Fr. Foncubierta, already back home in Port Mahon, but Fr. Febrer was there and had to administer the sacraments, even if he did not possess the powers of a Vicar General.

Fr. Febrer was extremely annoyed at this restriction of powers. Taking advantage of his favour with the Secretary of the Governor, Fr. Febrer did not hesitate to threaten those who had opposed him with expulsion from Gibraltar. There was an element of fear among the Catholic people who wondered what the new priest would do. The Elders could not stand him at all so they wrote to the Bishop to reinstate Fr. Foncubierta who was to pass by the Rock on his way to Lisbon. A Fr. Francisco Hinojosa appeared on the scene and supported this view.

The situation changed drastically with the arrival of a new Governor. The Elders saw the Governor on the current situation and the priest was immediately forced to mend his ways. When Fr. Foncubierta landed in

Gibraltar with letters from London he met the Governor and while the Elders hoped the meeting would result in Fr. Foncubierta staying in Gibraltar, it was found expedient for Fr. Febrer to remain in Office. The opposition put up by Mr. Gavino and friends was reason enough to refrain from further changes. hence Fr. Foncubierta left for good.[15]

With matters cleared by the new Governor's intervention, the Elders, who had earlier pleaded not to grant Fr. Febrer spiritual powers, now requested Don Thomas del Valle to grant him all the required titles and powers. It was precisely at this juncture that another Menorcan priest appeared on the scene and wrote to the Bishop in favour of Fr. Febrer.

Bishop Thomas del Valle wrote to the Elders expressing his sorrow at the strange behaviour of Fr. Febrer and how he had strongly persuaded him to resign from his Office and withdraw to his Franciscan Convent. The Bishop, furthermore, having decided not to consider Fr. Foncubierta the last Vicar General of Gibraltar, now grants Fr. Hinojosa faculties to administer the Sacraments among the people. It was his hope that the Governor would soon appoint him priest-in-charge. Fr. Febrer was counselled not to leave by Mr. Gavino who by now aspired to become the Spanish Consul in Gibraltar.

Fr. Febrer left for Port Mahon in March 1752 and with his departure tensions disappeared. Fr. Francisco Hinojosa was made priest-in-charge and ceremoniously installed while the Bishop of Cadiz did not hesitate to make him the Vicar of Gibraltar in May 1752.

Fr. Hinojosa and Spain

The Junta of Elders grew into an influential, if not a powerful body on the Rock. It was consulted and cultivated by the Governors. Its members were invited to the Governor's residence on royal occasions along with the Heads of the Jewish and Protestant communities. When, in 1756, the French expelled those inhabitants of Port Mahon who had been pro-British, and directed them to Gibraltar, the Governor asked the Junta to assess what lodgings were available and to make arrangements for the newcomers. People had already taken officers into their homes because of shortage of barracks; but, with the aid of the Junta, further room was found for the refugees from Port Mahon.[1]

The Junta was further proved an effective instrument and intermediary. It was consulted at least seven times in the course of the eighteenth century about the appointment of new priests. They had been definite in recommending Father Hinojosa as the most suitable of priests for the office of parish priest. Fr. Hinojosa obtained the faculties from the Bishop of Cadiz on 25 June 1751.

On 16 October 1765 a Spanish priest arrived suddenly at the church door to meet Fr. Hinojosa. The visiting priest was Fr. Francisco Colodoro de San Agustin. He was in charge of a Hospice in Meknes. He was carrying a message to the Governor of Ceuta on behalf of the King of Morocco.

It was obvious that the British Consul in Tangier informed the authorities in Gibraltar about this arrival, for quite unexpectedly Captain Brathwaite arrested him. Escorted by two soldiers the priest was taken before Governor Irwine. The priest had been found in possession of two or three pounds of tobacco. Asked why he had not gone to report to the authorities on his arrival, and having no excuse, he suddenly revealed he was bringing a message to the Governor of Ceuta. The letter was intercepted, read and returned. The tobacco was not.

When the whole search had ended the priest was asked to sign a form stating that he had not been badly treated and the other two priests were also asked to sign that the visitor signed the form freely.

When Fr. Colodoro arrived at Ceuta and reported to its Governor what had transpired in Gibraltar, there started a never-ending correspondence between the two governors. The Governor of Gibraltar simply pointed out the irregularity of the cargo the priest was carrying quite against the interest of

Spain and that he was not improperly treated, as the two priests testified. The incident was shelved, but orders were given to the Governor of San Roque that Fr. Hinojosa was to be captured as soon as he was caught sight of in Spain. It was to put such things right on the Rock that the authorities in Spain wanted to send an ecclesiastical mission there.

The next Governor of Gibraltar, General Edward Cornwallis, received a letter from the Governor of San Roque on 6 March 1768. It was written on behalf of the Vicar of San Roque who wanted permission to enter the Fortress. Father Ribera had been commissioned by the Bishop of Cadiz to "inspect the works the Catholic Church stands in need of and other matters pertaining to the same".[2] The answer given was polite and friendly. The fact that the commission originated from the Bishop of Cadiz, said Cornwallis, was an obstacle to his desire to oblige his fellow Governor. The question of jurisdiction aside, however, he would do whatever was in his power, if only the Governor of San Roque would advise him of what was amiss, and he would even allow Fr. Ribera in to examine the structure of the building.

The Spanish Governor expressed surprise that, in view of Article X of the Treaty of Utrecht, the Vicar of San Roque could not go to the garrison to execute the order of the Bishop of Cadiz. Surely, he argued, there could be no objection to the Bishop of Cadiz, to whose diocese the Church and the Roman Catholics of Gibraltar belonged, wanting to find out how matters stood as regards the Church and the consciences of the said Catholics, he being their legitimate prelate? There was no question, he said, of interference with matters of government, which were reserved to His Britannic Majesty. It was, after all for the Bishop, not a Spanish Governor, to deal with the Church. He was merely supporting the Bishop's wishes, and he professed himself always ready to help the Governor of Gibraltar, should the latter ever need his assistance. He still hoped that this reasonable and just request would be granted and that he would not have to refer the question to the Spanish Court.

Cornwallis replied immediately, saying that he saw no violation of the Treaty in his refusal. The people of Gibraltar had the free exercise of their religion in accordance with the Treaty. As far as he was able to ascertain, any claims to such jurisdiction over the previous 64 years had been constantly rejected. The Bishop had not in all that time appointed either a vicar or a curate. A previous Governor had obtained a priest from Menorca, and after his death, the Catholic inhabitants had been allowed to choose between two candidates. No obstacles had ever been put in the way of repairing the church. He pointed out that he had been ready to allow Fr. Ribera in, if the Governor had anything specific he wanted looked into; but he did not intend to enter on disagreeable disquisitions about power. If the matter did go to the Spanish Court, then he, Cornwallis, would likewise inform the British Court of the whole affair. He hoped, finally, that the personal relationship between the two military commanders would continue on the same friendly terms as before.

The matter was referred to the two higher authorities in Spain and Britain. Lord Selbourne finally supported the stand of Cornwallis, deciding that the exercise of foreign ecclesiastical jurisdiction in Gibraltar would be contrary to British sovereignty over the fortress.

Father Ribera was, in the end, allowed to enter Gibraltar as a visitor, and not as a delegate or official of the Bishop of Cadiz. Nevertheless he took advantage of his stay to tear out of the baptismal register the remaining pages covering baptisms up to 1704 and carried them off to San Roque.[3] When the Governor of Gibraltar heard of this – probably through the Junta – he decided to penalize Father Hinojosa for allowing it. Whether Father Hinojosa learnt of the Governor's displeasure and guessed what the outcome would be is not clear, but the fact is that Father Hinojosa, who never went to Spain, suddenly decided to go there. As a result of his entry into Spain he was immediately apprehended by the Spanish Authorities. The British Authorities who would have otherwise made loud noises to recover him simply kept silent on the incident and finished with him this way.

The new Vicar appointed by the Governor with the help of the Junta was the former assistant priest, Father Raphael Messa, an Augustinian, an older person, with doctorates both in theology and law. His assistant was to be Father Pedro Velasco, who took over the duties of Father Raphael when the latter died in January 1771.

By then the two other priests had arrived on the Rock: Father Francisco Messa, a brother of the late Vicar, and Father Pedro Reymundo, a priest related to an old Gibraltarian family. As the elderly Father Velasco was not likely to be appointed by the Governor, Father Reymundo set about forestalling the possibility of Father Messa being appointed, and wrote to the Bishop of Cadiz to that end. At all events, the Bishop asked the Spanish Court to take steps to prevent the appointment of Father Messa.[4]

Father Messa, however, in the meantime found favour with both the Governor and the Junta, since he was British and had a doctorate in theology. He was made Vicar in 1773 (March). The Governor then wrote to Lord Grantham informing him of what he had done and why: "The priests have always been appointed by the Governor. If the Bishop of Cadiz has given them a spiritual sanction it has been *en cache* to carry on the show of jurisdiction. . . . His Majesty's orders forbid my taking notice of the Bishop of Cadiz. The Roman Catholic inhabitants have never, during the ten years of my command, complained of interruption in the peaceable exercise of their religion as provided by Treaty". The Governor was unaware, however, that the Spanish Court had been in touch with Lord Grantham, asking that this priest be passed over.

The Spaniards received a more favourable hearing than usual, for their approach soft-pedalled the question of jurisdiction and suggested that the best way to solve this long-standing problem was for the Bishop of Cadiz to supply to the Governor a list of names, from which the Governor should choose one: and, if the person proved unsatisfactory, he would be replaced by someone else. The British decided that, while fulfilling the clauses of the Treaty to the letter, the Governor should take particular care to name as Vicar one of the King's subjects, but to act in concert with the Bishop of Cadiz on those points where there was no question of jurisdiction but merely one of the proper qualifications for the due discharge of the duties of Vicar.

The British Government's message had come too late. The Governor had simply consulted the Junta and that sufficed. In any case, the final appointment had been left to the discretion of the Governor. He did not, therefore, implement the suggestion that Father Messa be given "some reasonable gratification for his trouble in coming from Menorca and his return there" and be replaced by the cleric proposed by General Johnson. Father Messa remained in charge of the Catholics on the Rock.

The Genoese priest resented being assistant to Father Messa. He began to squabble with the parish priest, demanding a bigger salary, until their differences became public gossip and reached the ears of the Governor. The latter then asked Mr. de la Rosa, a member of the Junta, to get that body to settle this clerical dispute and draw up rules calculated to prevent such scandals and preserve due harmony. Father Messa himself presided over the meeting of the Junta, and his assistant was allowed to be present. The solution arrived at, after lengthy discussion, was that the parish priest should pay Father Reymundo eight dollars a month, while the latter was to give the parish priest three reals out of every stipend received for sung Mass.[5]

Father Reymundo, however, remained dissatisfied, and within one month another meeting had to be called. The Junta duly reported to the Governor and made different suggestions: all alms given to the Catholic Church in Gibraltar, plus other income from fees, funerals, baptisms, weddings, oaths, Masses and confraternity celebrations, etc. should be divided into three. Two-thirds should go to the parish priest and the remainder to the curate (exception being made of a portion to be devoted to the upkeep of the fabric). Alms received for the blessing of houses on Holy Saturday were to be given to the lenten preacher, while the non-preaching priest might accept whatever alms were freely offered him by the faithful. All the aforesaid monies were to be collected by the collector for the fabric, and to be passed on to the official Treasurer who in his turn would apportion whatever was due to the parish priest and to his assistant along with their respective accounts. Alms received personally by both priests were to be surrendered to the Treasurer for the sake of avoiding disputes and confusion.

The new suggestions also touched on the manner of voting annually for new members of the Junta. All the confraternities were to be called together by the parish priest; these would then vote for the three senior Brothers, three Treasurers, and three Collectors, active and capable of performing their duties; the men elected were to accept their duties under penalty of a one-dollar fine; an account of the amount collected was to be presented every year to the whole assembly; such money could be applied by the parish priest to the upkeep of the fabric or could be passed on to next year's confraternity members; no confraternity was to spend more than four dollars without the approval of the parish priest and that of the three Brothers in council. Both sets of regulations were accepted by all concerned.

The new Governor, Robert Boyd, was given prior instructions by St. James'

Court concerning the steps to be taken should Father Messa cause trouble. If any more complaints were made by the Court of Spain on his behalf, he was to be got rid of and to be replaced by a priest who was a British subject. One of the first things the Governor did after his arrival in 1773 was to investigate Father Messa's background. Among other steps, he wrote to the Superior of the Augustinians in Menorca for confidential information. From this source he received such a good report that he was inclined to favour Father Messa rather than Reymundo, the other priest.[6] During his investigations he became aware of the parish priest's difficult financial circumstances and generously got the British Government to award him an annuity of 100 doubloons a year, plus food for two persons, free of charge, from military stores.

It was really the Bishop of Cadiz, Don Thomas del Valle, who had been responsible for complaints from Spain reaching the Court of St. James. He opposed the appointment of Father Messa, but, when the latter applied for faculties, he had no alternative but to confirm him in his office of parish priest. It went against the grain for the Bishop to grant such concessions, and he pointed out to Father Messa that an appropriate stipend should have accompanied his request. But to have sent money out of the colony into Spain would have harmed the friendship that was developing between Fr. Messa and the Governor. Indeed, any transfer of money to Spain by a British subject would have aroused suspicions in the minds of the authorities in Gibraltar. The latter disliked even the idea of correspondence being sent to Cadiz whenever there was a question of obtaining dispensations for marriages or solutions to problems of conscience.

It was customary for the parish priest to allow the Governor to see letters that were destined for the Bishop's eyes. Letters concerning cases of conscience, however, he witheld. It was also customary for the parish priest to inform the Governor of impending marriages and to request permission to carry out the ceremony. Gradually, however, permission was only insisted on in the case of the marriage of non-residents.

It was the non-compliance with the mutual understanding in such matters that led to a cooling off of friendship on the part of the Governor.[7] Father Messa at one period was surprised to find that orders had been given not to allow him into the Convent (as the Governor's house was called). Even when he received an invitation, as representative of the Catholic Church, to attend a garden party, together with Mr. de la Rosa, on the Governor's birthday, he did not succeed in meeting the Governor. The estrangement lasted a whole year before the cause of this coolness reached the priest's ear via the Governor's Secretary. Father Messa had officiated at the marriage of someone who was not a resident and had no papers. As it turned out it was a case of the young man deceiving Father Messa rather than the priest slighting the authorities.

The priest wrote to the Governor apologising for having too readily taken the young man's word and neglecting to examine carefully his papers. He had acted in good faith, he said, and not out of disrespect or other ulterior motive.

This letter of apology and the priest's expression of good wishes for the Governor's welfare helped to repair the breach in their relationship.

In October 1774, Fr. Messa received a letter from a certain Don Jose de la Rosa, asking him for a meeting. This gentleman claimed to be the "Commissioner of the Holy Office for the City and Port of Gibraltar". He had been sent on a mission by "their Excellencies the Apostolic Inquisitors of the Faith" in Sevilla. He had certain documents to hand over to the parish priest, but as he found it awkward to get into the garrison, he suggested a meeting between them at a point beyond military guard on the Isthmus linking Gibraltar and Spanish territory.

Father Messa showed the letter to the Governor. Later the priest received a note from the Governor stating quite bluntly that the "Court of the Inquisition is a thing unknown in the British dominion and prohibited in any territory of the King". The Governor not only forbade him in writing to go outside the Colony to meet Don Jose, but also made it clear that any stranger, no matter how distinguished, who might come to town and embark on some action at the orders of the said Inquisition would be treated as a spy; and any Gibraltarian, lay or cleric, daring to help such a person would be treated as a traitor to King and country.

The letter was probably meant to safeguard the priest, vis-à-vis the Bishop, more than anything else, for the Governor informed Fr. Messa that Don Jose could be invited to the Rock as the Governor's guest, but not as a representative of the Inquisition[8] Fr. Messa sent Don Jose the Governor's letter and a covering letter of his own, pointing out that the Governor was in the right. From then on the Bishop of Cadiz left things in Gibraltar severely alone.

Two years later, the Governor was again caught up in socio-ecclesiastical affairs. For various reasons the people of Gibraltar preferred to have their loved ones buried inside churches rather than in cemeteries, at the Campo Santo Cemetery in North Front, or in St. Jago's Cemetery, or Sandpits, or Red Sands Meadows. It was now suggested to the Governor by the Junta that there were certain irregularities in the system of burials.

The Governor asked a commission of three army surgeons to examine the ground and the procedure used in Catholic burials.[9] They discovered that with the current practice, there was not enough room in St. Mary the Crowned; and that the dead bodies were sometimes removed in a state of putrefaction from under the aisle to a place called the Casa del Carnero, where they were allowed to go on rotting away without any adequate covering of earth; and all this in order to make room for other corpses.

They considered this to be a dangerous practice. They recommended that quicklime be put in the grave at the time of burial, and that no bodies be disturbed for at least four years after burial; nor should the grave be less than five feet deep. The Carnero should be filled with earth, and no such practice be carried out in the church or elsewhere in town.

The rumour spread with the speed for which Gibraltar has always been noted that the Junta was trying to put a stop to burials in church. Public

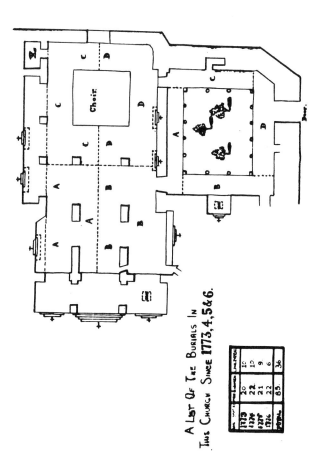

Sketch of the Spanish Church shewing the manner by which it may be divided into Four Parts, for intering the Bodies of 70 Persons in each Division, mark'd A, B, C, and D, exclusive of the Altars and Vaults belonging to the same.

Groundplan of the Church drawn by 2nd Lieut. W. Booth, R.E. 1776.

A List Of The Burials In This Church Since 1773, 4, 5 & 6.

YEAR	MEN & WOMEN	CHILDREN
1773	20	10
1774	22	10
1775	21	9
1776	22	6
TOTAL	85.	36

protests followed, as well as the posting up in public of comments on members of the Junta. The comments on Messrs. de la Rosa and Porro in particular were tantamount to libel. They were accused of embezzling money from the Poor Fund.

The Junta replied in kind. They supplied the authorities with visible evidence of the attacks on them, and they produced a copy of the Poor Fund's accounts, properly audited and signed, thus defending themselves against the charges. They were not trying, they said, to do away with burials in church – there was still room for more, but there was also plenty of room in the Campo Santo. Indeed, Fr. Messa had in the past assisted at burials in that very place. It was pointed out that, of course, the custom of burying people in church was a lucrative business for the priests!

The Governor simply published the findings of the commission and made them compulsory; quicklime to be put in the graves at the time of burial; none to be opened for four years; the Carnero to be filled with earth, and only a specified number of bodies to be buried in each of the four sections of the church decided on by the surgeons on the basis of the average number of deaths that had occurred in the previous four years.

The Junta cashed in on this decision with diplomatically worded letters declaring themselves to be His Britannic Majesty's loyal and faithful servants, and promising that they would punctually adhere to the wishes of His Excellency. They turned the incident to their advantage and further strengthened their position in the Church.

General Boyd was a far-sighted man. With Spain and France supporting the rebellious colonists in America he took precautions to strengthen the garrison's fortifications. He got local shipping firms and merchants to import bricks and stones. Barracks were repaired and fortified and King's Bastion was begun. He even gave thought to what might happen in spiritual matters if communications with Spain had to be cut off in the near future. Fr. Messa was asked to draft, on behalf of the Governor, a letter to the Pope, requesting that the Church in Gibraltar be made independent of the Diocese of Cadiz. This might seem a heavensent opportunity for Fr. Messa to strengthen his own position. On the other hand, it was a natural thing for the Governor to make this request. He would hardly know along what lines to address the Pope or whoever in Rome was to be addressed. According to the notes supplied by Fr. Messa, Vicars had always and at all times been named and appointed by the Governor of the Garrison, and the faculties subsequently obtained from the Bishop of Cadiz. Difficulties were bound to arise when there was need to correspond with the Bishop in cases of conscience: the secrecy involved might bring upon the priest suspicions of treachery.

The Governor used these details in sending His Holiness the Pope a letter asking him "to bestow on the Reverend Parish Priest, Father Francisco Messa of the Order of St. Augustine, full and ordinary powers as are customarily held by Vicars-General" so that he would be able to exercise as far as possible the powers that Bishops themselves have, "freed from all links with the Spanish nation, and linked directly to Your Holiness' Holy and Apostolic See, giving him for this purpose the dignity and title of Apostolic Protonotary and Vicar-General of this city of Gibraltar and Monte Caspio".[10]

He also put before the Holy Father the alternative suggestion of changing the Church of St. Mary the Crowned into an abbacy, of which the parish priest would become the abbot, "giving him all the powers necessary and all the honours, privileges and regalia which subjects honoured with such dignity are accustomed to possess." In any event, the procedure for the appointment of parish priest in this colony might be as follows: The Governor to propose three Roman Catholic priests as candidates, and the Pope to select and confirm one of them. The Governor did not realize how slowly Rome moves on matters of such a nature. Neither he nor his successor was to receive any reply. Some reaction squeezed through sixteen years later.

Life for Father Messa and for all the inhabitants of the Rock changed drastically with the outbreak of war on 11 July 1779, a war which saw the Great Siege of Gibraltar. The siege was embarked on by the French and Spaniards with a view to recapturing the Rock. The thinking behind the attempt was that, as England would be preoccupied with preserving the colonies in North America, little attention would be paid to Gibraltar, and its defences would thus be weakened. The war was to last nearly four years – until 12 March 1783.

Everything on the Rock had to be adapted to the needs of the fortress[11] The Church of St. Mary the Crowned, or part of it, was requisitioned by the authorities for storing victuals. While a large portion was taken up by the store, Father Messa was satisfied that enough space was left for religious services to continue there. Later on the Governor gave orders that all church-towers had to be lowered to impede the enemy's sightings. The belfry of St. Mary the Crowned was lowered with the guarantee that it would be reconstructed once the war was over. The heavy bombardment from Spain was such that the inhabitants took to the flat ground at Windmill Hill for refuge. When Father Messa saw that even the church was at peril, he and his sister's family followed suit and looked for safety. The Vicar, however, seeing that the church was ablaze and the precious articles in it would be lost, returned to it and braved the flames to save as many things as he could carry. He even saved the statue of Our Lady of Europe from being totally destroyed and carried it to Windmill Hill. The people there received Her with a tumultuous ovation.

As the war progressed and provisions became scarce, Governor George Eliott ordered the inhabitants to be evacuated. Only men in essential jobs were to remain. (This was something that the inhabitants of the Rock were to experience once more during the Second World War.) Only a few hundred men were left behind. As a result of the splitting-up of families, men suffered stress. Father Messa's brother-in-law became acutely depressed, causing the Vicar great hardships.

With the cessation of hostilities in 1783, the people returned to what had been the main town from the temporary one in the outlying districts such as New Jerusalem, Black Town, Hardy Town, Windmill Plains and New Mole

Entrance to the Spanish Church, Gibraltar.

The Entrance and Belfry after The Great Siege 1782.

Parade. They found scarcely a house intact. They had to continue living in their huts and tents while setting about the reconstruction. They were not allowed to use any new sites, nor were the military allowed to help in the rebuilding. It was only when the evacuees returned from Menorca, Portugal, Leghorn, Genoa, and London that real progress began. With the minimum of planning, houses began to spring up, replacing the buildings that had dated back to times when Gibraltar was inhabited by subjects of the King of Spain. All that remained of the Church of St. Mary were the four walls and the vaulted ceiling above the High Altar and the two side altars. If the rebuilding of the town was slow, the reconstruction of the church was even slower. By 1785, only the principal altars had been restored. Most important for church building was the welcome influx of skilled construction workers from Menorca and the return of Father Reymundo.

Apart from the fact that the rebuilding of the Church of St. Mary came low in the list of priorities, there was a great lack of money. It was this that led the Junta – it was made up of the same members as in 1778 – to decide that the church ceiling should be lower than it had been and that the building itself be less lavishly decorated. The Junta was, of course, anxious to re-establish its former position. It asked the priest to hand over to them the valuables still in his possession. Fr. Messa refused, on the grounds that he had risked his life to save these things when he had been left all alone to witness their almost certain destruction at the time of the bombardment. The Junta, without more ado, went to complain to the Governor, and the latter took their side. The parish priest, now old, weary and ill, was censured and kept under house arrest until he surrendered the valuables to the Junta. He died in 1792, and his successor, appointed by the Governor, was none other than the Genoese Fr. Reymundo, who had been a thorn in his side for so long.

CHAPTER FOUR

Fr. Reymundo, Protonotary Apostolic

The scene in Gibraltar had changed tremendously at this juncture when Fr. Reymundo took charge of the Catholic community. The inhabitants had already been repatriated from Menorca, Leghorn, Portugal and England. With them they brought many other sympathizers who were undoubtedly taken in by these people's "praises of life in Gibraltar". It is, however, well established that coinciding with this influx of people came a large colony of Genoese patricians. They did so not only in response to the British authorities invitation to settle on the Rock and assist in the economic revival of the city, but also because, with their foresight and sense of history, they feared that the Napoleonic forces would create havoc in their territory and cause them once again to suffer the ordeals of war.[1] To escape from it all these patricians, who alone were allowed to own ships and trade, took advantage of their personal fortunes and means to travel to and reside in Gibraltar.

At long last, Rome answered the petition of the previous Governor. Thus it came to pass that Fr. Reymundo became, by decree of Pope Pius VI, Vicar General and Protonotary Apostolic of the Holy See in Gibraltar: no longer would he as parish priest have to turn to the Bishop of Cadiz for faculties necessary for the care of souls on the Rock. By ecclesiastical law, however, Gibraltar still remained part and parcel of the Diocese of Cadiz.

The Protonotary Apostolic was able to work closely with the Junta. At the close of the century he suggested that the time had come for a change in selecting the members of the Junta. A unanimous decision was reached that they should no longer be chosen from the confraternities, but rather from among men of means who had a permanent abode in Gibraltar, who were British subjects, and who could afford annual subscription fees in order to be on the electoral list. What lay behind this move is not quite clear. Perhaps it was thought that members of spiritual confraternities were not necessarily intelligent or effective in getting things done, whereas business men were more likely to be so, though, of course, there was no assurance that all those who qualified for membership of the Junta would necessarily be pious persons as members of the confraternities presumably were.

From the Governor came a proposition in 1800, concerning the rebuilding of the church of St. Mary the Crowned. The Government itself would take over responsibility, it said, for repairing the rest of the church and for building

32

the tower as promised at the time of the siege, when it had been taken down; and would contribute £1000 towards the project, if part of the church were sacrificed in the interests of improving the highway – the aim being to link Church Street to Waterport Street and thus create Main Street. A third of the body of the church would disappear as well as a large part of the Moorish Patio de los Naranjos. The Junta and the priest agreed, and the Royal Engineers set to work on the project. The new building was finished in 1810. It possessed a splendid organ above the High Altar and the finished building displayed a strange mixture of architectural styles. The church authorities never received the promised £1000.[2]

Fr. Reymundo had noticed that a young man, John Baptist Nosardy Zino, of Genoese extraction, had a vocation to the priesthood and sent him to Rome to study. After six years' training, the young priest returned to Gibraltar and was to prove the most zealous of priests. Since the new priest was too young and Fr. Reymundo was rapidly getting very old there was an urgent need to look to the future and plan who was going to take over from Reymundo. The Junta and the Vicar fortunately recalled that Francisco Joyera, a Franciscan

Vaulted ceiling of High Altar showing delicate stonework

33

SECTION thro' A.B.

PLAN thro' C.D.

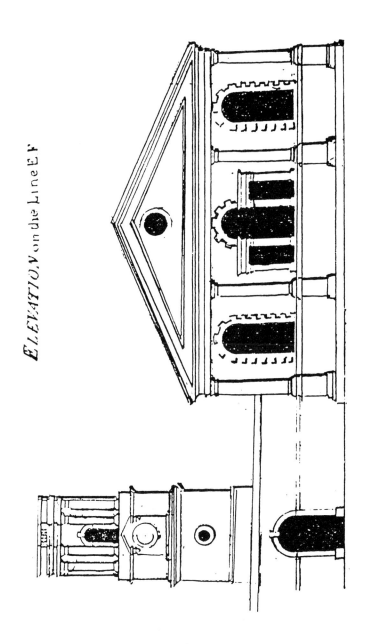

ELEVATION on the Line E F

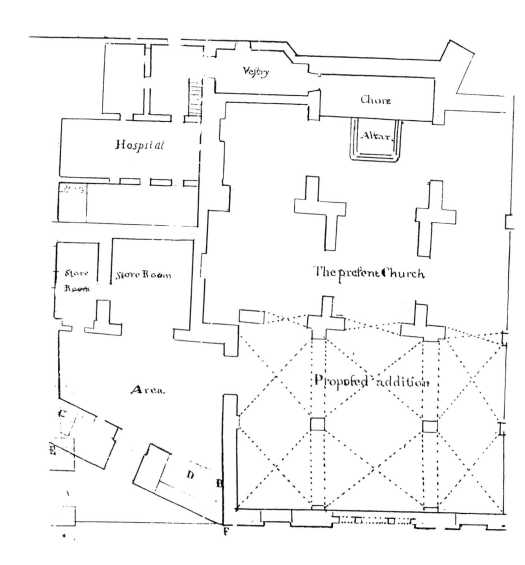

PLAN, ELEVATION and SECTION
the Spanish Church, as ordered to be alterd by
General Charles O'Hara Governor of Gibraltar &c &c.
10th September 1800.

Vestry

Chore

Altar

Hospital

The present Church

Store Room

Store Room

Proposed addition

Area

D

E

F

Plan, Elevation and Section of the Spanish Church as ordered to be altered by General Charles O'Hara, Governor of Gibraltar, 10th September 1800.

friar, lived in Malaga. They all knew him for his powers of preaching and learning. They approached him on the subject and he agreed to work in Gibraltar. Permission was, first of all, requested of His Excellency the Governor for the priest to enter the Rock to preach the Lenten conferences which lasted six weeks. Once the friar was in and proved to be to the liking of everyone, and with the proper qualifications and dispositions, the Junta pressed the Governor to name Father Joyera an assistant to Father Reymundo. The Governor agreed to do this so long as the priest was prepared to take an oath of allegiance to the Britannic Majesty.[3]

Meanwhile the Junta had approached the Sacred Congregation of Bishops and Regulars in Rome to obtain from the Holy Father the authority for Father Joyera to accept and comply with the mission conferred on him, remaining in Gibraltar independently of the Religious Superiors of the Franciscan Order, while retaining his religious habit. The affirmative reply arrived less than three months later on 16 July 1802.[4] Father Joyera won everyone's confidence and love, not only with his inspiring words but also with his enthusiastic involvement in everything that was going on.

When bubonic plague spread through the south of Spain and hit Gibraltar it killed 4,864 inhabitants. Father Reymundo caught it and died. Father Joyera who, together with Father Zino, attended the sick, was affected by the plague and was also killed by it. With the assistance of another priest, Father Zino attended the sick as best as he could. There were of course, no hospitals for the poor in Gibraltar at the time. The only assistance they had was a hospital set up by the priests at the rear of the church in Cannon Lane. The military had their own physicians and establishments to see to their needs, but the destitute only had this hospital which could take in approximately thirty persons. During the epidemic people were crammed into the building and laid out on the floor.

As time elapsed, Fr. Dominguez noticed that the Elders were not looking on him with favour. Assuming that they suspected him of being too pro-Spanish and not loyal enough to the British interests, he did not hesitate to point out what he had done for the troops.[9] When the Corpus Christi procession was organized to take place on the feast day, he discovered that the Catholic troops refused to march in it because they did not have decent helmets. Fr. Dominguez immediately sought the necessary funds to purchase them so that they participated in it. He was very proud to see them march so smartly.

Fr. Dominguez clashed with the Governor, General Don, around the years 1814–1815, and this ended with the Vicar's resignation. It was relative to the church hospital. Mr. Boschetti who headed the Junta in 1814 was also an architect. As a result of the epidemics the residents had experienced, and the manner in which the church hospital was overtaxed, he proposed to Fr. Dominguez ways and means to improve the hospital structurally and allow greater scope for emergencies. The Vicar would not agree. He would not allow the Junta to intervene in hospital affairs. This was his sphere. One day, when he least expected it, Fr. Dominguez heard in the street that a new hospital was to be constructed with the collaboration of the Governor. Whether Fr. Dominguez assumed that his hospital was to be pulled down and a new one constructed, or that his work would no longer be required we will never know. But, he wrote a letter to Governor George Don for enlightenment. To his astonishment the Governor replied with a most unexpected and explosive demand. General Don requested Fr. Dominguez to produce documents of ownership or lease of the hospital and a report of accounts.[10] The Vicar Apostolic knew he had none of the documents requested and no financial reports to present. He asked to see the Governor to explain to him personally exactly what he wanted to get clear in his first letter. The Governor insisted on the necessity of having those documents at hand if there was to be any meeting. The Vicar did not know where to turn. He did not want to turn to the Junta. He felt, deep inside him, that Boschetti and someone else were conspiring with the Governor against him. He noticed that things were no longer as they were before. He went his own way and the Junta theirs. He sensed tension developing within him, and an inability to cope with the situation. On Sunday 29 October 1815, Father Dominguez, at the age of 54, announced at every Mass said in the church that he had resigned as Vicar Apostolic.[11] He was leaving Father Juan Baptista Zino and Father Panizza to continue the work among the Catholics. He in fact hoped Father Panizza would succeed him as Vicar Apostolic. He said that he was resigning for health reasons and to recuperate. He left Gibraltar for Malaga where he took up residence. The news that the outgoing Vicar had shown preference for Fr. Panizza spread all over the Rock. The Junta considered this too presumptuous and rejected the candidate mentioned by the ex-Vicar. They wrote to Propaganda Fide giving their preference and naming Fr. John Baptist Zino, an Italian-born student of Propaganda Fide, well acquainted with Gibraltar affairs and a person who had shown his mettle during the hard times of the three dreadful epidemics by the care he had shown for the sick in the church hospital.

As the strain and horror of the plague subsided and there was a need to fill the position of Vicar, the Governor, General Henry Edward Fox, quite unexpectedly approached the Junta telling them he was naming Father George Staunton as the successor to Father Reymundo. Father Staunton was an Irish Augustinian priest who had never been to Gibraltar and no one knew him or about him. Out of deference to His Excellency's insistence and word they refrained from carrying out the customary screening of the candidate. While Father Staunton worked in the church, the Registers there show that he did not administer any of the sacraments until March 1805. Meanwhile, Father Zino and Father Ferrando, a visiting priest, administered to the people with the faculties granted them by the late Vicar.

It appears that Father Staunton antagonized many of the faithful and, worse still, the Junta of Elders. The latter did not hesitate to ask the Governor, General Henry Edward Fox, to dismiss Father Staunton from his office as Vicar, and furthermore, appealed that in future the selection for nomination should be left to the Junta. Father Staunton, when released from his charge·

as Vicar remained working as an ordinary priest, thus causing great embarrassment and irritation to the Elders.[(5)]

Mr. Breciano, now heading the Junta, recalled the recommendation given by the late Father Joyero of a Dominican friend in Malaga, Father Isidoro Dominguez. The latter was approached by Mr. Breciano who sounded him out on the subject, manifesting positive signs of his willingness to take on the office. The Junta put to the Governor their choice of candidate for nomination. The answer was, as expected, in the affirmative and Fr. Dominguez was named by His Excellency the Governor as the succeeding Vicar.

Little did the Elders expect objections to come from Fr. Dominguez. When the latter was asked to present himself in Gibraltar and take possession, a brief ceremony was held at the Patio de los Naranjos of the church, where the Governor presented the Vicar with the keys of the church. Fr. Dominguez refused to accept. He felt in conscience that unless he received the power and authority from a proper ecclesiastical authority his taking over would be an intrusion and his activities null and void.[(6)] No matter how much Mr. Breciano pleaded that he imitate Fr. Joyero, who received the powers once he was on the Rock, the Dominican priest insisted on a prior ecclesiastical mandate.[(7)]

The Elders, meanwhile, had already petitioned the Sacred Congregation of Propaganda Fide for the faculties and powers required by a head of an independent Catholic congregation. Simultaneous with this request to Rome the Bishop of Cadiz, Don Javier de Utrea, solicitous for the well-being of the Catholic population of Gibraltar and, like his predecessors, anxious that his canonical rights over the parish of Gibraltar continue to be recognized by Rome and the Court of St. James, was quite prepared to grant Fr. Dominguez the required faculties, even temporarily, so as not to endanger the spiritual welfare of the people[(8)]. The Nuncio in Spain received the decree from Rome written in July 1806, making Fr. Dominguez Vicar General of the Bishop of Cadiz in Gibraltar. He was also granted the extraordinary privilege of administering the Sacrament of Confirmation. Only when he received such an authority did Fr. Dominguez take up his appointment.

Large numbers of Genoese and other Italians, escaping from the onslaughts of the Napoleonic troops advancing through their countries in the Italian Peninsula, swarmed into the relative peace and security enjoyed by British Gibraltar. But Gibraltar had not been equipped for so many people whether hygenically or by way of accommodation. These unfortunate immigrants were the first to be affected by the plague when it reached the Rock in 1804. Strict orders were issued for Genoese and other Italians of French-occupied territories to abandon Gibraltar immediately. There was little response. When the other epidemics came in 1813 and 1814, they swept away 899 and 246 persons respectively. Even the Governor, Lieut. General Colin Campbell died in the last one.

As was to be expected, the destitute sought assistance at the church hospital. Fr. Dominguez immediately opened himself to the misery of the sick in the hospital. As he found it, the hospital could take in about thirty patients but, by moving the priests to other quarters, he enlarged it to a forty-bed institution. Once this change was accomplished he purchased the beds, mattresses, blankets and necessary linen to prevent the sick from having to lie on the damp floors. All these things he did without in any way consulting or involving the Junta. Questions like "Where is he getting all that money from?" "Is he presenting to the Junta a correct statement of accounts?" were going through the minds of the Elders. It was obvious the Junta did not like the manner in which he was doing his work without bringing them in.

When the French occupied Spain and the War of Liberation began many of the Spanish grandees took refuge in Gibraltar. (This was to recur when the Civil War took place in Spain in 1936.) In 1810 the people of San Roque came en masse and took up residence at Catalan Bay. Fr. Dominguez saw to it that these people were in no way deprived of spiritual care. When the war ended there was a thanksgiving service at the church of St. Mary the Crowned at which were present His Excellency the Governor, Lieut. General Colin Campbell and all the Spanish grandees, generals and colonels. Fr. Dominguez preached an extraordinarily long sermon which, while boring most of the people present, proved to be interesting reading in the handout printed especially by the El Calpense printing firm later on.

As time elapsed, Fr. Dominguez noticed that the Elders were not looking on him with favour. Assuming that they suspected him of being too pro-Spanish and not loyal enough to the British interests, he did not hesitate to point out what he had done for the troops.[9] When the Corpus Christi procession was organized to take place on the feast day, he discovered that the Catholic troops refused to march in it because they did not have decent helmets. Fr. Dominguez immediately sought the necessary funds to purchase them so that they participated in it. He was very proud to see them march so smartly.

Fr. Dominguez clashed with the Governor, General Don, around the years 1814–1815, and this ended with the Vicar's resignation. It was relative to the church hospital. Mr. Boschetti who headed the Junta in 1814 was also an architect. As a result of the epidemics the residents had experienced, and the manner in which the church hospital was overtaxed, he proposed to Fr. Dominguez ways and means to improve the hospital structurally and allow greater scope for emergencies. The Vicar would not agree. He would not allow the Junta to intervene in hospital affairs. This was his sphere. One day, when he least expected it, Fr. Dominguez heard in the street that a new hospital was to be constructed with the collaboration of the Governor. Whether Fr. Dominguez assumed that his hospital was to be pulled down and a new one constructed, or that his work would no longer be required we will never know. But, he wrote a letter to Governor George Don for enlightenment. To his astonishment the Governor replied with a most unexpected and explosive demand. General Don requested Fr. Dominguez to produce documents of ownership or lease of the hospital and a report of accounts.[10] The Vicar Apostolic knew he had none of the documents requested and no financial reports to present. He asked to see the Governor to explain to him personally exactly what he wanted to get clear in his first letter. The Governor insisted on the necessity of having those documents at hand if there was to be any meeting. The Vicar did not know where to turn. He did not want to turn to the Junta. He felt, deep inside him, that Boschetti and someone else were conspiring with the Governor against him. He noticed that things were no longer as they were before. He went his own way and the Junta theirs. He sensed tension developing within him, and an inability to cope with the situation. On Sunday 29 October 1815, Father Dominguez, at the age of 54, announced at every Mass said in the church that he had resigned as Vicar Apostolic.[11] He was leaving Father Juan Baptista Zino and Father Panizza to continue the work among the Catholics. He in fact hoped Father Panizza would succeed him as Vicar Apostolic. He said that he was resigning for health reasons and to recuperate. He left Gibraltar for Malaga where he took up residence. The news that the outgoing Vicar had shown preference for Fr. Panizza spread all over the Rock. The Junta considered this too presumptuous and rejected the candidate mentioned by the ex-Vicar. They wrote to Propaganda Fide giving their preference and naming Fr. John Baptist Zino, an Italian-born student of Propaganda Fide, well acquainted with Gibraltar affairs and a person who had shown his mettle during the hard times of the three dreadful epidemics by the care he had shown for the sick in the church hospital.

PART TWO

The New Vicariate Apostolic

The Very Reverend John Baptist Zino, Vicar General Apostolic.

CHAPTER ONE

Fr. John Baptist Zino

While the Sacred Congregation of Propaganda Fide considered the Junta's proposal, it was in the interest of Rome to discover what exactly was happening on the Rock. It appears that once Fr. Dominguez had left for Malaga, some Junta members discredited the ex-Vicar with the accusation that Church monies had not been accounted for. Fr. Dominguez naturally not only wrote back to publicly defend his good name, but also corresponded with Rome as to the accusation and requested the clearance of his name. Rome once again requested the assistance of the Bishop of Ceuta who had by now become Bishop of Jaen. Monsignor Esteban replied with definite impartial recommendations which Rome might or might not adopt.[1] He suggested: that the future Vicar Apostolic should be endowed with episcopal powers; that Rome should clearly outline the rules the Junta should follow in the selection of candidates for Rome to approve: rules for the manner in which the poor were to be assisted; that there should be three candidates named by the Junta, for Rome to appoint one as successor; that the three candidates should know Spanish, and this would inevitably open up the opportunity for a Spaniard to become a Vicar Apostolic.

Rome received all this information and these recommendations but preferred to manifest a steady and conciliatory attitude towards everyone involved. Fr. Dominguez's name was appropriately cleared with a fitting commendation by Rome for his loyal, dedicated and able service to the people of Gibraltar and the Church. On the other hand, Rome ignored the accusations made against Fr. Dominguez, and appointed Father John Baptist Zino as the successor. Orders were given in Rome for the Brief to be sent to Fr. Zino as the new Vicar Apostolic "senza titolo, e carattere d'vescovile".[2] On 25 January 1816, the Principal Secretary of State for the Colonies confirmed the appointment. Gibraltar was once and for all severed from the Diocese of Cadiz. This happy news was coupled with another piece of news that year: Mr. Boschetti had designed the new Civil Hospital; it was constructed in record time and put to use immediately. It was built in conjunction with the three leading religious denominations on the Rock: the Roman Catholics, the Anglicans and Jews. The Hospital had three wards, one for each of the different denominations. Each religious community had to subscribe towards the upkeep of the ward put under its care. Here was ecumenism working in a unique manner. No one, regardless of religion, in need of medical attention was at a loss for a place.

As the head of the Junta, Mr. Boschetti did not hesitate to write to Propaganda Fide. He wanted guidelines for the Junta to follow so that the Vicar Apostolic and the Junta might know exactly where they stood.[3] They wanted harmony and good order. The reply from the Sacred Congregation was signed by Cardinal Litta on 17 July 1817, but it did not arrive till Father Zino (he insisted that people should continue to call him "Father") received his Brief appointing him Vicar Apostolic many months later. The document contained ten articles. The first eight dealt with the Vicar Apostolic's spiritual obligations, the last two gave instructions regarding the Junta:

"Art.9. . . . Inasmuch as the Elders, as well on their part as on behalf of the Catholic people of that community, have undertaken to pay the Vicar Apostolic a daily pension of three gold pieces, by quarterly payments, and also to provide him a house, built for the said Vicar in 1804, it will be their duty strictly to fulfill the obligations so entered on.[4]

Art.10. . . . It will be the right of the Elders to elect a Treasurer and Collector, who shall diligently exact whatever money may accrue either from the pious oblations of the faithful or from ecclesiastical impositions and taxes, and shall lodge same with the Treasurer, giving due credit for the amount in the returns. Out of this fund are to be taken all emoluments, as well of the Vicar Apostolic as of other members of the Church, assigned according to the scale arranged in 1810, and if there be any surplus, it is to be applied to the reparation and keeping of the church, and in aid of hospitals and poor, a certain deposit, however being reserved for emergency.

The Vicar Apostolic was happy with this arrangement as the Junta was reminded from on high to pay him a regular salary; as a priest in the past he had often gone without one. On the other hand, the Junta was also pleased because the document made the situation clear, and furthermore recognized their standing. A chart displaying the table of fees for the administration of the Sacraments was printed and exhibited in the church in two places.

Baptisms:	In stole, with organ	2 doubloons[5]
	In cope, with organ	3 doubloons
	Cope, organ, illumination	6 doubloons
Marriages:	In Church, with banns	8 doubloons
	With dispensation of banns	24 doubloons
	In the house	24 doubloons
	In the house, with dispensation of banns	24 doubloons
Banns:	Publishing banns, for those marrying out of the garrison	8 doubloons
	Marrying out of the garrison with dispensation of banns	24 doubloons

Funerals: Without pall-bearers and with
undecorated coffin no charge
If decorated 4 doubloons

Fr. Zino was to hold office in Gibraltar for some twenty-five years. He seemed to work hand-in-hand with the Junta, which enjoyed ever increasing influence in the life of the people.[6] The Junta appealed to Rome for a Papal award to be granted to Fr. Zino. They petitioned that he be given nothing less than the Knighthood of the Golden Spur. The clearance was made with the British Governor on the Rock and it was granted to him in 1818. Permission was also granted to him to build a church at North Front, thanks to the donation of Mr. James Galleano. Such a facility would enable ladies to attend church services at North Front, and not in the city.

As the civilians living in Gibraltar already enjoyed freedom to practise their religion by the Treaty of Utrecht, and as restrictions concerning employment in Government departments and certain aspects of commerce had been lifted in 1807, the Catholic Emancipation Act of 1829 did not directly nor to any great degree affect Gibraltarians. With the passing of the Act, however, the Irish Catholics among the servicemen on the Rock now began to attend services in the local Catholic church, which they had not up to then frequented, being bound by military regulations.[7] They thus experienced the difficulties suffered also by the English Catholic civilian families, in particular the use of the Spanish language in the sphere of pastoral care and in Sunday sermons. A request for the appointment of English-speaking priests to help in this matter was promptly answered, because a Father William Macdonald started working for Fr. Zino. There are references in the church archives to military chaplains working alongside the local priests from the early 1830s onwards.

The year 1829 was, however, of some importance for Gibraltarians as regards civil liberties, for Mr. Barron-Field, who had been appointed Judge of the Civil Court in that year, and had quickly become dissatisfied with the juridicial system of the day, prepared a new Charter that would be more appropriate for the fast growing community of native inhabitants, in view of expected developments in the commercial, cultural, legal and religious spheres. His draft was studied in Great Britain and accepted. On 25 October 1830, he himself read out the Queen's Order in Council confirming his suggestions; and he was then sworn in as the first Judge of the Supreme Court.[8]

Gibraltar was not destined to fall behind in the education sphere either. In the British Isles, in the second decade of the 19th century, the National Society for Promoting the Education of the Poor in the Principles of the Church of England, was stepping up its activities, and by 1814, it had 230 schools for day pupils. Parallel to this development was the spread of the schools run by the British and Foreign Schools Society, a dissenting body. The Catholics likewise in the 1820s and 1830s were breaking through to large-scale education programmes for their poor through a Sunday School system.

But even before these stirrings, an educational movement had started in Ireland as a result of a call by Dr. Hussey, Bishop of Waterford, a busy Irish port enjoying close commercial ties with England and the New World; a call to resist the proselytising efforts of various Protestant organizations at work in the field of education. It was indirectly linked with the foundation of two religious Orders devoted to the Christian education of the poor. One of these was the Order of the Christian Brothers, which was to play an important role in the story of Gibraltar, from the ecclesial point of view, over the next century and a half.

In Gibraltar, up to the 1820s and 1830s, the well-to-do families employed private tutors for their children's education, but there was no primary education for the poorer classes. Lieutenant Sir William Houston, the Governor, was struck by this lack, and in 1832, took the initiative of summoning a public meeting with a view to remedying the situation. The result was the Gibraltar Public Schools – one for boys and one for girls – which were to be managed by a body composed of two standing members from each of the main Churches, the Anglican and the Catholic, together with a representative lay member from each of the three denominations (the Hebrew, Anglican and Roman Catholic communities), to be chosen annually. The Schools were to be maintained by annual public subscriptions. Among the Fundamental Rules of the new institutions was a "conscience clause", whereby the religion of the children receiving instruction in these schools was not to be interfered with. It was agreed that in Scripture-study Catholics were to use the Douai translation of the Bible and the Church of England children the authorized version. The girls' school was in Flat Bastion Road and that of the boys in Castle Road.

Unbeknown to most people, a Mr. Rule had already started a school in the previous year, partially as a means of backing up a proselytising campaign. The Methodist mission had begun as long ago as 1764. Its efforts had been focussed mainly on the Armed Forces but the mission bore little fruit, due to the opposition of Anglicans and the obstacles put in its way. Mr. Rule saw the establishment of a strong Methodist community on the Rock as a stepping-stone to the spread of Methodist teaching throughout the south of the Peninsula.[9] He took advantage of the petition of a few ladies, who wanted their children instructed in the English tongue, to set up a class which soon turned into a regular school with thirty boys and girls in attendance. He made no bones about his religious intentions, and soon was able to influence those Catholic children to join the Methodists. It was when he sent them to the newly founded Public Schools that his activities and the influence he was having on the children came to the notice of the Catholic clergy, who paid regular visits to the Public Schools to ensure that the religious beliefs of the children were respected. When Mr. Rule found that the conscience clause would prevent him dealing as he had done previously with the Catholic children, and that the Methodists could not be represented on the managing committee, he soon withdrew those thirty children and resumed his own classes in the Mission school. There the children were certainly taught competently and strictly disciplined, so that he was soon to be operating three schools on the Rock, two in the south and one in the town. By 1839 he was to have nearly 400 children under his influence, most of whom had been baptized members of the Catholic Church.

A first attempt to discourage Catholic children from attending Mr. Rule's classes was made through a series of conferences given during Lent, on the errors of Protestantism. Mr. Rule reacted with open-air preaching, before large crowds, on errors in Popish doctrine. He even interrupted the Catholic Lenten preacher in Church, arguing with him in front of the whole assembly until some of the men present fell on him, beat him and dumped him in the street.

He found support and consolation in the person of the Reverend William Robertson, a Presbyterian minister, who came to Gibraltar around this time. This gentleman considered that the great number of Presbyterians among the soldiers, as well as the merchants who were of that religious persuasion had been sorely neglected until now; that the great number of Jews, natives of Spain and of Barbary, resident in Gibraltar offered a most important field of labour; and that the native population – he referred to them as Spaniards – "would gladly hear the truth". In his book dealing with his residence on the Rock, he later described it as the "extreme outpost of Christianity in this part of the globe – an outpost pushed far within the lines of the infidel", and he praised Mr. Rule as a zealous and able man, "with every inclination to assume the aggressive and to make known the truth as it is in Jesus both to Jews and Papists". He said he was impressed with Mr. Rule's success with Gibraltarian Jews.

The next official step to counteract proselytism was taken by the Vicar Apostolic, Fr. Zino, together with the Junta of Elders. They would run a Catholic school on the lines of Mr. Rule's establishment.[10] It would be managed by a sub-committee of members of the Junta presided over by the Vicar. But there remained the question of who would teach in this school and how it was to be paid for. The Elders repeatedly appealed to Propaganda Fide to assist them in obtaining teachers for their planned school.

CHAPTER TWO

The Christian Brothers

Events connected with this project moved fast in 1835, perhaps too fast. On 4 July, the Sacred Congregation of Propaganda Fide in Rome wrote to Mgr. Zino to say how deeply impressed the Cardinals were by the constant requests of the many Irish Catholics in the garrison for a priest of their own nation to give them the spiritual help they needed; also by the trying conditions under which the Catholics lived, being obliged to send their children to Protestant schools, on account of the lack of Catholic teachers. "The Cardinals have decreed that one or two priests, experienced preachers, be procured from Ireland and at the same time one or two Christian Brothers". On 14 July, the Sacred Congregation wrote to Dr. Murray, Archbishop of Dublin, asking him to arrange for the dispatch of two Brothers and one or two priests. On 8 August, Fr. Zino sent a letter to the Cardinals relating his plans, but not to their Eminences' satisfaction. On 28 August Dr. Murray was able to inform Rome that he had found two Brothers for the Gibraltar School and a priest, Fr. Meehan, for the adults. On 12 September, the Congregation wrote to Fr. Zino, commenting that they had found his letter vague as regards whether one priest would be enough, and vaguer still about the coming of the Christian Brothers – whether these would be well received and all their needs met. The question of education the Congregation considered to be much more important than the other "inasmuch as you yourself state that a Methodist school is already erected and that approximately fifty (sic) Catholic boys attend it, and that the Methodists are looking for a site on which to build a new school". It was also anxious to know the results of the collection made for the funding of the Poor School.

For some reason the Congregation found it necessary to advise that the cash be carefully guarded; and it even promised financial aid for such an important work, should the necessity arise. On 29 October, the day after the two Brothers had left Ireland en route for Gibraltar, Fr. Zino informed Rome of the steps he had taken to prepare for the Irish priest and the Christian Brothers. The Roman authorities were pleased to receive the belated news, but told him to drop the idea of imposing a "tax for the benefit of religion" on the captain of each ship of a Catholic nation calling into Gibraltar.

Brother Patrick O'Flaherty and Brother Thomas Anthony arrived in Gibraltar on 3 November 1835, bringing with them books, prayer books, catechisms and school requisites paid for by Dr. Murray of Dublin. Once the warm welcome was over and they began thinking about preparing to open school, they were surprised to be faced not only with the Vicar Apostolic, but the Committee of the Junta of Elders who worked with him. O'Flaherty soon came to think that the Junta controlled rather than worked with Fr. Zino. Indeed, after three months' experience, he was to report to his Superior in Ireland that the Vicar was merely a tool in the hands of the Junta.

The Brothers found that the building in Parody's Passage would not be ready for some months to come; and when they found that they would be working in a Pay School they were even more surprised, for, in Ireland at that time, there was a serious division among the Christian Brothers over the question of working in Pay Schools, and Br. O'Flaherty happened to be among those who were opposed to the idea of this type of school, unlike Brother Edmund Rice, the Founder of the Christian Brothers, who was in the process of seeking permission from Rome to open such schools in order to finance Poor Schools for the more disadvantaged. The Elders of the Junta had likewise planned for the Brothers to teach in a Pay School in order to gain money with which to support a Free School. They were quite prepared to alter the formulation of conditions for admission to the school so that the Brothers would be able to teach with an easy conscience in the Upper Class. The compromise reached was that persons contributing any sum up to 32 dollars annually (about £5) could present children to the First School, and those giving more than that amount annually could present either their son or the son of some poor citizen. Honour was thus saved, and the school could be regarded as a Free School; it was thus named in the memorial presented to the Governor when he was asked for his patronage. The reality turned out to be that boys attended whose parents could easily have afforded to send them to colleges; and the Brothers taught in the Upper Class, while the Poor School proper was taught by two lay men.

The Brothers found that, according to the rules drawn up and published before their arrival, the day's horarium for classes was different from that to which they were accustomed in Ireland. They objected to this, since the Junta rather naively had thought that the climate of Gibraltar would make no difference to them or their pupils. Even over this point the Junta gave way, but it remained adamant concerning its control over matters such as entrance to and expulsion from the school, and the general control of school affairs by means of weekly meetings. The Brothers were not allowed even to deal directly with the parents of the boys. They considered that all this would undermine their authority and endanger discipline. Their colleagues at home in Ireland were already coming into conflict with certain bishops over the Brothers' determination to have no outsider interfering with their schools. The power of the Junta was evidently going to prove a great stumbling block.

When the school finally opened on 3 February 1836, so many destitute candidates turned up that not even one half of them could be accommodated. A room had to be fitted up in which 100 boys could be placed under the care of a schoolmaster: out of this group future vacancies were to be filled. But when this room in turn was opened up, the Brothers were faced with more than double the number expected. O'Flaherty calculated that accommodation for 500 should have been envisaged, rather than the room for fifty which had been thought sufficient at first. At all events, before the end of the month there were 260 children in the whole establishment.

When writing home to Ireland, Br. O'Flaherty could boast that within a few weeks of opening school he was able to march 200 boys, all in uniform, through the streets on Sunday before the astonished gaze of nearly all the personnel of the garrison. Yet he was not at all happy about the undertaking. He had understood that the limit in the Upper Class was to be thirty pupils. When it exceeded sixty, he went so far as to draft a letter to Br. Rice, asking for an extra Brother. He found, however, that the Junta would not pay an additional £80 from the 2000 and more doubloons in the Fund. A secular schoolmaster was therefore obtained, no doubt at a cheaper rate. It was not only the numbers but the potential of the boys that made O'Flaherty pessimistic. Most of them, he reported to Br. Rice, did not understand one word of English. They were as ignorant as possible. The so-called first-rate English school some had attended before the arrival of the Brothers had been run by soldiers, but he estimated that only five out of 130 boys attending their classes knew English well enough to actually follow his instructions. "All the rest, poor and rich, will be instructed by an interpreter".

Although O'Flaherty appears to have been a dynamic person in general, the two Christian Brothers did not seem, during the first three months when they were free, to have made a serious effort to acquire sufficient mastery of spoken Spanish to enable them to conduct the school properly. Certainly the Vicar Apostolic complained to Rome that they were "unwilling to study Spanish, which is as easy to learn as it is serviceable, and to acquire a knowledge of it is indispensable for the progress of the children in the school". It is significant for the short-lived project of a Christian Brother's school in Gibraltar that before the school had been open for one month, Br. O'Flaherty wrote to Br. Rice suggesting that they "could do better in a country where our language is spoken".

As the months passed, the weather grew hotter and the Levanter took its toll. The Brothers began to look forward to their summer holiday. O'Flaherty wrote to the Junta to inform them of the Brothers' custom in Ireland of taking a summer break of four weeks around July/August. He also wrote to the Governor of the Colony, seeking permission to use the military's bathing facilities at Ragged Staff. Permission was politely refused, as garrison rules were against outsiders using army facilities. The Junta, for its part, decided against a summer holiday for the children, and hence against a vacation for the Brothers, as the school had been open for merely five months or so; there was still the danger of the Methodists reasserting their influence if the boys were free; in any case, the other schools were continuing right through the hot summer months. Not only was the Junta slow in reaching this decision, it was also slow in passing it on to the Brothers. It was conveyed casually to Br. O'Flaherty by a member of the Junta who had not even been given the specific charge to do so. O'Flaherty wrote to the Junta, complaining about the way he had been treated, and emphasising the points at issue: the Brothers in Ireland were accustomed to a certain number of holidays; interference with internal discipline was intolerable; and an extra Brother was badly needed in order to cope with the current situation. Some four or five days later, the Junta gave in writing its reasons for the decision it had reached: they thought that, for the time being at least, the situation required exertions and sacrifices on all sides which might later be dispensed with; they could not go back on the printed regulations already widely distributed, in which no provision had been made for vacations of the type that were being requested.[2] They argued that the habits of idleness which the school was in the process of curing might surface anew with a long summer break. They had intended their unanimous decision to be conveyed to the Brothers verbally by any member to whom the convenient opportunity might present itself; they regretted that this had not been done with all the promptness desirable, but they maintained that any seeming want of courtesy was unintentional and not premeditated. They also assured Br. O'Flaherty that their stance in no way stemmed from dissatisfaction with the work of the Brothers.

O'Flaherty wrote immediately (25 August) to Br. Rice, urging him to inform Propaganda Fide and Dr. Murray. Br. Rice delayed his reply as he could not contact Dr. Murray, who was in London. O'Flaherty, being unable to contain himself for more than a couple of weeks, decided off his own bat, to try the ploy of saying that he had decided to abandon the mission; and he wrote to that effect to the Junta on 12 September. He made his decision quite clear, shortly and sharply, giving two reasons: the Brothers could not live their religious life properly in consequence of local circumstances, as the want of a proper residence together with other inconveniences was weakening their health; and they could not fulfil their religious and education mission vis-à-vis the pupils on account of their lack of knowledge of Spanish.

This letter startled the Junta into replying by return of post. Their letter of 14 September spoke of the dangerous and possibly fatal shock the interests of religion would suffer if they departed in this fashion. The Vicar and the Elders would be most happy, they said, to make every satisfaction, if they had given the Brothers any just cause of complaint.[3]

The impetuous O'Flaherty was probably relieved to see the door had been left open for him to have second thoughts; and he wrote on 17 September, emphasising the Junta's lack of consideration over the holiday question and the likelihood of his own health, and more particularly his colleague's health, being adversely affected by overwork.

On 19 September, the Junta members of the committee, but not the Vicar, wrote to say that perhaps they had erred and reached the wrong conclusions. They asked for further explanations, having the sincere purpose of setting things right, in order to preserve from ruin an establishment so highly conducive to the religious instruction of the rising generation. There were few sacrifices they were not prepared to make, they said. It was their wish that harmony and goodwill should prevail at all times.

Brother O'Flaherty must have thought he had won at least part of his case and, perhaps, also that he could drive a wedge between the Vicar Apostolic and his Junta. On 20 September, he addressed himself to Fr. Zino in person and said he would comply with the Elders' desire to know the reasons for his decision to withdraw, but would only give them verbally and in the presence of Fr. Meehan.[4] He misread the situation, however, for the Vicar in his reply stated that he had convened a meeting of the Board of Elders for Saturday 24 September, over which he would preside. Fr. Meehan and Br. Anthony could be present. But he agreed with the suggestion of the Elders that O'Flaherty should furnish in writing a condensed form of the points to be discussed at the meeting.

Br. O'Flaherty wrote back post-haste asking for the time and the date to be changed, since Fr. Meehan would be busy on the occasion envisaged. He stated, moreover, that he had no intention of entering into any discussion. He could come to give a verbal answer to the letters which he had received of late from both Fr. Zino and the Elders, but that was all. A position of stalemate was thus reached between the two sides on the Rock.

Shortly after this contretemps, the annual meeting for the election of a new body of Elders was held; and the Brothers received letters from the Head and Vice-Head of their Order. These "severely" reprimanded the Brothers in Gibraltar for their impatience, pride and independence in acting so outrageously as to bring disrepute on the Order. Little had been found in their reports on the situation by way of concrete facts or insoluble difficulties that might justify their action.[5] The authorities had realized, from the tone of the very first letter received from the Rock, that these Brothers would be difficult to please; and thought had already been given to replacing them with Brothers of more accommodating disposition. They were told not to abandon their post until asked to do so by the Superior General.

But the Superior General, when writing to his own brother, Father Rice, assistant to the Superior General of the Augustinian Order, defended the two Brothers as best he could. He asked his brother to see that the matter was put before Propaganda Fide for a solution, since the Christian Brothers had accepted the Gibraltar mission on the undertaking that it would be under the fostering care and protection of the Holy See and the Vicar Apostolic of the Colony.

The clear directive from Ireland had a steadying effect on Brothers Anthony and O'Flaherty, and on 13 October the latter informed the Elders of his intention to continue with the school. He also requested them once more to consider the three outstanding points that had led to the trouble: interference with discipline, the summer vacation, and the need for another Brother. It fell to the new Junta to reply to this peace offering.

The Elders began their long letter of 15 October with the assurance that they wanted to promote the interests of the school, meet the wishes and suggestions of the Superiors of the Order and give due consideration to the Brothers' comfort and convenience.[6] They mentioned also that, in view of past events, they had taken soundings and sought for help in other quarters. They would not, they said, allow themselves to be outdone by the Methodists, who were always ready to hold out secular inducements to obtain spiritual conquests. As a body, they shared the Brothers' anxiety to see greater progress made in the field of religious instruction; and no expense would be spared nor exertion shirked in order to further that end, though they had no concrete proposals to make for the time being. On the other hand, while the new members appreciated in the abstract the convenience of the proposal to put a summer vacation into the school calendar, they would prefer in the concrete not to implement it, for already too much spare time had been granted to the children in the form of classless Saturday mornings (one of the concessions made by the previous Junta) and the many days of Obligation (on which the boys were free, once their religious duties had been fulfilled). Indeed, the members of the Junta were thinking of restoring the old custom of Saturday morning classes! They spoke vaguely of planning for the Brothers' relaxation when the summer weather came round again, but not for summer holidays. On the point of discipline, they promised always to uphold the authority of the teachers in the eyes of the boys and their parents. They could not, unfortunately, see their way to pay for another Brother, but, if either of the two Brothers were replaced, the Junta would willingly bear one-half of the expenses involved. In saying all this, they added, they felt no ill-will towards anyone, but looked forward to cordial cooperation with the Brothers from now on. The letter naturally aroused no great hopes or enthusiasm on the Brothers' side. The cooks might have changed, but the menu was the same, or perhaps worse.

The Founder's letters to Father Rice in which he related the "insults, harassments and unreasonable requirements" suffered by the Brothers had been passed on to the Sacred Congregation. Its Cardinal Prefect sought further information from the Vicar Apostolic of Gibraltar. Having heard both sides, the Cardinal informed the Founder (29 November 1837) that he had written to Father Zino asking him to settle differences with the Brothers, using the utmost gentleness, and to see to it that others did likewise, with all due courtesy. He also asked Brother Rice to exhort his men to be docile and respectful to the Vicar established in Gibraltar by the Holy See, and to do their duty with greater alacrity and zeal, not slothfully; and to put the Glory of God and the service of the neighbour before their own ease. Harsh as these words were, the Sacred Congregation said it could not "take calmly if it should see destroyed the work of the schools which had begun so well, and for which it had spared neither concern nor expense" (!) There was a final word of consolation: if the Brothers felt themselves overburdened in anything, they should explain the whole matter sincerely and specifically to the Sacred Congregation – and patiently await its decision.

With a sad heart, Brother Rice discussed the contents of this letter with Dr. Murray. He was somewhat consoled to hear from the Bishop the comment that, despite the small amount of progress made by the Brothers as a result of their ignorance of the Spanish language, they had already achieved a great deal by destroying the attraction of the Methodists' school, and breaking the proselytisers' hold over the children.

Brother Rice wrote to the Brothers in December, giving them the substance of the Cardinal's letter. He made it clear, however, whose side he was on, for he added: "as regards the summer vacation, we are determined that you must get that". He recommended them to do the best they could, under the circumstances, as regards the religious instruction of the children. . . . and he trusted that "God will draw good out of the whole business".

From the tenor of the new Junta's letter, it would seem that unless some real change came in 1837, hopes of success in this foreign mission would not be realized. During the first half of 1837, O'Flaherty twice wrote to headquarters describing the difficulties the Brothers experienced in getting the children to conduct themselves properly, and the lack of improvement in the practice of Christian piety on the part of the children. The Brothers were clearly not in the best of health either, for they had now been teaching in unaccustomed climatic conditions for more than a year without a decent vacation. In May, the Founder took the step of sending out Brother Francis Corcoran, a non-teaching Brother, to assist the others as far as possible. More complaints reached Ireland in early June, whereupon Br. Rice showed the firmer side of his character and his loyalty to his Brothers. He wrote to O'Flaherty, in reply to two letters of "a very disagreeable nature". "You must tell these gentlemen that they are not to interfere with you, nor with the children. Upon the whole, I very much fear for the success of the mission altogether. Besides what I desired you to inform the Elders of, you can tell them also that you are to have the usual vacation in some part of July or August; and, should they refuse, write to me immediately, and in the meantime take the vacation yourselves, and do not go to school for them". He asked Br. O'Flaherty to put in writing and send to him whatever answer the Elders gave about the vacation, etc., and finally, not to fail in courage "for the good seed will grow up in the children's hearts later on".

As soon as he received these instructions O'Flaherty wrote to the Vicar (10 July). He asked to know his will on the question of the holiday with the least possible delay as he wanted to write to Ireland by the next boat. He added that "my superiors direct me to say that no-one can be allowed to interfere between the children, their parents and ourselves, except yourself and that all communications respecting their children be made to and settled by you or us".

It was clearly difficult for outsiders to understand the set-up of the Junta: whatever it directed or decided also implicated the Vicar, as he was the President of the Committee. As a structure, the Junta was unique: it was unknown to the usual run of Catholics living in Europe. On the other hand, there really was a danger of proselytism in the situation; and it was a fact that summer vacations for school children – be the idea good or bad in itself – were unknown in Gibraltar before the coming of the Brothers. Perhaps the educational practice of the latter was in advance of the times in some respects.

The very day that O'Flaherty's letter arrived (10 July) the Vicar hastened to state by letter that "no change whatever has taken place in the opinion which was expressed to you by the Elders and myself" – he was not going to allow a wedge to be driven between him and the members of the Junta – "that the allowing of such a vacation would produce the most serious prejudice to our schools. . . . We would be giving a great advantage to the Methodist mission and other rival establishments where no such vacation is allowed. . . . and such a step would be equivalent to shutting up the schools altogether". He spoke of the disagreeable necessity of objecting most positively to the proposed vacation.

O'Flaherty therefore wrote to Br. Rice telling him of the renewed refusal, but said that the Brothers would attend school until they heard from him. Br. Corcoran, who had been sent to help them, was now in need of their help: he had fallen sick with the heat and was confined to bed for several days. With this extra burden to bear, O'Flaherty dismissed the children, telling them to return within a fortnight. In making the decision he trod much more circumspectly than in the past, and addressed himself respectfully to Fr. Zino, once again trying to separate him from the Junta. He could not, however, resist putting into his letter a sting that belied the outward respect paid to the Vicar. The letter is worth quoting in full, for it reveals the tensions and feelings beneath the surface – not that there were not good reasons for the action taken by O'Flaherty.

24 July

Very Revd. Sir,

I am sorry that the exhausted and daily declining state of my health and that of my religious confreres obliges us to take the vacation ordered by our Superior earlier than we had intended. It grieves me still more that your protestation against obedience to our Superiors should be so strong and inculcates something opposed to that unity of purpose and action which is the best pledge of maintaining good order in every religious society.

Your judgement, Very Rev. Sir, on that as well as on every other occasion, I most sincerely respect, but twenty months of unremitting labour force us to take the little relaxation which is necessary to fulfil better the duties we have undertaken.

We have dismissed the boys, and their tender minds generously sympathised with us in our enfeebled condition, and they wished a speedy renovation to us, and both they and their parents showed a solicitude about us which we never in any way experienced from those for whose cause we left flourishing establishments in Ireland, and we were bound and called upon to protect our interests here.

If strength enables us, we shall return to resume our labours before the expiration of the usual vacation.

I remain, Very Rev. Sir,

Yours respectfully

P. O'Flaherty.

Perhaps Br. O'Flaherty thought he had a good case. There was an element of ambiguity at the end of the letter which, when the latter was placed before the members of the Junta by Fr. Zino, made them think long and carefully. They had their misgivings, but they evinced no immediate reaction to O'Flaherty's decision. Nine days later, however, they sent him their decision in a letter signed not by the Vicar, but by the Elders only.

3 August

Gentlemen,

The Very Rev. Vicar Apostolic has placed in our hands your letter received by him after your departure from the place, in which you inform him that the state of your health has obliged you to take the vacation ordered by your superiors earlier than you had intended and that you have dismissed the boys.

Your conduct in thus taking upon yourselves to abandon the schools without the slightest intimation of your intention imposes on us the painful duty of informing you that we cannot admit of any further interference on your part with regard to our schools and that we have taken prompt and, we trust, efficient measures for speedily procuring new teachers from England.

The Elders locked up some of the Brother's property in the school storeroom, got a person to take charge of the children for the time being and advertised the vacancies in the local press. They made Fr. Meehan responsible for the furniture of the house.[7] Two of them also sent an insulting letter to O'Flaherty, who reported this to the Vicar and sought an interview with him. It was not granted. The Brothers, then having no means of livelihood or other funds, took advantage of a favourable opportunity about the middle of August to take a boat back to Ireland.[8] The founder, undoubtedly saddened by the outcome in Gibraltar, wrote his feelings on the subject to his brother in Rome.[9]

Fr. Meehan later reported that after their departure, a worn-out soldier, whose discharge had been purchased, was employed in the lower school at a salary of £60 a year and had been given an assistant. "In the Upper School is a clumsy fellow – he has £70 and has an assistant also. It is said that the Londoner, if such he be, does not please them (the Junta)". It is also recorded that the local priests took on the teaching of the children in the Upper Class. It is difficult to know how much credence to give to Fr. Meehan's account. He was no friend of the Junta – though he still had to get his salary from them – for he referred to them as the "worst kind of Masons, a sort of half-sacrilegious kind of group".

Applications for admission to the Poor School increased so much that it became necessary to enlarge the premises. The Junta acquired a building next to Parody's House, but this purchase left them without resources to pay for the teachers or repair work. Fr. Zino appealed for help to the Governor late in 1837, without receiving a reply. Another letter some months later did result in a favourable answer, and a Government grant was promised, to be calculated on the basis of the total amount of money collected each year in the subscription fund. The amount would be equal to one-third of the total sum collected from the citizens. The first of these grants was made in 1838 to both the Gibraltar Public Schools and the Catholic School (later, the Methodists also received a grant). It is worth noting that the first Government grants in England (20,000 for building only) were not made until 1832, and were divided between the National Society and the British and Foreign School Society. Once more Gibraltar was at least keeping up with developments elsewhere in British territory in the education sphere. Catholic Schools for the poor in England were not to receive Government aid until 1847.

The departure of the Christian Brothers did not solve the Junta's problems. A new Protestant school, called the Christian Knowledge Society School, was established in 1838. It was staffed by teachers from England and managed by an ex-Catholic priest. Great numbers of children who could not find places in Catholic schools began to attend this new one: and before long, the Society set up another school at the other end of the Rock.

In the statutes of these schools there was no "conscience clause" to prevent proselytism: it was assumed that Catholic parents, by sending their children there, agreed to religious instruction being given along Protestant lines, since the overt aim of the schools was to "educate poor children in the doctrines and duties of Christianity as taught by the Church of England". The education was free and given in the Spanish language.

Instruction was given in Spanish also in Mr. Rule's school: the day was hallowed by prayer; the Bible read as a class-book; the Wesleyan Conference Cathechism was learnt; and all the children were assembled every day for divine worship. On local feast days, Catholic children were still expected to attend classes. "No concession whatever has been made to popular prejudice", Mr. Rule reported.

In October 1839, the centenary of John Wesley was celebrated with pomp. Mr. Rule organized a great public party "in real English style", and he got four hundred boys and girls to march in procession along the Main Street, singing hymns and carrying banners announcing in three languages that "Hitherto the Lord hath helped us". This was interpreted as a boast that he had gained this great number of adherents from the Catholic Church. Fr. Zino, who had just received news from Rome that a new Vicar Apostolic had been appointed for Gibraltar, immediately reported to him all that the Methodists had been doing as well as the general situation and the inroads being made by proselytizers.

The Right Reverend Henry Hughes, O.F.M.,
First Vicar Apostolic
Episcopus Heliopolitanus: 26th March 1841
Resigned: left Gibraltar 1856.

CHAPTER THREE
Henry Hughes O.F.M.

The weight of the complaints sent by Dr. Murray, Archbishop of Dublin, Brother Edmund Rice and his priest-brother, then resident in Rome, had a profound impact on the Prefect of the Sacred Congregation of Propaganda Fide: in its view the Junta was behaving in a most unorthodox manner and was made up of many freemasons. It was un-Catholic, and hence it had to be stopped. The wheels of change started moving within the Sacred Congregation and, with the further assistance of the Archbishop of Dublin, the set-up in Gibraltar was to be given a different form. The new Vicar would have episcopal powers with authority and the right to possess all the temporalities of the local Church.

Before Fr. Zino heard of all these manoeuvrings, Dr. Murray found the candidate he considered suitable for the difficult task. Once Propaganda Fide heard of the new candidate they informed Fr. Zino of Rome's intention. He was to be relieved very soon and he was to leave the place immediately after receiving a generous grant from the Junta.[1] As was to be expected, Fr. Zino was dumbfounded at the orders received. So was the Catholic population. There was a split among the people.[2] Some very eloquent people grouped together to blame the Junta for what had happened. They insisted that the Junta should immediately make representation to Rome to stop the injustice that was being done to Fr. Zino. They wanted no one but Fr. Zino to govern them in Gibraltar.

Was Gibraltar to forget the many hardships Fr. Zino had experienced for their sake during the War and later on in the three epidemics? Forget his work for the sick in the church-hospital? The Junta was pressed to do something about it. The Junta could do nothing at all. They had no reply to these expressions of support for the old priest. What could they do? This was in fact the first time since the Junta was formed that a new Vicar was chosen without their involvement one way or other. Rome had preferred to ignore the Junta in selecting a successor. They were being criticised for what happened when in fact they had no inkling of such a move. The people continued to harass the Junta and even blamed them for the many children who were leaving the Catholic schools to attend the Protestant ones.

The Junta, hurt by Rome's sudden disregard for them, nevertheless did not show disrespect for Rome's decision. Publicly they showed submissiveness and loyalty to whatever decisions emanated from the Eternal City. These educated men were, however, not to miss the point of the new change. They knew that with episcopal powers and the right to possession invested in the Vicar Apostolic, the Junta's days were numbered. The writing on the wall was all too clear. The Junta was to be done away with. Still the Junta preferred to wait and see how it would be done. It would not be easy because the Junta had certain civic commitments to fulfil. Then, too, the Vicar Apostolic might want to use the Junta for some other purpose. Who could tell, then? They simply waited.

At the suggestion of Dr. Murray of Dublin, the forty-nine year old Provincial of the Franciscan Order in Ireland, Fr. Henry Hughes was appointed. He had a good knowledge of Spanish, having trained in Salamanca, and had already shown great talent and zeal in his priestly and pastoral life. He was consecrated in Rome in 1839 by Cardinal Franzoni. The title given him was Bishop of Heliopolis. He was also put into the picture as regards the problems of Gibraltar in the sphere of education by the same Cardinal Prefect of the Sacred Congregation for the Propagation of the Faith.

Bishop Hughes arrived in Gibraltar in January 1840. He received a warm welcome. Great pomp marked the occasion of his official installation. The Junta was to the fore on both occasions. The Bishop allowed the Junta to continue functioning: he collaborated with its members, presiding over their regular meetings.

In that same year the Upper Class of the Catholic Poor School had to be closed as the local priests were unable to carry on teaching in it. This withdrawal meant less secondary education for the children of the wealthy and hence the drying up of a source of much needed income if classes for the poor were to be continued. Moreover the government grant was bound to diminish in proportion to the decrease in voluntary contributions. The Treasurer, Mr. Bartholomew Mascardi, left no home unvisited in his attempts to raise alternative funds.

In the spring of 1840, the Junta reported to Bishop Hughes that the Catholic children attending the Gibraltar Public Schools were being forced to use Protestant religious books in the Religious Instruction periods. The Bishop thereupon asked the Colonial Secretary to call a meeting of the school's Managing Committee. This was held on 8 May 1840. Chief Justice Barron-Field presided and Mr. Benoliel represented the Hebrew community. Dr. Hughes drew the committee's attention to the second rule of the Institution that "no attempt shall be made to interfere with the particular beliefs in which it may be the wish of the parents to educate their children". The committee finally agreed that the Vulgate translation should be used by Catholics instead of the Authorized Version, just as the Douai Catechism was used instead of the Protestant Catechism. A week later, however, Dr. Burrows, one of the committee members, withdrew his agreement, and suggested that it might be better if the two Christian Churches sorted out both funds and scholars and began two separate schools, each to be conducted on denominational lines. The Jews would then be left with a choice between the two. The suggestion was not adopted and Dr. Burrows resigned from the managing board.

Much as Bishop Hughes appreciated the Junta's warning regarding the danger of proselytism, he very soon realized that the ongoing activities of the Junta itself constituted a spiritual cancer within the Church. In fact, he was quicker than most to see the intricate network of forces operating on the Rock. So while presiding at the Junta's meetings, he had secretly ordered his priests to quietly visit the poor people's homes and put their Christian lives in order, without charging them "un centimo".

The Bishop had discovered that there were at least three hundred couples living in concubinage on the Rock. To his astonishment he found that this irregular relationship had stopped people from bringing their children to receive baptism, and because they were not baptised, they were not entitled to a christian burial. In his endeavour to get to the roots of this state of affairs he discoverd that it was all due to the emergency law laid down by the Governor, General Don, some thirty years earlier to curtail the continuous flow of people into the Garrison of Gibraltar. Gibraltar's sanitary system and perennial housing shortage had earlier on in the century been utterly inadequate to cope with the masses of political refugees settling down in Gibraltar. This had resulted in a series of epidemics and over 6000 people were killed by them. General Don would not have another epidemic and so laid down the law to restrict the flow. One way of stopping the more subtle of the non-British foreigners was to refuse them marriage to local females unless a dispensation was granted by the Governor and a payment of twenty-four doubloons were paid out for it.

Father Zino had quickly seen the harm that would befall the poorer class of people. He lost no time in objecting to the imposition of the rule but it was of no avail. In contrast, the Junta of Elders, rather than support their Pastor, accepted the ruling even though it harmed the people's spiritual life, and took on the responsibility of collecting the fees for each of the weddings dispensed and carried out. In reality only wealthy non-British foreigners did get the dispensation and were properly married. The poorer people would not even apply for a dispensation because of the very high fees. Without the dispensation no priest could marry anyone on the Rock. The people, therefore, lived together and resigned themselves to the stigma of being regarded as public sinners and be deprived of the Sacraments of the Church.

Bishop Hughes would not tolerate this situation any more and accordingly sent his priests to marry and baptize people in their own homes, without charging for their services. There is no doubt that what was happening in Gibraltar was known to everyone, even to the Junta of Elders. There are very few secrets that can remain undiscovered for long in this town. Then two things occurred that upset this "modus vivendi" between the Junta and the Bishop.

One day in August 1840, a well-known man in Gibraltar died.[3] His wife had called for a priest to administer the Sacraments to him before he passed into an unconscious state. When he died and arrangements were made for the funeral he was carried to the church of St. Mary the Crowned. Suddenly the priest conducting the service abandoned the corpse in the church with the excuse that "the man could not be given Christian burial because he was a freemason". The crowd present and the whole of Gibraltar afterwards were scandalized by the incident. The Elders, after an emergency meeting which the Bishop could not attend, decided to inform the Governor, General Sir Edward Woodford, that they had played no part in the incident which they deprecated. On being told of the Elders' communication to the Governor, the Bishop changed his attitude towards the Elders. He started questioning their authority.[4]

While this issue was still being disputed one very keen priest, unknown to the Bishop, decided of his own accord to take down the TABLE OF FEES from the church walls. This was intolerable to the Junta. They blamed the Bishop for this and so decided there and then to show the Bishop who in the Church in Gibraltar had authority. The Junta challenged the Bishop over the removal. He pointed out that no order to this effect had been given: he had merely told the priests to administer the Sacraments wherever necessary, without asking for fees when insistence on these was impracticable. First things first: the spiritual life of the people was all-important. He patiently explained that, as Bishop, he had full powers over the spiritual and temporal matters of his Church, and the step he had taken was based on conscientious and pastoral motives. The Bishop took it for granted, as would any other Bishop of the Roman Catholic Church in any diocese, that the Elders could not force him to charge for the administration of the Sacraments. He ignored the Junta's insistence for some recognition of their authority on temporal matters. In view of the Bishop's unwillingness to yield to their demands they took the matter to the Supreme Court and thus cleared their lawful position.

The Junta's case was put by a lawyer. The Junta claimed that it had the right to the exclusive regulation and reception of all monies given by the faithful to the Catholic clergy in Gibraltar for the administration of the Sacraments and the performance of the various religious offices of the Church. It required of the Bishop all the money collected by him and also the £300 paid to him by the Receiver General of Gibraltar by order of Her Majesty. In addition, they wanted the Table of Fees put up again in public, in the church, as before. And so to support their arguments the Elders presented the well-known Mr. Francia to testify that the Junta's rights and practices were of long standing – "from time immemorial". They produced the decree of the Prefect of Propaganda Fide of 1817, in which mention was made of the duties of the Junta, and claimed that this communication was recognition of their rights.

The Bishop explained, through another lawyer, that as ecclesiastical superior lawfully appointed to the Roman Catholic Church in Gibraltar, he had full right, power and authority to manage and direct all concerns and affairs of the Church, and to administer its revenues according to the established rules and regulations of that Church. He maintained that no assembly of laymen had or should have any right to interfere in the management and government of the said Church. It was the Bishop's duty to regulate the accustomed dues and payments made to the clergy in such a way that there would not be any hindrance to the administration of the Sacraments and rites of the Church, through the exaction of amounts beyond the resources of the faithful. He considered the fees to be too high and in need of alteration and revision: the fees insisted on in practice by the Junta were more than could reasonably be expected from poor Catholics. It was his duty to rectify this situation for several reasons. For one thing, the past state of affairs resulted in concubinage: that was why he had directed his clergy not to make fees a condition for the performance of spiritual rites on behalf of those who sought them from the Church.

The Chief Justice studied the affair and the relevant documents. In October 1840, he gave his verdict, namely, that if the Bishop had examined the documents studied by the court he would have acknowledged the authority of the plaintiffs and have adhered to his practice at the beginning of his period of office when he cooperated with the Junta. He knew the Bishop fairly well, as he had worked with him for some time on the Public Schools Committee. The Chief Justice told His Lordship quite frankly, that, in the light of the documentation, the law was against him. The force of "custom" or prescription showed the Elders possessed rightful authority. The Chief Justice, therefore, recommended the Bishop to become once again the President of the Junta and to devote his rank and talents to the welfare and harmony of the Catholic Church and its community.

The Bishop lost no time in writing to Rome to give an account to Propaganda Fide of the strange situation. Rome was astonished to hear that the few laymen, the "so-called Junta", had taken the Bishop to a Civil Court. "The power which the mis-called Catholic Junta aims at arrogating to itself is an absolute usurpation" which could never be recognized by Rome. The Bishop was ordered to put an end to their jurisdiction and to tell them to dissolve their body. Their ignorance may have been an excuse in the past, but from now on they should know that they could not interfere in matters appertaining to the Church. They were exposing themselves to the danger of incurring the most severe censures, if they obstinately persisted in carrying on a battle against their Bishop by appealing to lay tribunals, contrary to Canon Law, in matters which solely appertained to ecclesiastical authorities. Rome was obviously annoyed as well as surprised.

Once the Bishop received Rome's reply, he did not hesitate to write to the Secretary of the Junta, Mr. Emilio Gonzalez de Estrada. In it he accused the Elders of insolence for interfering in purely ecclesiastical matters and for denouncing him to a protestant Governor. He pointed out that the Elders were destroying the peace and harmony of the flock with their usurped authority. He, therefore, had no alternative but to counteract them to safeguard the independence of religion, so necessary for the development of virtues.[5]

Since the Junta's case was being fought on the basis of the "force of custom" or "prescription", the Bishop argued at length to show that there existed no grounds for "prescription". He pointed out that since the Junta of Elders had been instituted it had changed form six times. There were no fixed laws governing its activities. There was no determined way of voting, methods were always changing, abolishing, renewing without any fixed or permanent objective, except an aversion to religion. If "prescription" was claimed, which of the different Juntas was being pointed out as having authority? They were all different. The current Junta was called "popular" by the Elders. Yet, the Bishop pointed out, only 100 of the 10,000 Catholic inhabitants were allowed to vote for the twelve men for two duros (which were often never paid in). The Bishop insisted that the Junta was not a popular one since it claimed to represent a people who never voted for it and who were never allowed to vote for it.

The Bishop did not mince his words in his condemnation of the Elders' activities:

> *"Believe me, Sir, you are not representatives of the Catholics of Gibraltar, but a few evil and irreligious men. You lament the evils that had befallen the local Church in the past while at the same time you allow sacred and religious vessels to be disposed of, out of sheer greed, by some members of the Junta. You have witnessed also how with the priests' money the members have carried out business transactions, buildings constructed and properties purchased. You have seen the poor punished with the widespread concubinage of hundreds of brother Catholics. Because I would not allow that the sustenance of nine or ten individuals in this church should fall in the hands of the Elders, you reproach my conduct and denounce me to the Governor; you call me before the Court of Law, and you declare prophetically: 'that the peace of this town will not be restored, while the present Vicar Apostolic remains. . . .' You threaten my imprisonment, as if the prison would terrify a Catholic Bishop, who labours to obey the rules and laws of the Church."*

Angered by the Bishop's letter the Elders wrote back and alerted the Chief Justice to the fact that the prelate had not complied with the instructions given in court.[6] The Chief Justice was forced, therefore, to officially declare on 22 January 1841 that the plaintiffs were the duly constituted Elders of the Church of St. Mary the Crowned. . . . "the Bishop should pay to the Treasurer all the fees and monies of the funds of the said church. . . . and to pay him monthly and every month all such fees and monies as shall be collected as funds of the said church. . . . and neither he nor the clergy nor anyone acting under his orders should interfere in the managing of the funds of the said church", and that the Bishop should pay the costs of the Court case.

The Bishop did not agree with the verdict and decided to present his case to the Court of Appeal which for Gibraltar then was the Privy Council. On 9 February, he asked the Chief Justice for copies of the proceedings in order to state his appeal. The Chief Justice gave leave for the appeal on 12 February, but insisted that the Bishop comply with the decree and pay the £500 in advance before starting on the appeal. The Bishop was clearly not used to English law – he wondered how he could appeal against the decree if he was forced beforehand to carry out its dictates. When he decided not to pay heed to this notice, the Court issued an attachment against him for contempt of court. On 5 March, the Bishop was committed to prison until such time as he cleared the contempt.

Catholics in England and Ireland reacted against these bizarre happenings. The clergy in Ireland sent a petition to the Archbishop of Dublin asking him to appeal to the Queen against the imprisonment. The Archbishop wrote to Lord Russell, the Secretary of State for the Colonies, claiming that the proceedings against the Bishop were oppressive and unlawful: and he prayed for redress. The reply came back from Russell that he had no power to deal with the case; it was for the Privy Council to decide. The Junta wrote a malicious letter to the *Dublin Evening Mail* when they heard about the steps taken against them, and a spate of comment appeared in various magazines, some of it smacking of the old anti-papist attitudes, which had progressively and happily been absent from Gibraltar since its capture from the Spaniards. One writer saw it as the beginning of an "affair involving the re-establishment of the old Romish domination over the western Churches of Europe". He hoped it would actually turn out to be "the vindication of the principle of civil and religious liberty against the combined assaults of Propaganda, the College of the Jesuits, and the Hiberno-Papal influence". Shades of the Counter-Reformation! Mr. Weld, a descendant of an old English Catholic family and Chairman of the Catholic Association, (whose son is to appear later on in the story) also made a strong representation in favour of the Bishop, obtaining for the Bishop the best English lawyer available. Daniel O'Connell approached the Duke of Wellington over the affair.

The Privy Council advised Her Majesty to grant the Bishop's petition, suspending the effects of the decree and also ensuring the release of the Bishop from prison. Even so, it appeared that this could not take place until the Elders had consented to it! The Junta duly held their meeting – without their president – and agreed to their president being released from goal. It may read like something from Gilbert and Sullivan, but it was deadly serious at the time. The Supreme Court handed over the Bishop the necessary documents and the Bishop then appealed to the Privy Council. . . .

The verdict of the Privy Council was that the Junta of Elders had an undeniable authority acquired by force of custom.[7] The Bishop was bound to accept their legal standing in Gibraltar and respect their obligations and duties.

In 1842, Dr. Burrows, formerly of the Gibraltar Public Schools Committee, himself started a new Anglican school for girls. Once again some poor Catholic families took advantage of the educational opportunity offered and sent their children to this school. Here too, these Catholic children were subjected to Protestant-oriented religious instruction. Dr. Hughes decided to go to the roots of the problem. With his experience of Irish affairs he was well aware of the successful developments there in the educational field both for girls as well as for boys.

He wrote to the Archbishop of Dublin, Dr. Daniel Murray, for assistance. Dr. Murray in turn, happy to be of some use and proud to have been instrumental in establishing the Irish branch of the Institute of the Blessed Virgin Mary in the person of Mother Frances Ball in Ireland, referred Bishop Hughes' invitation to her. With the readiness of a Spirit-filled missionary Mother Frances immediately accepted the challenge. Gibraltar was to be the second mission to be started in 1845 outside the British Isles. The other one was Mauritius.[8] Bishop Hughes was more than overjoyed when he heard the Loreto Nuns would be sent over. He therefore started thinking of the necessary arrangements for the newcomers.

Forewarned is forearmed; Bishop Hughes set about this new venture very carefully. He would have to get a convent as well as a school for the nuns – one of the complaints of the Christian Brothers in 1836–37 had been the inconvenience of their accommodation. The property would have to be big enough to accommodate both buildings, but funds were too low to enable the Bishop to rent, let alone purchase, a decent site. As a last resort, he had recourse to Propaganda Fide and was much relieved to receive a favourable reply. With the money sent from Rome he bought a property known as Gavino's Dwellings, just off Cornwall's Lane.

It was on 13 December 1845 that the three Loreto Nuns and the one lay-sister arrived in Gibraltar.[9] The whole town turned out to receive them. The Cathedral bells rung with joy, the troops lined Waterport Street up to the Cathedral and His Excellency the Governor together with the Bishop and the Junta of Elders waited on them to give them a formal welcome. Thus it was that a strong bond was formed between the Institute and Gibraltar, a link which has remained unbroken to this day. Where one man sows another reaps: it was a different Bishop who was to benefit from the coming of the nuns.

The uncomfortable atmosphere in which Bishop Hughes had to work and the climate of Gibraltar had its effect on him. All through his life as Bishop, he suffered greatly from bronchial trouble. It was during one of his convalescent periods at home in Ireland that he resigned his bishopric and recommended Father Scandella to Rome as his successor. His recommendation was accepted.

John Baptist Scandella

The Right Reverend John Baptist Scandella
Vicar Apostolic
Episcopus Antinopolitanus: 30th November 1857
Died: 27th July 1880.

John Baptist Scandella, born in Gibraltar on 19 September 1821, was a member of an old Gibraltarian family of Genoese extraction. He had been a pupil of the Christian Brothers during their short stay on the Rock (1835–1837) and from an early age had felt a vocation to the priesthood. He did his priestly studies at the Urban College of Propaganda Fide in Rome. He proved a gifted student: on one occasion, he of all his contemporaries was chosen to defend Christian philosophy in a disputation held before a panel of Cardinals. He completed his studies "magna cum laude". Apart from his native Spanish, he had a good knowledge of English and was fluent in Greek, Italian and Latin. He perfected his English, as Vicar General to Archbishop Nicholson, when he had close contact with the British forces in Corfu. After ten years in that capacity he came back to his home town in 1855 to become secretary to Bishop Hughes.

The people of Gibraltar were overjoyed at having an indigenous Bishop; Rome seemed to be saying that the Colony was now mature enough to have one of its own to govern it spiritually. Dr. Scandella was consecrated in England as Bishop of Antinoe by His Eminence Cardinal Wiseman on 30 November 1857. Before returning to the Rock he made sure to visit the Secretary of State for the Colonies. From the latter he obtained unqualified guarantees of support in his new office. Bishop Scandella made education his particular concern. To employ more teachers he increased the fees paid by the wealthy inhabitants for having reserved seats in the choir loft. Furthermore the fees for members who wished to enroll in the electoral list for choosing the Junta of Elders was now raised to six doubloons – seventy men enlisted annually for this distinction. With the new income the Bishop also opened a new school, St. Bernard's, at Rosia Parade. This was staffed by clergy as well as laymen. When the Bishop founded the Conferences of St. Vincent de Paul in 1860 to cater for the spiritual and temporal needs of the poor, he pressed them to foster the education of children. The S.V.P. actually opened two schools, one in Catalan Bay and another at Lime Kiln Road. These were increased by two more in the crypt of St. Joseph's Church when it was completed in 1865.

Notwithstanding the continuous efforts made by the Bishop and his predecessors to improve Catholic education in Gibraltar, Bishop Scandella received quite a nasty blow from a most unexpected quarter. The Anglican Archdeacon Sleeman in a sermon at the Holy Trinity Cathedral praised the newly created Anglican school, "but of how much importance is it when three-fourths of those children are Roman Catholics who would otherwise be left in utter ignorance of God's Blessed Word".[1]. An open debate ensued in the *Gibraltar Chronicle* which led to the release of the Bishop's official edict. In it he stressed that while the "conscience clause" is upheld in the Catholic schools, the Catholic children attending Protestant schools are made to receive a Protestant religious instruction.[2] Catholic parents were discouraged from sending their children to those schools. It was later on revealed by Archdeacon Sleeman that Catholic children were no longer forced to take Protestant Bible studies.[3]

Bishop Scandella, as a Gibraltarian, saw to it that the original statue of Our Lady of Europe held at Algeciras since 1704 was returned to the Rock. To recover it he had to commit himself to get an exact replica of the statue made so that the people of Algeciras were not left without an image for their devotion to Our Lady. The statue returned to Gibraltar in 1864 and a chapel was built for it at St. Bernard's Road where it was enthroned in 1866. It was in that same year that the Papal States were appropriated by the leaders of the "risorgimento". Dr. Scandella rallied the Catholic community around him to support the Pope imprisoned in Gaetta. Long articles were splashed in all the local newspapers defending the rights of the Holy Father and decrying the injustices to him and the Church as a whole. The Bishop went as far as petitioning the British Government to send official complaints against the humiliating treatment meted out to the Holy Father.

It was at this juncture that the Pope called the First Vatican Council as if to call the world to order. He had by now transferred to the Vatican. Bishop Scandella took advantage of this Council to go to Rome and make his "ad Limina" visit and also attend the Council. Whilst there he informed the Congregation of Propaganda Fide that the Junta of Elders was no longer in existence. He explained that after Bishop Hughes' court case people started to lose interest in the Junta. The Members gradually stopped paying their subscriptions and did not enroll in the list of electors. In December 1864, of the expected 100 members there were only 21 members on the list from which a Junta was to be elected. The following year the list was made up of barely 15 and in 1866, there were a mere five. It had died a natural death.[4]

The Bishop's interest in improving educational facilities never flagged. Right to the end of his days he was ready to improve schools. In 1869, when he had to go to Rome for the Vatican Council, he contacted the Holy Ghost Fathers, who were thinking of leaving their establishment in Santarem, Portugal, as there was little prospect of obtaining vocations there for their Congo mission. Bishop Scandella offered them St. Bernard's School as their field of labour. He also offered to help them with the teachers if they took it over. The Father Superior of the Holy Ghost community visited Gibraltar to investigate the situation and it was soon decided that the Holy Ghost community of St. Bernard would be established on a trial basis – the conditions being: development of the school, and the setting up of a scholasticate and a novitiate for Brothers, should vocations be forthcoming. According to the Bishop, a lot of Spaniards would come to the Rock to be educated as the result of the suppression of Religious Orders and their schools in Spain. The Fathers took over the school on 20 August 1870. Before the first year was over, however, they began to have their doubts. Many schools were opened in Spain by non-religious teachers and there was too much competition among them for anyone to think of coming to Gibraltar for education. No vocations seemed likely to appear either.

So, by 23 October 1871, the Fathers decided not to carry on and to leave by Easter 1872 at the latest. St. Bernard's was thereafter transferred back to its original premises and the Europa Road site was given to the nuns who had spent some twenty-five years working in town. These premises in the more healthy district of Europa Road, were to prove their permanent home. They were to grow from strength to strength in the spacious grounds now available to them. They renamed their school Our Lady of Europa Convent School, because of the shrine of Our Lady located behind it. They also opened another school in Pitman's Alley.

The Bishop took a justifiable pride in the educational facilities provided for the girls. He considered that Gibraltar had means of social instruction and personal sanctification such as few cities could offer. In his opinion, Europa Convent School could stand favourable comparison with any good school in other European capital cities.

Success in this sector made him anxious to make more adequate provision for the boys, whom he wanted to see capable of occupying respectable and important positions in society. He envisaged them taking up careers in law, medicine, engineering, architecture and the naval and military professions. Such a goal required a school where boys could study literature, physics, chemistry, higher mathematics, etc. – in other words, a middle-class educational establishment.

Naturally, he thought of turning to the Irish Christian Brothers who had exercised "such a tender kindness in his earlier years in the Castle Ramp Upper School". But the Brothers had developed a lot since 1837. Their experience, not only in Gibraltar, but also in England, Australia and Ireland, had left them convinced that, for the permanence and security of the Brotherhood, it was essential that they be independent of governments, bishops, clergy and school committees, not to say Juntas. Indeed, at that very time they were withdrawing from their foundations in England, as they judged their security was threatened by certain bishops, clergy and committees: "those connected with such establishments in England, be they committed or patron, lay or cleric, always contend for the power to *rule*, and hence are jealous of having all legal rights vested in themselves – consequently hold the Brothers always dependent on them".

Brother Barry, who was most keen on establishing the Order in England, said he "had had enough of being at the mercy of every successive patron or committee who assumed the responsibility of management of the financial and other affairs of the school". Bishop Scandella's repeated endeavours to engage the Brothers naturally proved fruitless.

The Bishop turned to other Religious Orders in France, Belgium and England. He also had hopes of persuading the Society of Jesus to take on this prestigious school. Father Weld, a Jesuit, and son of Mr. Weld, the president of England's powerful Catholic Association offered to take on the directorship of St. Bernard's School. The Jesuits would run it, but it was necessary that the Bishop should meet the General. A visit was made by the Jesuit General, and a Convention was held to draw up the terms of agreement. The Bishop set about organizing the project with the cooperation of the School Committee, the members of which were Father Constantino Stephanopolis, Messrs. Mascardi, Peter Amigo, F. Balestrino, D. Madden, John H. Recagno, James

St. Bernard's School
Bishop Scandella with some members of the Junta.

Terry, J. Spotorno and M. Verano. It was a simple matter to give the proposed school a name: The Institute of the Immaculate Conception – just one year before he came back to Gibraltar as a priest, the doctrine of the Immaculate Conception had been proclaimed by Pius X, and during the first year of his episcopacy the apparition of the Virgin at Lourdes was reported. It was to be financed in the same manner as the Poor School in Castle Ramp, namely public subscription. It would teach Religion, English, Latin, Spanish, General History, History of England, Geography, the use of the Globe, Arithmetic, Reading, Writing and notions of Hygiene. The extraordinary subjects included: French, Italian, Book-keeping, Drawing. Parents would pay 60 doubloons and be entitled to send their sons to the school. The donor of 32 doubloons would be entitled to send one student for the whole course. Non-Catholic children would be exempted from religious exercises and studies if parents so wished. There were as many as 70 applicants for the new school. The list of subscribers was completed with the utmost speed by Mr. Mascardi so as to qualify for the current one-third Government grant as in the past. The sudden increase of income caused a flutter in the Treasury, for the colonial estimates for the year 1871 had already been determined and only £160 had been earmarked for this particular sector.

Seeing that his explanations for the increase were unacceptable to the Government the Bishop did not hesitate to appeal to the Earl of Kimberley, Secretary of State for the Colonies. If the Imperial Treasury, he argued, could increase the amount earmarked for sanitary work in the interest of public health, then no obstacle should be put in the way of the education of the poor. He was persuaded that neither in Britain nor the Colonies was less done by the Government for education. Britain spent 9/10d per annum for each child whereas in Gibraltar the capitation grant was a mere 2/11d per annum. He asked the Government to adhere honourably to the terms agreed on in 1838 between Church and State where the subsidy was apportioned by subscription list, not by the yearly estimates. Unfortunately owing to the ensuing turmoil and the weak chances of getting Spanish boys, the Jesuits too decided not to take on St. Bernard's School.[5] The Institute was, in due course, got under way by making use of the local clergy as full-time teachers.

In the midst of his educational projects the Bishop got caught up in a controversy that caused him great pain and made the end of his life unhappy despite the great things he accomplished. The British Government had decided in 1865 to introduce an Order in Council providing for the appointment of a Body of Sanitary Commissioners to see to the public wellbeing. These included local ratepayers, not elected but appointed by the Governor. The rates which were subsequently imposed on landlords and merchants to defray the cost of setting up an adequate sanitary service was frowned upon by traders. When, in the following year, another Order in Council was imposed, the traders resolved to seek greater local involvement in the making of such laws: a committee – the Exchange and Commercial Library Committee (ECLC) – was selected by and among the business interests involved, to represent the "interests of the people", and it immediately petitioned the British Government to revise the Orders in Council relating to the Sanitary Commissioners. The petition bore no fruit.

The Official Gazette of December 1872 next announced an Aliens Order, based on advice given by the Sanitary Commission and the Attorney General. The Government view was that the welfare of the people of Gibraltar could only be ensured by restricting and controlling the entry of Spaniards to the Rock. The ECLC met several times and drew up many suggestions for amendments to the Order that would make it work in their favour. Mgr. Scandella also worked hard, his goal being to make the ordinances less harmful to the ordinary people.[6] The efforts proved worthless, because the draft ordinances became law thirty-one days after their publication, and, he, being ignorant of Parliamentary procedure, did not present his views within the time given. By the end of the year, however, the ECLC had met frequently and produced a memorandum to be sent to Lord Carnarvon, the Secretary of State for the Colonies: the traders wanted their committee to have time to consider any legal enactments before they became law. These first democratic initiatives made little impact: a whole year was to pass before any reply to the memorandum was received. Even then it was not at all satisfactory from the ECLC's point of view in its search for some modicum of democratic expression.

Some years later came the news that the British Government had decided to reorganize the Customs services in Gibraltar. This move was the result of pressure being brought to bear on Britain by Spain over the smuggling of tobacco from Gibraltar into Spain, and the loss of lawful revenue to the Spanish Crown. On March 5 (1877) the *Gibraltar Chronicle* summarized the effects of the draft Customs Order in Council:

Masters of vessels on arrival in the Port will be required to make a report of the ship and cargo, and no vessel or boat will be allowed to sail from the Port without clearance.

Licensed hulks in the Bay will be classified according to the description of goods intended to be stored in them.

Hulks in which goods liable for duty, or restricted goods, are stored will be made subject to special Customs Regulations.

It is proposed to impose duty on tobacco or any other goods imported or exported. The duties will be limited to spirits and other liquids, and a uniform wharfage toll will be payable on all goods and packages landed at the Waterport Wharf and Stone Jetty, North Front.

It is proposed to limit the importation and exportation of tobacco and cigars to vessels of a certain tonnage, and the exporter will be required to give a bond with surety for the due landing of the tobacco at the port or place for which it was intended for shipment. The export of tobacco by land is to be prohibited except under such regulations and conditions as His Excellency the Governor for the time being may direct. In the interest of the licensed wine-house keepers and tobacconists, it is proposed to prohibit the retail of spirits and wines on board vessels and hulks in the Bay, and to establish two kinds of tobacconist licenses, one for all importers and wholesale dealers in tobacco, and one at a lower rate for manufacturers and retailers, not being importers or wholesale dealers.

The *Chronicle* thought the scheme would not affect legitimate trade, but would very much affect the smuggling of tobacco. Some other place would now be found from which to carry on the illicit trading, but Gibraltar's role and gain from this occupation would decrease. The people of Gibraltar knew in fact that it would ruin the traders and inflict hardship on many employees. The Bishop had an interview with the Governor and spoke along these lines. He then decided that some alternative plan must be worked out; and that, in the case of the scheme being persevered with, thought should be given to the need for full and ample compensation. As a lot of money was involved, the question would have to come before Parliament.

On 7 March, the Bishop met the ECLC and other traders of all races and religions in the Cathedral Hall. He found, to his surprise that the traders were not anxious to have him involved in this matter. He was, someone remarked, really meddling in their affairs. He was told to leave such matters to traders and to stick to his ecclesiastical duties. The meeting was therefore fruitless. After it, the committee went to see the Governor, and, on the following day (8 March) held a meeting in the Commercial Library, to which crowds of people went. The resolutions adopted were to the effect that the proposed Order was contrary to free trade, and harmful to the businessmen who had invested large sums in building stores for trading purposes. A fund was to be started with which to run a campaign to dissuade the Government from carrying on with the scheme. This stand was communicated to the Manchester Chamber of Commerce, which then contacted the Secretary of State for the Colonies. The latter gave an assurance that the people of Gibraltar would have the required time to have their say before the draft became law. The Bishop meanwhile had put his arguments on paper and had sent them to the Governor, who in his turn sent on this letter to the Secretary of State.[7] Many Spaniards across the border did not want these restrictions imposed either. The newspapers in Britain, however, supported the Government's idea. They hoped that trading relations between Spain and Britain would thereby be improved. They looked on the Gibraltarians as smugglers pure and simple.

Lord Carnarvon's reply to the ECLC stated that the traders' claim that the order was contrary to the 1705 Order of Queen Anne was mistaken as several Orders had been implemented since then thereby repealing it. He referred to "the systematic smuggling into a neighbouring country": measures tending to prevent frauds upon the fiscal laws of Spain were therefore not at variance with international law. He admitted that those doing the smuggling were foreigners, resorting to the Port of Gibraltar for purposes of smuggling: the part played by the Gibraltar community being no more than to sell goods to those persons in open market as they would to any other purchasers. The committee members then decided to try contacting various ministers in Parliament directly to get a different decision.

Bishop Scandella got in before them. He arrived in London on 10 June 1877. He soon found that both Protestants and Catholics were of the opinion that Lord Carnarvon was right, and that the steps to stop smuggling should have been taken long before. He wrote to Gibraltar suggesting that the committee hasten to London as quickly as possible. The businessmen in Gibraltar, however, had in the meantime heard that a Blue Book was being printed in which some documents of the Bishop were quoted. They suspected that the reason for this was that the Secretary of State saw in those papers information which would endorse the Government's intentions. In the Blue Book there was mention of Scandella's alternative plan, namely, extradition for the "crime" of smuggling.[8] The Government document admitted that the alternative scheme would certainly repress smuggling, but said it would likewise have as great an effect upon local prosperity, and upon the Spaniards in the neighbourhood, as would the measures proposed by the Government but deprecated by Scandella. It was also pointed out that Scandella's admission that almost all the tobacco imported into Gibraltar ultimately went to Spain, even if by way of Oran, Melilla and Ceuta. The traders were angry at this revelation of information, up to then concealed. The Bishop was accused in the newspapers of supplying the Ministry with intelligence that favoured its case – either out of ignorance of business matters, or perhaps in the expectation of getting in exchange some financial guarantees for his schools. On 23 June 1877, Messrs. Francia, Thomson and Schott sailed for England as a deputation from the Library Committee.

Meanwhile, the Bishop was surprised to find that the Blue Book contained his own papers which he had meant for the eyes of the Governor alone. He therefore wrote to the Secretary of State, pointing out that the Government had at least indirectly encouraged and sanctioned the tobacco trade for a very long time, thereby contracting serious obligations. Moreover, the Gibraltarians merely sold their goods to the Spaniards, who at their own cost and risk introduced them by fraud into their country. By this new law, the real authors of the frauds on the Spanish Crown would escape any dire consequences, free from loss and punishment, but the inhabitants of Gibraltar – perfectly guiltless – would be the principal if not the sole victims. The charges against the Gibraltarians, the Bishop said, were entirely contrary to fact. The lack of criminals on the Rock was remarkable: every year the Chief Justice congratulated the Jury on the absence of crime in the Colony. But those persons and their families who were dependent on the tobacco trade would be plunged into the greatest poverty. He added that this conviction was shared by the *Gibraltar Chronicle*, which was run by a committee of officers and an editor who was a captain in the army and aide-de-camp to His Excellency. He thanked Lord Carnarvon for receiving his ideas about extension of trade with Morocco, but that possibility lay far ahead in the future.

When the deputation from Gibraltar arrived in London (on 29 June), Mr. Francia lost no time in meeting the Bishop. He was fairly friendly and did not mention the reaction in Gibraltar to the inclusion of the Bishop's documents in the Blue Book. The Bishop told Mr. Francia about his plan to meet as many Parliamentarians as possible. This he later did and succeeded in convincing them all of the goodness of the Gibraltarians' cause. On the other hand, the deputation got nowhere with their meetings. On 2 July, Francia pointed out to the Bishop the ambiguities in some of the things he had said to the Governor in his writings. The Bishop promised to write to the Secretary of State, explaining those points more clearly. Unfortunately, poor Mr. Francia concealed from the Bishop the expressed wish of the committee – motivated by some information given by Jerome Saccone and others – that he, the Bishop, cease from all intervention, as his initiatives had already proved prejudicial to the interests of Gibraltar. It was only later that Fr. Canilla got to know of this, and insisted that Francia himself return to tell the Bishop. Mr. Francia finally blurted out that the Gibraltarian traders were angry that the papers written by the Bishop had been used in the Blue Book to their disadvantage. The Bishop was hurt, and indeed angry, about this, yet he was prepared to give way. He promised to limit himself from then on to winning friends privately so that the new Customs Bill would be defeated in the House of Commons. Fr. Canilla even read out to Francia another letter the Bishop was in the process of composing by way of answer to the Secretary's reply to his previous one. Francia accepted the contents of this letter as being just what he himself thought and would be ready to support. He apologised for having been so harsh, saying that he had spoken in his public capacity as chairman of the deputation rather than as a private person.

But on the following day, 7 July, a telegram from the deputation was received in Gibraltar attacking the Bishop very seriously. Either Mr. Francia did not tell his fellow members what had happened on the previous day at the Europa Hotel, or else he failed to convince them of the truth of his own experience, and the others decided to attack the Bishop notwithstanding. *El Calpense* published the contents of the telegram and gave the general impression that the Bishop's activities were prejudicial to the interests of Gibraltar. Yet, when Francia met the Bishop on 14 July, no mention was made of sending any telegram. Two days later, the Bishop got a letter from Mgr. MacAuliffe and a copy of *El Calpense* in which the inflammatory message was printed. For the Bishop this was the last straw. On 17 July he wrote to the Secretary of State, asking him to consider as withdrawn all his remarks and requests, for he found that the persons whose interests he had so much at heart wanted him to cease from all further negotiation. On 23 July came a reply from Lord Carnarvon stating that nothing said by the Bishop had in any way affected the kind of answer that the Minister would in any case have given to the deputation. In a later letter the Secretary of State pointed out that when the Government puts before Parliament all the available information pertinent to a question, such a procedure is carried out without considering whether any particular papers tend to support or oppose the Government's own views. Even Mr. Ryland, the Minister chosen by the deputation to look after the interests of the traders of Gibraltar, put it in writing that the Bishop had done his duty especially on behalf of the poor employees in Gibraltar; and that the strong claims he had pressed upon the Colonial Office to be given favourable consideration were all to the good; this had in no way weakened the efforts made by the traders to influence Parliament against the proposed measure.[9]

On 26 July, the deputation was able to say that it had been successful: the Prime Minister had said the ordinance would not be enacted until it had been fully discussed in Parliament. The members of the deputation received a great welcome when they returned to the Rock. They lost no time in getting down to producing serious proposals for the Minister. When a certain Mr. Shakery suggested that the setting up of a Fiscal House in Algeciras was the best thing proposed so far, he was howled down – it had been one of the Bishop's suggestions. From now on, nothing the Bishop had said was good. Mgr. MacAuliffe felt that the only way of clearing up the affair was to bring the whole truth to light. But when he wrote to bring the information to public attention it only showed up the deputation and the Exchange Committee in a bad light. The final state was worse than the first: the people were not prepared to see the deputation blamed for anything – they were the traders, the intelligentsia, the employers, whereas the Bishop was just an ecclesiastic. Articles were written against him by someone who did not like bishops – the writer signed himself as "De Mal en Pis".

Mgr. MacAuliffe and Mr. Francia used *El Calpense* and *The Gibraltar Guardian* to argue with one another about what actually happened and when, and argued themselves to a standstill. It was evident that the chronology of events was different on both sides. A group of reputable gentlemen finally wrote to both of them asking them to put an end to their public disputation. When the Bishop got back, he too wrote to the Monsignor officially asking him to put an end to the controversy. The result was a private letter from the Monsignor to Mr. Francia and another from the latter to the Monsignor, in very strong terms, accusing the Bishop of factual errors and misinformation from MacAuliffe together with a final request that the Bishop should not meddle in things "that you do not understand and that do not appertain to your Ministry".

During that busy and critical period in 1877, the Bishop took advantage of his trip to London concerning the proposed Customs Bill, to visit Ireland in the company of Fr. Gonzalo Canilla. He hoped for a meeting with the Christian Brothers and the opportunity to make a personal appeal to them to attract them back to the Rock. He talked to them in terms of opening a free elementary school and a secondary school on the Rock, and he even mentioned an industrial school. But he made the visit at the very time when matters were coming to a head in Liverpool between the Brothers and the priest-managers of St. Nicholas' School, over powers of admission and expulsion. It was also a critical juncture in the controversy between the Brothers and the Irish Bishops; were the Brothers to remain independent of the hierarchy?

Bishop Scandella came away disappointed. He set off for Gibraltar, still hampered by the effects of a fall he had suffered in Lisbon and weighed down by apprehension about the reception he was likely to get in Gibraltar for his role in the Customs Bill affair. He called into Paris in the hope of getting the Holy Ghost Fathers to change their minds about the schools. He also tried to get other Orders in France to lend a hand. Finally he decided that his search was, for the time being, fruitless, and continued on his way home.

He re-entered Gibraltar overland, via the Spanish border, to avoid a clash with his opponents, who were expecting him to disembark from a ship. He was immediately confined to bed. There he felt that his physical handicap was a block to furthering the many developments he wished for his town. Yet from that same bed he accomplished many things, including a successful outcome to the attempts to get the Brothers back. From his sick-bed he wrote a very strong letter to Cardinal Simeoni in their support.[10]

Despite the then uncertain future of the Christian Brothers as an Order, two of them came out to Gibraltar – one of them being the headmaster of the famous Artane industrial school in Dublin – to examine the situation at close quarters, with a view to eliminating the kind of problems that had marked the 1836/37 venture, should the prospects prove favourable. They succeeded in making a satisfactory contract with the Bishop: the Brothers were to be given a furnished residence and £60 each per annum as salary; travelling expenses would be paid in advance by the Bishop; limits were set to the number of boys per class; the Brothers would be free to live in accordance with their rules and constitutions in Gibraltar as in Ireland. In their turn, they promised to conduct the schools to the satisfaction of the Bishop and the public in general.

On 11 January 1878, four brothers – three teaching Brothers and one lay Brother – arrived in Gibraltar. They settled into a flat in City Mill Lane, as their own residence was not likely to be ready for another two years. Having taken over the Castle Ramp School, the Poor School and the Institute of the Immaculate Conception as well as the day and night school, they were, inside a few weeks, teaching a daily average of 280 boys. The two young Brothers were reported to be "capital workers in school, and at studying Spanish". As all seemed to be going well, the Superior General of the Order, at the request of the Bishop, decided to send two extra men out in August for the elementary school.

The Bishop, however, in his eagerness to get things done, started preparations for the opening of a secondary school in August. This annoyed the authorities in Ireland, as they were not yet prepared to undertake such a task. The idea of teaching in a fee-paying school was still a sore point among the Brothers. They had, in fact, no secondary schools at all at that time, and were in the throes of getting geared up to the new Intermediate System of Education in Ireland. The Bishop almost lost the support of headquarters by running ahead of their plans, but, in the long run, he did get his way and a secondary school was opened on 2 September 1878. Not only did two extra Brothers come in August but a further pair arrived in October.

The Bishop's idea of a school adequate for Gibraltar's need was certainly all embracing and ambitious for that period. The public notices which he issued stated that "under the patronage of the Right Rev. Bishop Vicar Apostolic" this schol was being established to "afford an English commercial and liberal education to the Catholic youth of Gibraltar, preparing for professional or mercantile pursuits or for the Civil Service".

"The course of instruction comprises English Language and Literature; the Latin, Greek, French and Spanish languages; History, Geography, and Elocution; Arithmetic, Handwriting and Book-Keeping; Algebra, Geometry and other branches of Mathematical Science; elementary Physics and Drawing. Special attention is bestowed on the religious and moral training of the students.

Applications regarding terms and further particulars to be made to the Director, Brother Stanislaus, Castle Gully, Gibraltar.

August 1878"

The school was to be set up in Commercial Square (the site of today's New Haven Government Offices in John Mackintosh Square). When the school opened the Bishop was sick in bed, and from there he lent his valuable support to the Brothers in their appeal to the Holy See against the Bishops of Ireland, who interfered with their lives and work. The case was finally settled in favour of the Christian Brothers on 3 December 1878.

IN DOMINO CONFIDO

The Right Reverend Gonzalo Canilla
Vicar Apostolic
Episcopus Lystrensitanus: 12th June 1881
Died: 18th October 1898.

CHAPTER FOUR

Gonzalo Canilla

In the Spring of 1880, the Bishop's health was clearly failing, but he had the consolation of knowing that he had achieved what he had dreamt of for years – adequate educational facilities for all the children. On 23 July 1880, he called to his bedside an old priest friend, Fr. Ferdinand Moreno, who had been sent to him by Propaganda Fide and had faithfully served him for years, to sound him out as to the appropriateness of the last of his plans for the Rock, namely, the appointment of another indigenous Bishop from among the local clergy, one who would have the good of the people of Gibraltar very much at heart, and would replace him very soon because he intended to resign.[(1)] The old priest was taken aback at the idea of the Bishop resigning, and suggested that he should instead ask Rome for a Coadjutor. The Bishop was not convinced by his friend's reasoning, and went on to express his line of thinking in greater detail. His successor should be a British subject, not a stranger to the laws and customs of Gibraltar; he should be fluent in both Spanish and English; and, with a view to the establishment of an indigenous clergy in this local Church, he should be chosen from among those who were already priests in the Vicariate. The Colony had given six ecclesiastics to the Church: Fr. Sciacaluga had died, and there remained four others besides the Bishop himself. One of these, he thought, really had the qualities he had outlined. This was Fr. Gonzalo Canilla, the thirty two-year-old priest he had taken with him to London and Dublin as secretary when preoccupied with the Customs Bill and the attempt to get teachers for his schools.

The young priest belonged to a wealthy family which ran a successful tobacco business. He had been privately educated with a view to his entering the family business, but due to his close acquaintance with Fr. Stephanopolis who strongly counselled him to think of the priesthood, he decided to become a priest. He first went to study in San Pelagio in Cordoba, and later on to the Good Shepherd Senior Seminary in Hammersmith, London.

When the Bishop became somewhat indisposed by the accident he suffered in Lisbon, Fr. Canilla had to take over an array of meetings with various important personalities. He proved himself to be an able ambassador. The Bishop had chosen him for his secretary on the strength of his culture, common sense, and fluency in English, Spanish and Italian. Fr. Stephanopolis and Fr. Canilla were always together and inseparable in everything.[(2)]

The Bishop was more ill than his friend Fr. Moreno had imagined. A few hours after the departure of the latter, the Bishop fell into a coma, and on 27 July, four days later he died. He was buried in the Sacred Heart Church, which he had done so much to get started, but which was still without a roof at the time.

Two days after the funeral, the Acting Vicar Apostolic, Mgr. Narcissus Pallares, summoned all the clergy to inform them officially that he had told Cardinal Simeoni of the Bishop's death. Before embarking on his duty of describing for the Roman authorities the current situation and needs of the Vicariate, he wished to take counsel with his fellow priests. It was at this juncture that Fr. Moreno revealed what the Bishop had said to him shortly before his death concerning the successor he hoped Gibraltar would have. All those present with one exception – Father Constantino Stephanopolis – agreed with the Bishop's reasoning and choice. Fr. Stephanopolis would only accept "a native priest" so there was no possibility of having an Englishman or an Irishman as Bishop, a cleric who would be a total stranger to local rivalries and differences. This was a most unexpected remark from Fr. Stephanopolis. Of all people, he should have been profoundly happy that his close friend had been so highly thought of by the late Bishop. Instead he was so hurt at being passed over that, very definitely, he would not agree to Canilla. He had to say something: hence "not a native priest" but an Englishman or Irishman. Fr. Stephanopolis had been fifteen years in Gibraltar at that time. He had been specially chosen by Propaganda Fide as a good classicist and linguist. He was intelligent and capable. He had been made chaplain to the Poor School Committee and was highly regarded by a large number of influential Gibraltarians. He had been spoken of as a likely successor to the Vicariate. Some said that he actually believed himself to be destined for that position. Mgr. MacAuliffe suggested to Monsignor Pallares that Fr. Stephanopolis's opinion should be included in the report to be sent to Rome, so as to give an overall view of the clergy's thinking. Fr. Stephanopolis, while maintaining his stance, objected to this procedure.

At all events, Mgr. Pallares sent his official account to Cardinal Simeoni. Mgr. MacAuliffe, as one who knew Roman protocol well, having studied in the Urban College of Propaganda Fide, thought it only right to tell the whole story. He also requested a friend of his – the Rector of the English College in Rome, who happened to be on a visit to Gibraltar at the time – to let him know privately whatever developments took place in Rome concerning the matter.

Soon it transpired that Fr. Stephanopolis was visiting his friends and acquaintances, collecting signatures in support of his view that what the colony needed at this time was a person who was quite unconnected with the conflict between churchmen and civilians. Exactly one week after the death of the Bishop, the local Spanish-language newspaper, *El Calpense*, carried a pointed leading article and a warning.[3] It reported rumours that the local clergy had suggested a certain local priest as a replacement for Scandella – "a stupid mistake", it called this idea – saying that Catholics should oppose this "en masse". The new man should be of outstanding talents and be either English or Irish: otherwise a terrible struggle was liable to take place, and scandalous scenes reminiscent of what happened thirty years before might well occur. "May this communication serve as a preliminary warning to those who entertain such a thought".

The following day, *El Calpense* carried the information that steps were being taken to send a deputation to Rome to counteract the proposal of the said clergy, "partly made up of foreigners". The paper trusted that all Catholics of standing would sign the memorandum to be taken to Rome: "We will fight the candidature to the end", it added: "this is a most opportune moment to re-establish the old Body of Elders to handle the affairs of the Church" – traces of the motivation behind the opposition were already becoming apparent.

Young Fr. Canilla, the target of this opposition, made his feelings clear in a letter to Mgr. Pallares. He thanked him and the other priests, saying that while he appreciated their desire to carry out the wishes of the late Bishop, he did not want to lose the peace and independence which he now enjoyed. His thoughts were far from honours and titles; and he would only accept such a position in obedience to the express wish of the Holy Father.

Mgr. Pallares thought it well to publish this semi-official letter in *El Calpense* of 2 August, in the hope of revealing to people that the movement to make Fr. Canilla bishop did not stem from any ambition on the part of the young priest himself. The paper's sarcastic comment was that Canilla's act was long overdue. Yet it was only one week since the clergy's original meeting after burying their Bishop. Father Stephanopolis had stirred up feelings of bitterness and resentment that would grow stronger yet, and lead to untold suffering for many persons. He was no fool, and had persuaded many people of sound character to think that the clergy had acted wrongly in not consulting the general public. People were led to believe that they had been unfairly treated and deliberately outmanoeuvred from exercising a right that was properly theirs. This may sound strange even in post-Vatican II times, but Gibraltar was, and still is, unique in some respects, as must have become evident by now.

By autumn, Fr. Stephanopolis had collected a thousand signatures to petition the Holy Father to disregard the clergy's recommendation – an unusual request to a Pope. This petition was to be sent to a Pope whose predecessor had been through the trauma of finding himself attacked by the secular power, but supported by the closing of ranks on the part of the ultramontane clerics. Fr. Stephanopolis himself took the memo to Rome to present it personally to Cardinal Simeoni.[4] What transpired at the meeting is still a secret, but the priest came back a changed man. Not even visiting Bishops, or higher ranking clerics count for much in Rome and the priest was put in his place. But things were out of his control now.

Bad feeling continued to simmer amid rumours and doubts until, on 11 February 1881 unofficial news of the Holy See's decision sent by Fr. MacAuliffe's friend, was intercepted in the communications sector of

Gibraltar. The official recipient of the message immediately informed the Vicar General of the contents of the telegram. Together they decided not to divulge the contents until after the arrival of the Papal Brief itself. They should have known better. Twenty-four hours later, Fr. Femenias, Parish Priest of St. Joseph's, came to St. Mary's to congratulate his colleague, Gonzalo, on being appointed Bishop. The news had come to him from people in the street! The forces of opposition had not been idle; they had instructed individuals in the appropriate quarters to keep a look-out for relevant news and report to them. They therefore got the news as quickly as the addressee of the telegram.

Rumours of the appointment got into the *Gibraltar Guardian*; and on the following day, 11 February, *El Calpense* reminded its readers that it had from the start qualified this idea as a stupid mistake. It claimed that the majority of the Catholic population shared this view and had petitioned the Holy Father to appoint an Englishman or an Irishman, "believing this to be fitting and necessary for the good of the Church". It added that the paper's attitude should not be taken as reflecting enmity towards Reverend Father Canilla: "We have always admired and respected him for his great qualities, but for the present we do not consider him the appropriate person to take charge of the Vicariate". It is not impossible to concede that the paper was still fighting a Bishop, now dead and buried some eight months.

Mr. Francia had already arranged for a public meeting to be held at the Theatre Royal on 15 February, to discuss the still unconfirmed "nomination". The local press and door-to-door canvassing were used to encourage a full attendance. On the day before the meeting, Fr. Canilla, on the advice and with the help of Mgr. Pallares, published a statement in the *Gibraltar Chronicle* in the hope of calming the tense atmosphere. It was his intention, Fr. Canilla said, to refuse the office of Bishop if it were conferred on him, since so many persons objected to the idea. He was even more concerned than his fellow citizens to oppose the hypothetical appointment. Nevertheless, as every Catholic was bound to submit to mandates of the Holy Father, and as priests should give example to the faithful in this and other matters, he would have no alternative, if the Pope finally insisted he should keep his oath of submission, but to obey, even though this might entail for him unpleasant consequences to the end of his life.

A letter, in the same edition of the *Guardian*, from some anonymous contributor, accused all the clergy except Fr. Stephanopolis of making use of the English hierarchy to achieve their aims. The writer had nothing but praise for Stephanopolis as having shown better judgement than the rest. The writer agreed with him that the imposition of Fr. Canilla as Bishop would be prejudicial to the Vicariate. He went on to suggest that the meeting on the 15th should also consider the restoration of the Body of Elders to administer the temporalities of the Church, thereby revealing once again at least some of the forces which lay behind the whole movement of protest.

The meeting at the Theatre Royal was chaired by Mr. Peter Amigo (his son was later to become Archbishop of Southwark, London). Once an ardent supporter of Bishop Scandella in supporting the Holy Father during the "risorgimento" was now stating that "our rights and wishes have been ignored by Rome and we are here today to express publicly our great discontent and displeasure at the announced appointment". Fr. Canilla was not in possession of the requisite qualities for a Bishop. A respectful message was to be sent to Pope Leo XIII asking him to accept Fr. Canilla's resignation. It was further resolved that the commission representing the Catholics of Gibraltar should be made up of Mr. Peter Amigo, Mr. Bernard Mascardi, Mr. Manuel Verano and Mr. Thomas French.

All pro-Canilla manifestations locally received abusive reaction from the opposition, and these were enfuriated when a La Linea newspaper branded the opposition's attitude as "monstrous and malicious", and "irresponsible and disobedient". These remarks provoked the *El Calpense* to write something surprisingly different: "in the event that the Holy Father did not consider our petition and Father Canilla remained Head of this flock, we would simply submit to the decision of the Universal Pastor of the Church".

However, when the Papal Brief arrived on 5 April there was a mighty rumpus in several parts of the town. The church entrances were crowded and clergy insulted. An effigy of Canilla was hanged from Amigo's house in George's Lane. The newspapers announced that people would stop supporting schools and would not attend services. Meanwhile, Fr. Canilla kept his word and sent his written resignation to the Holy Father. The fact that he wrote in it that he would "abide by the Pope's final decision" was taken by the opposition as an indication that Canilla never wanted to refuse the appointment. Continuing to use the *El Calpense* as their mouthpiece and resenting the Spanish newspaper's interferences, the opposition wrote: "Why bring about such an explosive situation to the detriment of our religion, making us a laughing stock of our enemies? Are not the blessings of a City of greater value than the glitter of a mitre?". . . . "It should not be thought we are rebelling against the Church. We uphold with the Church the right that is given us to be listened to on such important matters that concern our own spiritual well being."

The Holy Father confirmed the appointment and some members of the opposition, Mr. Francia and Mr. Mascardi submitted to the Pope's decision – *Roma locuta est, causa finita est*. Other opposition members insisted that until Dr. Canilla was consecrated and installed he was still without jurisdiction. There was therefore time to press the Pope to change his mind.

The opposition found a new leader in a Mr. Luis Imossi. He was a rich merchant who never interfered in Church matters. He had been persuaded by Fr. Constantine Stephanopolis that the clergy had taken to themselves the powers exercised by the Junta in the past; that the candidate chosen, and his family, had been too deeply implicated in the struggle against the Customs Bill; that Canilla was not learned enough; that he was ambitious. Imossi also felt sympathy for the people whose communication to the Pope had been given such short shrift so another meeting was arranged for 17 May in the Theatre Royal.

Mr. Luis Imossi chaired this meeting and he enlarged on the evils likely to ensue from accepting a spiritual head who was *persona non grata* with the majority of Gibraltarians and insisted on the right of the people to ask for a pastor who satisfied their aspirations. A telegram was to be sent to Propaganda Fide stating that eight-hundred persons assembled there objected to the appointment and refused to submit to it. The Clergy was to be censured for recommending Fr. Canilla, and the Governor was to be asked to restrict Dr. MacAuliffe to his role of Catholic Chaplain to the Forces. He was to be told to leave Gibraltar. That the majority of Catholics denied the clergy's claim to administer the temporalities of the Church, that the Body of Elders be re-established to administer such temporalities, since church property belonged essentially to the whole Catholic people of Gibraltar. The Pope and local authorities were to receive the Minutes. The press published the resolutions.

When the Chairman and Secretary tried to enter the Church with the new resolutions they were rejected by Monsignor MacAuliffe, Fr. Dotto and Fr. Bossano. All the insults and calumnies thrown at the clergy made Mgr. MacAuliffe still more resolute in stopping the opposition entering the holy place. Because MacAuliffe stood out in defence of the clergy's handling of the succession question he became the object of the opposition's attacks. Letters were written to the Governor to have him removed from Gibraltar. The Governor declined to interfere in the affair.

Meanwhile Fr. Gonzalo Canilla sailed for England in the S.S. Australia. He was to be consecrated Bishop by Cardinal Manning at Westminster. His title was to be Vicar Apostolic of Gibraltar, Bishop of Lystra. When Cardinal Manning replied, commenting on the resolutions sent to him by the opposition, these did not publish it. The Clergy on the other hand made certain that the Cardinal's views were published in the press thus incensing the opposition to a state of frenzy. And so another, the third, meeting was held on 18 June in the same theatre to elect the Junta of Elders. Since the meeting turned out to be uneventful a commission was set up to take appropriate measures should Fr. Canilla return before the Body of Elders was formed. He had to be shown that the Catholics did not accept him as Vicar Apostolic. It also transpired at the meeting that a certain lawyer named Hector Varela had committed himself to defending the opposition's viewpoint in Rome, where he happened to be stationed.

During the last three weeks of June, three different leaflets were distributed all over the Rock asking for prayer, peace and acceptance of the Holy Father's decision as Supreme Head of the Church. The fact that the authors – who made use of pseudonyms – could not be identified infuriated the committee. Its members were especially annoyed by the leaflet that was printed in La Linea, probably by a Spaniard, accusing them of being irreligious, irreverent and even schismatical. Their only answer to this was to insult the author and to challenge him to call a meeting or organize a poll to ascertain whether or not a majority was for or against Dr. Canilla. The point at issue, they maintained, was not loyalty to the Holy Father – everyone revered him – the point was the Holy Father had been misled by the clergy. What the committee sought above all, was that religion should not decline into the state that had been characteristic of the first forty years of that century.

Many people, fearing victimization if they took the side of the Bishop-elect, stopped going to religious ceremonies in the church. Children were taken across to La Linea to receive the sacrament of Confirmation from the hands of the Bishop of Cadiz. It was such trends that most of all worried the clergy. This certainly would damage the growth of the Church in Gibraltar.

One day, in July, when the church bells rang out with an enthusiasm that had not been noticed for twelve years past – when they marked the return of Bishop Scandella from Vatican Council I – the opposition party really thought that Dr. Canilla had returned surreptitiously from London. They were relieved to find that the pealing was to welcome the arrival of the Bishop of Cadiz, Mgr. Jayme, and his secretary, who had come to settle this disaffection in the Church. Mgr. Pallares lodged the visitors in the priest's house and distributed leaflets announcing that the Bishop wished to meet Catholics at 12.30 on the following day.

On the morrow, by noon, there were so many men assembled that the venue had to be changed from the Hall to the church itself. The visitor came on to the altar precisely at the time fixed. After a few moments of private prayer before the altar, in front of the packed congregation, he sat on a chair in front of the communion rails and took out a piece of paper from his pocket. He recalled the happy visits he had already made to the Rock, to launch the campaign for the building of Sacred Heart Church and later to lay the foundation stone of that same church. He had words of praise for the non-Catholic British Government, which showed itself so tolerant of religious freedom. He had come this time, he said, with a smile as he waved the telegram, in obedience to the Holy Father. He was there to learn about the crisis and the reasons and motives they had for not obeying the Pope. His task was to try and bring about peace among them. He did not intend to make this holy place a platform for discussion, but he would willingly put himself at their disposal. They were free to come and see him either individually, or as a group, or as representatives, in the Bishop's Hall upstairs.

Mr. Imossi could not contain himself and he blurted out:

"My Lord, I speak on behalf of the majority of the Catholics of Gibraltar. I agree with everything you have said. We want unity. We want peace. We want happiness and we want to practise our religion peacefully. But neither I nor any of the Catholics will accept Dr. Canilla as the Vicar Apostolic of Gibraltar".

The Pope's delegate commented that he found Mr. Imossi's statement very inopportune. He gave a hurried blessing and went off to the sacristy, leaving the audience temporarily stunned. Someone made the suggestion that they should all assembly in the church-yard under the windows of the Bishop's Hall. There they began to shout and make uncomplimentary remarks about

Dr. Canilla. They only dispersed on being told that the Bishop would hold another meeting on some other day. They hoped that the demonstration in the yard had served to manifest to the Bishop their strong feelings against Dr. Canilla; that it would show him that Dr. Canilla would never be able to exercise spiritual or moral influence over the people.

That same night, Mr. Imossi, along with a representative group, visited the Bishop and apologised for the interruption of that morning. No offence had been intended! Thereafter they gave their reasons for their opposition, arguing that the whole of the population was behind them.

The Bishop expressed the opinion to them that they should have made all this known to the Pope before he made his decision. He also expressed his doubts as to this group having the full support of the whole population. The fact was, unbeknown to the persons before him, he had already interviewed members of the Catholic Schools' Committee and the St. Vincent de Paul Society, not all of whom supported the opposition, even though they admitted the situation was grave. Some, indeed – including Mr. Lugaro and Mr. Ferro – were altogether on the side of Dr. Canilla. The afternoon visitors had shown him the type of thing that had been published in the newspapers. Mr. Imossi and company finally went away unconvinced and dissatisfied, but determined to play things calmly.

The Bishop spent three days fruitlessly listening, and arguing that it was essential that all obey the Holy Father for the good of the whole Church. The opposition thought that if they stuck to their guns without getting angry, they would finally wear the Bishop down. They felt they could impress him with their prestige and respect people had for them as good and truthful persons. They even wanted to give the Bishop a resounding farewell when he was going away. But the Bishop had had enough: he left Gibraltar quietly without being noticed. They were left standing.

In the meantime, Dr. Canilla had been consecrated by Cardinal Manning. He spent some days with the Cardinal and also contacted the Prime Minister, the Earl of Kimberley, who received him cordially and discussed the crisis in Gibraltar. On his way back to the Rock, the Bishop called into Lourdes in France. From Marseilles he telegraphed Mgr. Pallares, to say he would arrive on 11 August. The Vicar Capitular in his turn asked Mgr. MacAuliffe to inform the authorities of the date and time, and to ask them to give the Bishop adequate protection and to ensure good order, so that nothing would prevent the Bishop from being installed in proper fashion. Assurance was given that the authorities would do all that was needed to ensure good order.

Dr. Canilla was welcomed by his brother and brother-in-law in the presence of a few policemen. Instead of taking a coach to the church, the trio walked all the way there – about a mile – with its police escort following behind. The Bishop found a large crowd assembled outside the church, but the doors of the church were closed. When he tried to walk through the crowd to the doors, he was held up by Mr. Imossi and other leaders of the opposition. The policemen were no longer to be seen. The crowd began to shout at him, telling him to go away and not to try and enter. So great was the hubbub that the Bishop decided to give up his idea. He walked instead to his parents' home in Rodger's Ramp, (now known as Hospital Steps).

It is not clear what official arrangements had been made to receive the Bishop, but the clergy inside were certainly not expecting to see, when the doors were suddenly opened by the men standing at the back of the church, a rowdy, dangerous-looking mob rush in instead of the Bishop. The younger clergy quickly moved out of reach, but Mgr. MacAuliffe stood his ground in front of the altar, wearing his confessional stole over his alb.

But the crowd came right into the sanctuary, and called on him to leave the church. Seeing he would not obey, they tried to push him off the altar steps. He resisted and had his stole partially pulled off in the mêlée. He called out to them, reminding them he was a priest, and this was his place. He ordered them out of the sanctuary. The reply he got was that it was all their property, not his, and they threatened him "Get out or be thrown out!" Still protesting that he would not go until he received orders from his superiors, he saw a policeman pushing his way through the crowd. From this man, too, he heard a recommendation to "leave this place". Then, amid the hullabaloo, someone produced a note purporting to be from the Vicar General, asking him to abandon his efforts to stay on the altar. Having read it, he pushed his way back through the mob into the sacristy.

The rioters laughed and cheered at their victory. They then set about breaking up the church chairs and benches, and they cut the ropes of the church bells. They tried to get the keys of the church from the old sacristan, but he refused to part with them, and ran off to tell the Vicar Capitular what was happening. The mob followed and threatened the Vicar that if he did not surrender the keys, they would change the locks and in that way take over the control of the building. No policeman made any attempt to prevent the damage being done by the rioters or the disorder they caused.

After this incident, the opposition leaders came together in their usual meeting place – Mr. Garibaldi's pharmacy, opposite the church itself. It was decided to hold a formal meeting on the following day. They sent a message to *El Calpense* to this effect. A commission made up of Messrs. Schott, Coll, Bassadone and Carrara then went to the Bishop's family home in Rodger's Ramp. The Bishop agreed to see the group. They merely wanted to know what his plans were now, in the light of the taste of opposition he had experienced. His answer was: he intended to wait a few days until the tension had disappeared, and would then walk to the church to be officially installed. He was resolved not to shrink from the responsibility laid on his shoulders by the Holy See. This reply was interpreted as further proof of his arrogance and ambition.

Once again, on 12 August, the Theatre Royal was packed for an anti-Bishop meeting. A Body of Elders to adminster the temporalities of the Church was elected. It claimed to have power to interfere in all matters connected with the Vicariate. It consisted of Messrs. Imossi, John Garese, Candido Savignon, Emilio Castro, Nicholas Femenias, Avelino Gaggero, Adolfo Conti, James Bado and Felix Benvenuto.

These men were given the task of taking whatever steps they thought necessary to get the appointment annulled, and to ensure that Bishop Canilla did not exercise the duties of the office conferred on him. At the end of the meeting, Mr. Imossi asked for the staging of a demonstration outside the church on the following Sunday, in case the Bishop might attempt to go there and preach to the military personnel who regularly attended the nine o'clock Mass. By the time news of this "possible" move reached the ears of the Governor, this rumoured project of the Bishop sounded as if it were fact. The Governor did not want the army mixed up in any ecclesiastical struggle, so he called the military chaplain to him. Monsignor MacAuliffe explained that the Bishop had neither decided on this step nor even entertained the idea of addressing the forces. The Bishop himself then issued a communique denying the allegation.

Nevertheless, on that Sunday, a huge crowd gathered outside the church and disturbed the military congregation inside with its noise and excitement. The soliders showed great restraint and forebearance in not taking steps to put an end to the uproar. In fact, this noisy demonstration won the support of the soldiers for the Bishop. They sent him a document congratulating him on his appointment and on it were recorded all the prayers and Masses that had been offered for his success.

An announcement was made, two days later, by the new Body of Elders, or Administration, as they also called themselves, that they would officially take possession of the temporalities of the Church on 19 August.

As reason for this, they alleged that the funds had been inefficiently administered in the past by Bishop Scandella, to the detriment of the Catholic body as a whole. Dr. Canilla, still residing with his family, heard of this and wrote to the Governor through the Colonial Secretary, telling him that members of the Junta intended to present themselves at St. Mary's and take possession of the church and of the archives, etc. belonging thereto.

"Under these exceptional circumstances, besides appealing directly to the acting police magistrate, I feel it my duty to lay the matter of such a proposed outrage at once, through you, before His Excellency.

I am requesting His Worship to post a sufficient number of the police officers within the sacred edifice, and the archives office, as well as in the yard and other precincts. . . . . . . .with a view to the preservation of the said Church and of the Clergy attached thereto and in possession thereof, which they have peacefully enjoyed . . . . with the full sanction of the Government, and with which none but the Government who left it for Catholic uses in 1784, can in any way claim any right of interference". [5]

The Bishop was assured by both the Colonial Secretary and the Acting Police Magistrate that the "police magistrate and his officers will be prepared to afford you and the Clergy of your Vicariate all the protection and assistance in their power. . . ."

The march to the church did not take place. The opposition gave no reason for this change of plan. Instead, they began preparing people's minds to reject the pastoral letter the Bishop intended to have read on the feast of St. Bernard, the town's Patron Saint.

They asked the clergy not to read out the letter on that day. The clergy, of course, disregarded the suggestion.

In this Pastoral letter, the Bishop spoke of the serious responsibility placed on him by the Head of the Catholic Church. He referred sadly to the lamentable reception he got when trying to enter his own church. He spoke of the apparent impossibility of fulfilling his ministry to the people with the freedom and quiet that he desired.

"At all times a Bishop, by reason of his ministry, is called upon to endure much adversity and opposition in the discharge of his duty, but in the present situation those troubles are multiplied in an astonishing degree, and render his life a prolonged martyrdom."

He declared before God and man that he had never even thought of the possibility of being elected to the episcopal dignity, let alone sought it. He had even asked to be relieved of it, but his appeal was not accepted. The Holy Father had decided otherwise, and his investiture as Bishop was an act of submission to the Supreme Head of the Church. As he now represented the authority of the Sovereign Pontiff, opposition was logically disrespectful to His Holiness:

"We therefore entreat all Catholics to depose their animosity for our humble self and think only of the authority that we represent".

It was his duty, he said, to defend the rights and prerogatives of the See of Rome, and he did that through no paltry motive of ambition, haughtiness or a desire for authority. He had again written, just recently, to the Cardinal Prefect of Propaganda Fide, explaining the situation and had asked that he be superseded in the office to which he had been appointed, because of the impossibility of quietly discharging the duties attached to it. From the bottom of his heart he wanted the rights of the Holy See to suffer no diminution and the interests of the Church no wrong.

"Our mission is one of peace and conciliation, and we cordially invite all Catholics so to believe it in all sincerity, and be convinced of our ardent wishes to protect the interests of the Church by all conciliatory means in our power".

In a final appeal, he begged all Catholics not to let themselves be carried away by predilections or partialities, but to unite in expressing their adhesion to the teaching of the Church:

"We are prepared for all the personal sacrifices which shall be required of us,

and we will omit nothing that may in any way assuage and mollify the present situation, provided that the sacred rights of the Church and the Holy See are not impaired. Come to us, therefore, all who may consider themselves aggrieved by our elevation, be their social station what it may, we shall receive them all and hear them with the greatest charity. We are certain that they will find us determined to make all possible sacrifices for the good of this Vicariate. Our earnest desire is that peace may be restored to all Catholics, and that there be no dissension among us, so pernicious to religion and morality".

The appeal fell on deaf ears as far as the opposition was concerned. They discussed and analysed each paragraph, and found nothing but indications of Dr. Canilla's ambition and eagerness to become Vicar Apostolic. By letter, they presented a formal protest to the Bishop, stating that the people were still against his appointment and that he should not therefore exercise any powers as Bishop of the Vicariate. If he did, he would be responsible for the consequences.

Not all Gibraltarians, however, reacted negatively to the Bishop's appeal. On 2 September, a group of men from St. Joseph's Church (Messrs. John Sciacaluga, Joseph Danino, Laurence Morello, Telmo Dodero, James Sterico and John Chiappe Jnr.) published a statement supporting the Holy Father's decision and warning off the Elders from extending their activities and claims to the South of the Rock.

"Since the foundation of St. Joseph's, its material interests have been exclusively discharged by the priest in charge. We will not allow any alteration in the present custom, and we strongly protest against all attempts by any corporation, no matter what its title or origin, to interfere with the administration of control of such interests. We deplore the incidents that occurred in front of and inside the Church of St. Mary on 11 August".

The Elders' reaction was to call a meeting for 6 September and to declare once again their intention of proceeding to take possession of the Church's temporalities. Mgr. MacAuliffe immediately wrote to the authorities warning them about another possible breach of the peace. This time the civil authorities ensured that the meeting went off quietly and that no march was made on the church. The organizers were told to choose more appropriate times for their meetings and to avoid any action that might meet with resistance.

Within a day or so it was rumoured that the Bishop intended to enter the church on the night of the 8th. On that evening large groups of men waited outside the various entrances to the church, intending to block the Bishop's way. They remained there until darkness fell. When a horse-drawn coach was heard coming down Cannon Lane, the men at the Main Street entrance rushed around to join those at the back of the church. They stopped the coach and tried to open the doors, but failed to see who was inside. All they got was loud laughter from within; and the driver managed to get quickly away.

Suspecting that they might have been vicms of a jape their leaders went to ask the Vicar Capitular about the Bishop's intentions. Finding they had been made fools of – probably by idle young men – and that the Bishop had no plans to come that evening, the mob abused the clergy and threw stones and shoes at the windows of their residence.

The Bishop wrote to the Colonial Secretary, reporting this rowdiness and requesting protection for himself and the clergy. He was sure, he said, that if only His Excellency would forbid such assemblies, the agitation would soon fade away. The note was not even acknowledged.

On that same day, the opposition party sent a memorandum to the Governor for transmission to Her Majesty's Government. They wanted the latter to request the Holy See to revoke Canilla's appointment. This memorandum was dispatched immediately to the Secretary of State.[6]

The Bishop, however, got very little satisfaction from the authorities when he passed on to the Colonial Secretary a letter he had received from his clergy as a group, complaining of the lack of peace and security. These two elements, the clergy said, were essential both for them – in order to carry out their sacred functions – and for the laity, if they were to attend divine worship regularly and with proper devotion. The cause of the trouble, in their eyes, was the propaganda that had led the public to believe that all ecclesiastical property was the people's by right, and that the clergy residing in the priests' house were merely the people's tenants, living there on sufferance. Clergy and faithful were afraid of the masses of men, mostly of the lower classes, who had of late been gathering around and within the principal church in a threatening attitude. They felt they had a right to a measure of protection inside and outside the church: a sense of security had up to now been one of the greatest boons conferred upon them by British laws. The Governor, in his reply, emphasised again that the authorities, while ready to assist the clergy in every way, could not agree with the suggestion that public meetings such as those which had taken place recently be suppressed.

The Bishop suffered additional disappointment when Mr. Mascardi resigned from the position of Treasurer of the Poor School Fund: it would become impossible to run the schools without money from the better-off section of the community, and many of these families had ceased to contribute as part of the campaign against the Vicar Apostolic. The latter was, of course, blamed for the resignation of the Treasurer. The Bishop was ready, it was said, to let even the poor suffer provided that he achieved his ambition.

When the Spanish Bishop reported his failure to win over the opposition, Rome decided to send an English Jesuit to the Rock. Fr. Weld arrived *de incognito* only the Bishop knew of his presence – stayed in a small hotel in City Mill Lane, and spent a fortnight or so mixing with the people and finding out for himself how matters stood.[7] He discovered that more than 400 persons in the town itself, as well as a large number in the southern part of the Rock and all the inhabitants of Catalan Bay were clearly not against either the Pope or his Vicar Apostolic. He had heard from the Bishop that all the lawyers who were consulted assured him he had every right to enter the church and suggested he make another attempt to gain entrance. Fr. Weld therefore went to the Governor to tell him of his mission, of his findings, and of the Bishop's intentions.

On 23 November, the Bishop officially informed the Governor and the Police Magistrate that he intended to enter St. Mary's on the following day and asked for their protection. Captain Blair was told by the magistrate to have a few policemen patrolling the route the Bishop would take to the church: the Captain himself and two policemen were to stand near the church entrance but not to go inside unless a breach of the peace were committed. The Attorney General, Mr. R. French-Sheriff, had no objection to these arrangements, but emphasised that the police should not interfere in any way, apart from maintaining order. They were not, for example, to open the doors, if the Bishop found them closed against him, nor force a passage through the crowd for the Bishop.

The opposition leaders did not become aware of the Bishop's intention until late in the evening of 23 November. They were however able to rally their followers to be present at nine o'clock on the following morning. When the Bishop alighted from his coach, Mr. Imossi was there to confront him. He was told by Imossi to go away, but Captain Blair stepped forward to warn Mr. Imossi not to obstruct the Bishop. Imossi thereupon appealed to the crowd, on whose behalf he claimed to speak and act: "He is imposing himself against our wishes and I will not allow it", he shouted. The Bishop tried to reason with the noisy crowd, saying that he had not come to impose himself but to carry out the wishes of the Holy Father. Mr. Imossi's interruption at that point sounded very much like lèse majesté vis-à-vis the Pope, but the crowd became ever more noisy and restless. Captain Blair advised the Bishop and his companion to return home, for he feared he would be unable to control the people present, and worse scandal might occur should the mob force its way along with the Bishop into the church. Dr. Canilla took the advice and made his way back to the family home. The church was occupied by the crowd for the rest of the morning. Speeches were made in the sacristy and insults offered to the clergy.

On the following day, the Bishop wrote in desperation to the Governor, to say that he could not see how he was ever going to fulfill his duty as Vicar Apostolic, duly appointed by Rome and recognized by the British Government, if the support given him by the local authorities continued to be as inadequate as it had proved on the previous day. The Governor replied that inquiries were being made into the incident. It was regrettable, he added, that such short notice had been given of the proposed move.

Two days later, at Fr. Weld's suggestion, the Bishop was installed as Vicar Apostolic privately in what we have seen was a very sacred place for Gibraltarians – the Chapel of Our Lady of Europa.[8] The nuns who had charge of the Shrine were present at the ceremony, as well as Mgr. Pallares, Fr. Weld and Fr. Femenias of St. Joseph's. The event became public knowledge by means of a notice in the *Gibraltar Chronicle* of 28 November. The opposition called it a fake ceremony, and remained adamant that the

Bishop would never be allowed to enter the principal church on the Rock. In the days that followed, Fr. Weld of course became a target for criticism. The Papal emissary, however, had gone off to visit the Bishop of Cadiz immediately after the ceremony in order to consult with him about the future.

Clearly, the Governor's determination not to take sides left the clergy in a vulnerable position. The Bishop therefore adopted a different line of action: he would himself try to bring the law to bear on the crisis.

It had been decreed a long time before, by Earl Granville on behalf of the British Government (20 September 1869), that churches and chapels in Gibraltar be handed over to the various communions. In a letter of 26 September 1872, the Colonial Secretary had suggested to Bishop Scandella that in this context a Church Body of Trustees be set up by charter of ordinance. A public meeting had been duly held on 21 March 1876, and a resolution unanimously passed that a group of men, acceptable to the whole community, be chosen to hold in trusteeship all Catholic church property. It had also been agreed that this body should consist of the Vicar Apostolic, the Vicar General, the Deputy Governor of the Catholic division of the civil hospital, the senior member of the Board of Trustees of Gavino's Asylum, and the Treasurer of the Catholic Poor School. Thereafter, an ordinance had been drawn up and approved by the British Government, but it had remained in abeyance while all the other clauses of Granville's original suggestions had been implemented. The Bishop now suggested to the Governor that this ordinance should be given the force of law without delay. In the case of further disorders on the part of persons who were no longer canonically Catholics, the trustees would be in a position to adopt measures to secure the peace necessary for God's house and its use.

Lord Napier parried this attempt to resolve the difficulties in the community, arguing that no instructions had been received from the British Government to enact the ordinance. Even if he were directed so to do, it would none the less be expedient and proper, after so long an interval, to replenish the draft for general information, to give the Roman Catholic community an opportunity to make a fresh selection of church trustees. This suggestion came as a surprise to the Bishop, but what surprised him even more was to find the Governor saying that no complaints had reached him concerning the kind of disturbances referred to. The Bishop therefore wrote back directly to the Governor, giving him details in case he really had been misinformed or uninformed all along the line. He cited specific occasions, especially those of 11 August and 24 November, to back up his previous statement that "any moment men might with impunity and in the presence of the police, first, create a disturbance in and around the church; secondly, repel the legitimately appointed Vicar Apostolic; and, third, insult the clergy as often as they think proper".

An incident was soon to occur which brought out even more clearly the depth of animosity entertained towards Bishop and clergy by certain Gibraltarians.

When Fr. Weld returned from Cadiz, instead of stopping at his hotel he went to St. Mary's, where at Mgr. Pallares' suggestion, and with the Bishop's permission, he occupied the rooms normally used by the Bishop. The opposition party soon heard of it and objected to this "abuse" – the people had not given permission for an enemy of theirs to live in the presbytery. Mr. Imossi warned Mgr. Pallares of possible dire consequences, should the Jesuit be allowed to remain. The next day, when Mr. Weld was reading in the Bishop's Hall, he could hear a crowd milling around beneath the window. On looking out, he was seen and was told to leave the place. For safety's sake, he locked the outer doors of the apartment and the doors of the Hall. In the meantime, Messrs. Imossi, Garese and Conti found Mgr. Pallares, and asked him to get the Jesuit out of the house. The Vicar General suggesed they should wait until noon of the following day, and left them. The trio then sought out Fr. Stephanopolis, who also informed them that the Jesuit would be gone by the morrow. They objected even to this, however, and Fr. Stephanopolis agreed to go and speak to Fr. Weld. Mgr. Pallares and Fr. Dotto accompanied him, but they could get no reply from Fr. Weld, since both doors to his quarters were locked. While they were still trying to attract his attention, a group of trouble-makers invaded the house. At that point, two of the priests retired to their rooms. Stephanopolis stayed, but when he failed to calm the intruders, he went downstairs to consult their leaders. In the meantime, the intruders broke the glass of the outer doors, and this caused Fr. Weld to shout from the window for help from the police. The one policeman available turned away with indifference when he heard what was happening. The intruders then broke down the oak inner doors and rushed into the room. They failed to hold the priest fast, and he escaped into the bedroom where he locked himself in. His pursuers lifted one of their number shoulder high and made him get into the bedroom by the window above the staircase. Jumping in, he attacked the priest with a stick, while a second man climbed through the window and opened the door, with the result that the priest was at bay before an angry mob. They pounced on him, knocked him down, and dragged him by his feet out of the room and down the flight of marble steps. He was finally dragged across the yard and out into the street, where he was left lying on the ground. A police inspector came up and asked everyone to leave the poor man alone. He then suggested to the priest it would be better to go and stay in Mrs. Petit's hotel where he had lodged on a previous occasion. Fr. Weld walked there, shoeless and hatless, in the company of the policeman and Messrs. Pitman and Dumoulin. Plenty of space and abusive language were devoted to this incident in the following day's newspapers. The general tone of the articles was that this should truly demonstrate to the Bishop and clergy that the people of Gibraltar were not to be trifled with in the exercise of ecclesiastical jurisdiction. That same day, the Police Magistrate began a thorough investigation, taking sworn statements from policemen and clergy alike. His verdict was that a disgraceful disturbance had undoubtedly taken place in the Church of St. Mary the Crowned. The relevant law was read aloud in court in English and in Spanish: no-one had the right to take the law into his own hands. The eight men arraigned were fined 295 pesetas.

The ringleaders, however, were not charged.

The Governor had received from the Magistrate an account of what had happened even before the verdict was pronounced. Immediately he wrote to the Bishop, via the Colonial Secretary, to the effect that, in view of the troubled state of the community, it would have been far more judicious not to have allowed Fr. Weld to stay in the presbytery in the first place. Thus, even in the case of a blatant breach of the peace, the poor Bishop was made to feel guilty. He could not see why he should have acted otherwise than he did. Why refuse hospitality – especially to a priest who was highly respected both for his family origins and his personal qualities; and a delegate of the Pope, to boot? In any case, that particular apartment had been occupied by the clergy of the Catholic Church in Gibraltar ever since the occupation of the Rock by the British – why should the Bishop not offer it to whomsoever he please?

In writing back to the Governor, the Bishop refrained from dragging in such considerations. Instead, he reported that Fr. Weld had something to communicate to the Governor. The answer came that whatever Fr. Weld wanted to say could be conveyed through the Bishop. Fr. Weld therefore wrote a letter to the Governor on 17 December, and the Bishop sent it with a covering note of his own stating that his views coincided with what was expressed in Fr. Weld's letter:

> *"This is not a dispute within the Catholic Church. It is no longer a question of Bishop Canilla. It is the effort of a mob directed by well-known individuals, to assert a power over ecclesiastical property and its administration in this town. . . . I submit that it is no longer a question of religion, but of law and order. . . . It is because the mob has been taught that the property is theirs and have been instructed to use physical force against those whose principles forbid them to use it. . . . Your Excellency has more than once referred us to the ordinary course of the law. May I be allowed to state that on 24 November, when Mr. Imossi stood at the head of the mob to bar the entrance of the church, his conduct was witnessed by the Chief Inspector of the Police and other members of the force, and yet we were informed on that occasion by the police authorities that they could neither arrest nor proceed against him. It seems, then, to be evident that to have made a complaint to the police would have been of little use, and that some further protection is needed."*

An appeal was again made to the Governor to restore order and to put an end to the opposition's policy of obstruction, aimed at preventing the Vicar Apostolic from performing his duties.

A day or so later, a letter for the Bishop arrived from the Prefect of Propaganda with a personal message for Fr. Stephanopolis. The result was that both Fr. Weld and Fr. Stephanopolis left Gibraltar for good on 21 December 1881. Fr. Stephanopolis went to Brazil later on. From there he passed on to Argentina as Vicar Apostolic of Panaria, then became the parish priest of Villaguay in the Province of Cuatro Rios.

The various reports and appeals reaching London had caused some ripples of interest in the Foreign Office. No steps were taken, however, apart from passing on the documents to the British Attache in Rome, who then offered them for comment to Mgr. Massotti, the Secretary of Propaganda. The latter's attitude was that any complaints against the Vicar Apolistic concerning civil matters should be tried before the proper tribunals; but objections to Papal appointments were simply not acceptable – appointments were only made after due reflection and in accordance with ecclesiastical protocol. *Roma locuta est.*

Lord Napier's full report to the Secretary of State (December 1881) concerning the trouble among civilians inside the Fortress of Gibraltar, were to be taken more seriously. Having recalled the opposition to Dr. Canilla's second attempt to enter the Church of St. Mary's – already reported by him – the Governor mentioned the installation of the Vicar Apostolic carried out in the Chapel attached to St. Bernard's School. He also spoke of Mr. Francia's suggestion that the R.C. Church Ordinance of 1876 be enacted, Fr. Weld's support for this line of action, and the Vicar Apostolic's written submission that this plan be carried out. The Governor pointed out, however, that the persons acceptable as the people's representatives in 1876 were not necessarily so acceptable now. He explained that the attack on Fr. Weld was probably motivated by the suspicion that some attempt was to be made by him to install Bishop Canilla in the Church of St. Mary. In this context, he criticised the unsatisfactory conduct of the police. At the same time, he had some hard words about the untimeliness of Fr. Weld's action in a situation that was very tense. The Governor thought that this dispute needed settling once and for all. But, from the records of the case against Bishop Hughes, he found that the Roman Catholic community apparently did have some share in managing temporalities until the practice was suppressed – he was not sure how – by Bishop Scandella! He reported a general feeling of dissatisfaction about the manner in which this had been done, and the temporalities subsequently disposed of. He thought it desirable that the Roman authorities should somehow meet the people's wishes, if trouble was to be avoided between either party and the non-religious authorities in Gibraltar.

After dispatching his report, the Governor summoned various persons to meetings with himself, the Colonial Secretary and the Attorney General, in order to seek some definitive solution to the problem. The meetings bore little fruit, however, apart from the emergence of a suspicion that Dr. Canilla had been recommended as a successor to Scandella in order to prevent exposure of doubtful financial transactions carried out in Scandella's time.

The Bishop, in his interview with the Governor, asked him who really did own church property in Gibraltar. The Governor gave a non-committal reply, and suggested that the Bishop should consult legal advisers as to the steps to be taken to get the answer to that question. But in mid-January, the Governor received clearer guidance from London as to how he should act in future. "I desire", wrote the Earl of Kimberley, "that measures be taken at once for enforcing order and obedience to law, and for enabling the Vicar Apostolic and any other duly constituted ecclesiastical authorities to have full and free access, without molestation of any kind, to the Cathedral and presbytery and those other buildings which have been used by them or their predecessors. . . . It would be desirable that public notice be given, warning all persons that any attempt at renewing those disorders will be summarily repressed."

These orders came just when a letter from the Bishop to the Earl of Kimberley was on its way to London requesting "absolutely the presence of at least two constables in the church courtyard during the hours that the church is open to the public, and a sentry during the night between the outer doors". The Bishop pointed out that those who had broken into the presbytery had not been sought out by the police nor penalized. Nor had any action been taken to restrain libellous statements and insults against him in the press. The opposition leaders in particular, had got off scot-free. He argued that, if only the Ordinance were passed, the Churches of St. Mary, St. Joseph, and the Sacred Heart and the property connected with them would all be rendered safe. Disorders would cease if firm steps were taken by the local authorities: there was no need for the police to wait for complaints to be lodged by offended parties before apprehending delinquents who were guilty of misdemeanours committed in the very presence of the police. The newspapers should be restrained from publishing threats or inciting people to violence: the local Spanish newspaper had virtually recommended Fr. Weld to leave the presbytery in order to forestall the violence that was likely to break out at a certain hour in the evening. Much as he regretted having to appeal to London, said the Bishop, he was bound to avail himself of every means in his power to ensure respect for the office entrusted to him: it was a matter on which the very existence of the Catholic Church in Gibraltar depended.

The Bishop's letter went to the Secretary of State via the Governor and the Attorney General.[9] The comments added by the latter agreed that it was regrettable that no individual had been summoned when access to the Church had been blocked, but he thought that the Bishop was the proper person to take legal proceedings against those who had caused the obstruction. The Attorney General also agreed the Body of Administration was wrong to suppose it had the right to evict Fr. Weld. As regards the Ordinance, he submitted that His Excellency could not act immediately for reasons already given, more especially the non-representative character of the trustees as defined in the existing text. It would be the responsibility of the Secretary of State to decide on the necessity or expediency of forcing Dr. Canilla upon the community against its conscientious objections. He ventured to point out, however, that it could bring the local authorities into direct and certain conflict with the inhabitants. Installation of the Bishop did not automatically imply acceptance by the people or safety for the Bishop. There were legal tribunals in Gibraltar to which Dr. Canilla would have recourse before expecting the Government to interfere between himself and his flock. The Attorney General added that, in point of fact, no religious services had ever been disrupted. Fr. Weld's open defiance of the leaders and his refusal to produce credentials from the Pope had only made the situation worse. As for the Body of Administration, it had merely embarked on a lot of talk. Mr. Imossi and his eight colleagues were not a valid body at all. Legally the churches and buildings attached to them were never owned by either the Junta before it was dissolved in 1863 or any of the Bishops. The decision of the Privy Council in 1842 merely recognized the existence of a Junta and its right to administer the temporalities of the Church of St. Mary. In the meantime the Secretary of State wrote to the Governor specific orders for establishing order.

The twelve men who had constituted themselves the Body of Administration, all unaware of the directives from London, the Bishop's request to London and the Attorney General's advice, summoned a meeting for 30 January 1882 for the purpose of affirming publicly the people's right to elect a Junta of Elders. The Bishop, knowing the Governor would not forbid the meeting, asked him at least not to give official recognition to any resolution passed at such a meeting. The meeting was duly held and during it Mr. Imossi ran over the history of the ancient Body of Elders as he saw it. He recalled how they had won their legal struggle against Bishop Hughes. He then gave his account of all that had been attempted against the will of the people in recent times, and read out a telegram and a letter addressed to Cardinal Simeoni protesting against the removal of Fr. Stephanopolis: he implied that the priest had been removed as a result of false reports laid against him in Rome, and thus aroused the audience to express its indignation.

A modicum of praise was given to the Governor for his kind reception of members of the opposition. But strong criticism was levelled at Mr. Francia for declining to head the group. The next item on the agenda was the election of a new Junta. The following were chosen:
Lewis Imossi (President), Michael Pitman (Treasurer), John Garese (Secretary), Candido Savignon, Henry Levy, Emilio Castro, Adolphus Conti, Nicholas Femenias, Avelino Gaggero, James Bado, Felix Benvenuto, Claudius Marin.

A resolution was passed insisting upon this body's ancient rights, as decided on 17 October 1840 by the Supreme Court of Gibraltar. Any rules and regulations made since then and inconsistent with those rights were declared null and void. The usurpation of the Elders' functions of receipt and disposal of church funds – from which, it was alleged, abuses and scandal had resulted – was also said to be null and void. The Body just elected was given the task of taking over and performing those duties until January of the following year. It was also charged with the employment of lawful means to take over the church and the buildings connected with it, the archives, emoluments, monies, and other temporalities. A declaration was then agreed on that "Vicar Apostolic" was a title defined by Bishop Scandella, and that the "Vicar Apostolic of Gibraltar" had no legal or other status on the Rock except what was accorded by its Catholic inhabitants. Those present at the meeting then renewed their firm refusal to grant Rev. Gonzalo Canilla any such status.

It was finally resolved that the Governor be asked for a copy of the draft Order in Council of 1873, with a view to having the Order enacted and the

Junta confirmed in its ancient rights and privileges. The proceedings of the meeting were published in full in the *Gibraltar Chronicle.*

On 15 February, the Secretary of State, having heard of what took place at the meeting, reiterated to the Governor his directive that disorder must not be countenanced, despite the Government's determination not to take sides. He pointed out that while the Crown had allowed the Catholic community the use of the church for worship, it had not so far transferred any property rights. He ordered the Governor to warn those opposed to the Bishop that any attempt to take over the church would be resisted by Government forces.

Following this lead, the Governor then made it clear to the opposition how he viewed the latest meeting and its resolutions. He also gave his answer to the deputation he had received on 6 February. He regretted, he said, the remarks that had been made in public about the Vicar Apostolic and the disturbances of the peace connected with the Church of St. Mary. He pointed out that it was only the reluctance of the persons aggrieved to identify the guilty parties that had saved the latter from fines and imprisonment with hard labour. He issued a serious warning against further disorders, together with the suggestion that redress for alleged grievance be sought through legal means. He did not consider the committee elected at this latest meeting to be representative of the Roman Catholic community, and under no circumst-ances would its members be allowed to possess themselves of the church or its precincts, or in any way to molest the clergy. They should know that the legal status of the Vicar Apostolic had been recognized some forty years before by the Supreme Court of Gibraltar, by the Privy Council and by the Junta itself.

Finally, he added that, as he had no instructions to release any copy of a draft Ordinance, he must decline to do so.

This clarification of the situation by the Governor came as a bomb-shell to the opposition. It blew all Mr. Imossi's plans and hopes sky-high. The opposition was resolved, nonetheless, not to allow Dr. Canilla into the principal church. But how could they succeed in doing this without breaking the law? They were in danger of losing face, after all they had promised and threatened.

When priests were invited to Gibraltar to preach special sermons and to hear confessions, in the season of Lent, for example, it was common form to fix on a regular outline of topics. Delicate matters which might offend members of religions other than the Roman Catholic were always avoided: such topics could be dealt with more suitably by pastoral letters written by the Bishop. In February 1882, Father Sanchez, a Franciscan from Seville, was invited as guest preacher and confessor. He was, of course, told not to broach any of the current problems in the Vicariate. But when he spoke in one of his conferences of papal authority and the duty of Catholics to obey, umbrage was taken by the leaders of the opposition. Mr. Garese, signing himself as Secretary to the Junta, complained to the Vicar General and issued a veiled threat to the local clergy of dire prospects should they fail to warn the preacher to keep off topics that could be interpreted as applying to the ecclesial situation in Gibraltar. The Bishop immediately pointed out to the Governor the similarity of this language to that of the warnings issued prior to the outrage committed on Father Weld in the previous December.

He emphasised that the utmost care had been taken to avoid any reference to Vicariate affairs, but even in expounding the most elementary Catholic doctrine there was every likelihood, in the case of persons who were acting in direct opposition to the Church's teaching, of seeing allusions being made to their conduct. He therefore asked the Governor to take steps to prevent whatever outrage might be in the offing. The Governor, after consultation with the Colonial Secretary and other responsible persons, decided to put an end to this 17-months old situation of stalemate or worse.

On 27 February, the following Government Notice was published:

"In pursuance of instructions from Her Majesty's Government with reference to the recent disturbances of the peace at the Church and Presbytery of St. Mary the Crowned. . . . all persons are hereby warned that any renewal of similar disorders will be summarily repressed, and any who attempt to obstruct the Right Reverend Dr. Canilla, Vicar Apostolic, or any other minister of religion, from having full and free access to the said Church and Presbytery, or who may attempt to molest or interfere with the Vicar Apostolic, or other Clergy in the exercise of their sacred functions therein, will be prosecuted and will render themselves liable to the heavy penalties of fine and imprisonment in such case provided by law.

His Excellency the Governor calls upon all well disposed inhabitants of Gibraltar to use their best endeavours to prevent any further disturbances of public order.

By command of His Excellency the Governor."

The Colonial Secretary wrote to Dr. Canilla informing him officially of the warning and asked him to give 24 hours notice of his intention to proceed to the Church of St. Mary, and to restrain his clergy from making any further comment about the Vicariate question. Such a request was a gift from Heaven to Dr. Canilla. He sent the Governor his written thanks on the same day, assuring him he would get the clergy to steer clear of the slightest word or action that could cause irritation. Indeed, they would be even more conciliatory than they had already been. He informed the Colonial Secretary that he would like to proceed to the church on 2 March at midday.

Mr. Garese's reaction on behalf of the so-called Junta was made known to the Secretary of State by telegram and to the Colonial Secretary by letter.

"The Roman Catholics respectfully submit that the Governor's Notice imposing on them Dr. Canilla as Vicar Apostolic is a depreciation of their rights and against the wish of the whole community who cannot conscientiously accept Canilla. The Catholics implore your Lordship's protection."

Apprehension was expressed concerning the consequences of the publication of this Notice. After three days of meetings in Garibaldi's Pharmacy, all the opposition could think of doing was to tell the Colonial Secretary that there was intense excitement among the Catholic community, that they considered "the rights and privileges enjoyed from time immemorial" had been abrogated by the Government's support of Dr. Canilla, and to reiterate their view that any serious consequences that might ensue would be the Government's responsibility. Plans were also drawn up by the group to fill the church at 7.00 a.m. on the Tuesday morning and, after Mass, to close the doors to prevent the entrance of the Bishop at midday.

The Attorney General sensed that the time was ripe for suggesting to the Colonial Secretary that some military presence was called for, to forestall any violence being directed at Dr. Canilla, and to back up the none too reliable police on this occasion. He emphasized that he did not want either the police or Dr. Canilla to be hurt or any blood to be shed. Mr. John Clements, the Police Magistrate, working with the Bishop, decided that the shorter the route to the church, the better; hence the Bishop would go by way of Governor's Street and City Mill Lane into the Main Street, and then into the church. He freed extra police by cancelling all court duties, and asked the Governor for the help of the military police.

On the day itself, between 7.00 a.m. and 7.30 a.m., the church filled up though the particular Mass for this day (a Foundation Mass) had not been attended by anyone for years. At the end of Mass, the crowd in church split

Asi me den con un porro,
lo que es yo.... no suelto el GORRO.

"I will not let go of the hat
Even if they hit me with a bat."

up. One group forced the clergy up into the presbytery attic and locked them in. A second group went to the belfry to cut the ropes and put the bells out of action. The others barricaded the doors with benches and chairs. The loyal old sacristan escaped and went to Rodger's Ramp to inform Dr. Canilla. The latter sent him on to the Governor with a letter asking for help. The Governor immediately contacted the Police Magistrate, who sent out his whole force – thirty-three officers and constables – to free the church from this occupation. The task took them one and a half hours. Twelve of them finally used a ladder to get into the building through the Bishop's bedroom window, and then proceeded down to the churchyard.

A fight ensued between police and occupants. The police in the long run were able to make their way to the gates and open them up to the rest of the police force and the military police. Forty-eight arrests were made and the men were sentenced by the Magistrate as they arrived at the Court house. Despite the efforts of Mr. Cornwall, the barrister, most of them were either heavily fined or sent to prison.

Meanwhile, the wife of Constable Davis reported hearing Mr. Imossi say in the pharmacy that he would shoot the Bishop as he entered the church. The Police Magistrate, being told of this, went with two policemen to warn the proprietor and to search Mr. Imossi. The latter appeared to have no gun on his person, but two constables stayed there to see that nothing amiss would occur.

At 11.30 a.m. companies of piquets from three regiments were in position along the Bishop's route. Strategic points were blocked off to give the Bishop unimpeded access to the route and the church. The Berkshire Regiment lined both sides of Main Street from the Exchange to the Spanish Pavilion. At 12.20 p.m., when all was ready, the Garrison Town Major gave the Bishop word to enter his horse-drawn carriage. But there was no crimson splendour or cope or mitre or crozier to be seen – the Bishop was dressed in his black cassock and cloak. With him were Fr. Femenias and the Lenten preacher. Walking behind were his brother and Mr. Juan Baggio and a score of civilians and military. No cheers, no bells, no music.

When he paused at the church entrance the Bishop looked sad. Around him he saw only soldiers. He was however, welcomed by "cccc saccrdos magnus" from a scratch choir as he entered the church, and was escorted by police to the high altar. Mgr. Pallares produced the papal appointment and Fr. Dotto read it aloud. The Bishop then proceeded to the throne, where he donned the cope and was given the crozier and mitre. Prayer followed, and at the end of the short ceremony, Dr. Canilla gave those present his first episcopal blessing – that is, to six persons, apart from his own relatives and the police. The whole congregation including the choir amounted to about seventy persons.

After a short chat with the Vicar General in his episcopal apartment, he got back to his carriage, and escorted by police, returned to his parents' home. Nothing, after all, had happened apart from a few comments from high-up windows and the odd shout to "get out", "fuera". A few squads of soldiers

An artist's impression of Bishop Canilla's Entrance into the Church escorted by the Army.

roamed the town afterwards just in case any disorder might break out.

The newspapers next day – with the exception of the *Chronicle* – were full of comments about the events of the previous day. The language was somewhat inflated. "Let all Europe learn what has happened in Gibraltar" – the people's requests, entreaties, prayers had been met with contempt and dishonour by Propaganda. The soldiers of the most liberal of countries had taken up arms and imposed on Gibraltarian Catholics what their consciences rejected. Field guns had been posted, the bridges of the fortress drawn up, 400 men armed with rifles had been put on guard, all regiments placed under arms, the squadron at anchor in the bay had been alerted, the signals station put at the ready – all this amounting to a state of siege – and why. . . . to impose on Catholics a Vicar whom their consciences rejected. There followed descriptions of the removal of Catholics who were occupying the church –

much easier than dislodging the Boers, be it noted: "The Commanding Officer and Superior Officers being mounted and in continual motion, displaying an intrepidity which recalled to our minds Napoleon's at the battle of Austerlitz". There was mention of the deathly silence, the reign of brute force, the quiet of non-existence, the stillness of desolation, the suppressed breath of Catholics who from their homes protested not with their lips but with their hearts, as perhaps some dictator approached.... "Was it Attila, or Nero?.... No, Dr. Canilla.... ridiculous display of force.... a most eloquent display of repugnance and contempt during the triumphal passage of the rejected Vicar...." "Families wailing for their children and relatives sent to prison, the inviolable rights of the natives of Gibraltar trampled under foot, antagonism and anger excited between the civil and military elements.... England giving to the world an example of despotism of the Middle Ages, imposing on the Catholics a Vicar whom their consciences rejected...." "Doctor Canilla has not only wounded our dignity, but has been the cause of our deprivation of the most cherished right now possessed by the civilized world, the right of liberty of conscience"....

Two days after the installation of Dr. Canilla, the Colonial Secretary informed Garese that, once attempts at riotous proceedings had ceased, consideration would be given to reasonable representations about the administration of church buildings put at the disposal of the Roman Catholic community by the Crown.

This peace offering got short shrift. The Elders, having got precious little satisfaction from Governor or Secretary of State, appealed to the Houses of Parliament for protection and the establishment of Gibraltarian Catholics' rights and privileges. One member of the Junta, Mr. Pitman, wrote to the Earl of Kimberley, criticising the Governor. He objected, he said, to the phrase "attempts at riotous proceedings". Gibraltarians had never embarked on such lines of conduct, he asserted. Moreover, while Roman Catholics in Gibraltar had been carrying out Her Majesty's commands, the Governor had not. The sanctity of the Church had been violated by Protestant soldiers, and peaceful Roman Catholics had been ejected from the church *vi et armis* – on the very day a vile assassin had made an attempt on the Sovereign herself! Hence, thousands of Roman Catholics had been forced to go to a foreign country to attend divine worship for fear of further attacks from Protestant bayonets. Mr. Pitman said that, as an Englishman, he regretted the Governor's ineptitude and despotic proceedings; they were "an opprobrium upon the honour of a British Officer and on the age in which we live". He demanded the setting up of a "Royal Commission to investigate the Governor's conduct and that of other menials in office".

Patiently the Secretary of State explained that the church in question was still the property of the Crown. The Junta had been voluntarily dissolved in 1872. Just as the draft Ordinance had yet to become law, so a new Junta had to await approval from the Government.

The Governor was pleased to announce to the Earl of Kimberley on 24 March that no further disorders had taken place since the day of installation.

The Bishop had said Mass for the military on the following Sunday and he had taken up permanent residence in the presbytery.

The presence of police around the church and priests' house was gradually lessened, and terminated altogether at the beginning of April. Those who still disagreed with the Bishop's presence went to La Linea for Mass. Some who owned benches in the church removed them to La Linea. Others were afraid to come to services lest their action might indicate support of the Bishop and something unpleasant might happen to them. The Maltese living in St. Joseph's parish and the Catholics who belonged to the Armed Forces did, however, support the Bishop by attending St. Mary's regularly.

The opposition leaders brought pressure to bear on people who were bereaved to drop the custom of having an absolution given in their homes, followed by a second and a third blessing at the church and in the North Front cemetery. A number of laymen volunteered to conduct funeral services. Mr. Manuel Montegriffo, Secretary to the Gavino's trust and in charge of the Catholic ward in the Civil Hospital, was one of these. He would collect the corpse at the house, accompany the hearse to the church, recite the appropriate prayer there without actually entering the church itself, and then conduct the procession to the cemetery. He reported these secular burials to Rome, expressing a hope that the Cemetery Committee would disallow such unprecedented burials.[10]

The Bishop very much regretted this form of burial, but he had other troubles to bear. In October 1882, Mgr. MacAuliffe left the Rock.[11] The priest had proved too outspoken a person to be able to remain and die upon the Rock, though he had given to the people living there some twenty years of service. He felt deeply the insults and humiliations inflicted on him by the opposition.

The greatest blow of all for the Bishop was the death of Mgr. Narcissus Pallares. He was found dying among the archives with his throat cut. His death, however, had nothing to do with threats from the opposition. As archivist, he dealt with marriage problems, education, weddings and baptisms. He also acted as almoner. A young man who wanted to marry Miss Clemencia Saccone – though he had never spoken to her – often urged Mgr. Pallares to fix up the marriage for him. The priest neither could nor would do anything to help, as the young fellow was unbalanced and the Saccone family was anxious to protect the girl from the boy. The priest was prepared, all the same, to listen to the young man's ramblings, and made use of delaying tactics to put him off as diplomatically as possible. On 3 February 1885, the youth became impatient with the priest's stalling, and stabbed the Monsignor in the neck with a carving knife. A young boy who had come in looking for alms saw what happened and shouted for help. Dr. Canilla came down and gave the victim the last rites of the Church. The boy was able to identify the killer, who was then tried for murder, declared to be insane, and was removed to a mental hospital. The Bishop thus lost another friend. Yet he seemed to benefit from Mgr. Pallares' death, for many of his opponents came to the burial service in St. Mary's where the body was laid to rest in all solemnity.

Hearing that some leaders of the opposition had been present at the Funeral Mass, many people who were attending religious services at La Linea began to attend St. Mary's once again and returned the benches.

The last time the Bishop had to withdraw from some projected plan because of continuing opposition was when he proposed to say Mass at the cemetery for all those who had been buried in a secular fashion without the presence of a priest. At the first sign of resistance to the idea on the part of Catholics, he withdrew from his project, even though he had written to the Governor asking for advice about its advisability. With the passage of time, people began to desert the opposition leaders and became resigned to the status quo and the young Bishop's presence. Mr. Imossi was probably the last to agree to a reconciliation, which took place at his daughter's wedding. Layman and Bishop shook hands.

By then, Dr. Canilla had suffered a lot. At his first *ad limina* visit to Pope Leo XIII, the Pope commiserated with him on this point. Yet the Bishop also accomplished a lot. He founded an additional home for aged men and women of all creeds next to Loreto Convent, and put the Little Sisters of the Poor in charge. Twelve of these cared for seventy old people. Their resources came from alms begged by these humble sisters whose strict rule of life forbade them to possess money or property. When the Jews left this home for the newly built Hebrew Home in 1907, the Little Sisters of the Poor Home became totally Catholic and remained in operation until World War II. It was later restarted as a different home for 140 persons but put in the care of the Franciscan Sisters, Missionaries of the Divine Motherhood.

The Harvey Report on elementary Schools and the Rules and Regulations for Annual Grants – based on inspection and payment by results – had been received by Dr. Scandella when he was ill. Some thirty months later, as a result of the Bishop's death and the troubled early period of his successor, nothing had been done about them. The Anglican and Methodist schools having adopted the Rules, were thus in receipt of grants from the Imperial Treasury, whereas the Catholic Schools, though still functioning, received nothing by way of monetary aid. This situation was made even worse by the campaign waged against subscriptions to school funds by the opponents of Dr. Canilla. As soon as the latter was officially installed in the Cathedral, however, he rallied whatever members of the Poor Schools committee were available to deal with these Rules.

Those who drew up the new regulations were evidently not familiar with the problems of many of the poor children of Gibraltar. The severe rules about punctuality, for example, were unsuitable; very many children were involved in the working life of their parents, whose jobs might require the children to bring them their breakfast or lunch, in which case the children might not be able to come to class before 10.00 a.m., or might have to leave before noon. Some children could only attend one class per day. The Bishop did not see why children caught up in such difficult circumstances should be penalized. Payment by results also tended to militate against the interests of some children, as a lot of them spoke only Spanish, and an idiomatic kind of

Spanish, so that the operation of such rules would require an Inspector well versed in the idiomatic peculiarities of the children. Again, the Bishop could not agree with the treatment meted out to religious instruction in the Rules, for he did not want to see the denominational system weakened in any way. Neither he nor the Religious Orders could accept the exclusion of religious instruction from the syllabus. He sought the Government's agreement to allow three half-hour periods per week for this subject; and wanted prizes given for it too. The requirement that teachers should undergo an examination to qualify them to teach under the new system was likewise unacceptable; it clashed with the Bishop's existing agreement with the Sisters and the Christian Brothers, who were the mainstay of his schools.

Despite the enthusiasm of Mr. Buckle in pressing for the strict observance of the Harvey Rules, the Bishop stuck to his guns. So long as the problem was unsettled, no grants were forthcoming. It was finally resolved by the Government's agreeing to accept an assurance from the Bishop that Religious Orders would only send members with the requisite teaching qualifications to Gibraltar. The regulations were amended to read accordingly, and the Government lost no time in granting the necessary subsidies, once the religious superiors guaranteed that no members of their Orders would be sent except those who had been well trained to teach.

Bishop Canilla was anxious to realize his predecessor's plans for the fast developing area higher up on the Rock near the Sacred Heart Church. The monastery behind the church for the Christian Brothers was finished, but funds were lacking to execute the construction of the two wings containing the classrooms. By 1885, however, the south wing was completed at a cost of £1200, the Government contributing £500, and the Bishop providing all the requisite furniture. The north wing was not finished until 1890. At its opening the Government donated a large open space behind the school for use as a garden. That same year, the nuns likewise opened another school in Johnston's Passage.

The Day-Pay-School which the Brothers opened in Commercial Square in 1878, with 36 boys on the roll, had developed so well that it had to move, first of all, to City Mill Lane in 1881, and finally to Line Wall Road, to a property bought from Mr. Jerome Saccone in November 1887 for £2,200. A further £2,000 was spent in alterations and building an extra storey. It was known as Line Wall School. Though this school was established for the youth of Gibraltar, its excellence gradually attracted the sons of military and naval officers stationed on the Rock. It also became popular among the sons of many wealthy families living in Sevilla, Malaga, Granada, Algeciras, Tangiers, Madrid and San Roque. The school was pulled down in the spring of 1986. Another small boarding school (St. Stanislaus College) was opened at Scud Hill in 1893, and was affiliated to the Instituto de Jerez, and took examinations for the Spanish bachillerato. It had as many as thirty boarders and a hundred day boys, but it lasted only until July 1897 as accommodation problems proved too difficult. It carried on as a Day College, however.

Under pressure from Spaniards who wanted to learn English, a further attempt to run a boarding school was made at the Line Wall establishment. A house was acquired next to the day school and the reconstructions effected made it possible to house some 26 boarders. The places were always taken up, even though they were not advertised. Over the years, several of its pupils became priests, and among its most enthusiastic supporters was Don Pedro Merry del Val, brother of Pope Pius X's Cardinal Secretary, whose nephews attended the school. The Bishop said Mass every week for the community in the college chapel, and he had such confidence in the community that he never required their pupils to be examined in Religious Knowledge before the reception of the Sacrament of Confirmation. This college, though looked on as the chief educational establishment in Gibraltar, did not come under Government inspection.

Bishop Canilla was still not satisfied with the few schools that existed in the southern district of the Rock, and in 1886, he asked the Brothers to open yet another school for boys in St. Joseph's parish. The Government also asked the Bishop to take over a school which had been opened in 1841 by the Wesleyans, and run by them for thirty years, and then by the Church of England until this offer was made. He took it over from the Anglicans with a lease of 99 years and spent £200 in alterations and improvements before putting it into use for Catholics. Even the previous Protestant teacher at this school had his son attend it under Catholic auspices and take Catechism and Religious instruction.

The Bishop spent much time with the children, visiting each school once a week and trying to get acquainted with each child. He also paid regular visits to the hospital, and called in to see his mother who lived just a few yards away from it. A hospital run by the Brothers of St. John of God had existed on the same site before the coming of the British to Gibraltar. With the departure of the Brothers to Spain, the building was turned into a barracks, which was later reconstructed on the lines planned by Mr. Boschetti, to provide the colony once again with a hospital, divided into separate parts for the Jews, Protestants and Catholics. The governors of this institution were selected from each of the three communities. The Catholic division benefitted greatly from the will of Mr. John Gavino. It was the Catholic division, of course, that was most of all in use; not even Spanish workers or Spanish residents from La Linea were excluded from the care dispensed there. Such service was recognized by the King of Spain himself, who, during the outbreak of an epidemic when Gibraltarians went to live in huts on the British side of Neutral Ground, sent provisions and other help to those afflicted by the disease. In 1889, as the diocese was finding it ever more difficult to cope with the expense of running the Catholic division, the Government took over the task and renamed the block the Colonial Hospital.

It was about the time of this take-over that the Bishop's brother, Sebastian, was diagnosed as having an acute cerebral illness that would surely paralyse him, if not kill him. Dr. Canilla accompanied his sick brother to Lourdes, where bathing in the waters of the Grotto had a remarkable effect on the patient's health. In fact, he recovered totally from his sick state. As a result

113

of this the Bishop installed a statue of Our Lady of Lourdes in each of his four churches, and he renamed the Chapel of St. Francis in the Cathedral the Chapel of Our Lady of Lourdes. He also put up a statue in his mother's new house, to which was given the name "Villa Lourdes". The feast of Our Lady of Lourdes was thereafter celebrated in Gibraltar with novenas and great solemnity. The Bishop also gave the same name of Lourdes to the last school he was to open – at Castle Road – paid for by an endowment from Mr. William Eschauzier, a Gibraltarian who had amassed a fortune in South America and retired to Sevilla with his wife, the daughter of Mr. Terry. When the Lourdes School was established, the Christian Brothers took over and transferred to it the poor boys they had been teaching at Castle Ramp. By 1897, the Brothers were in charge of six schools educating almost 2,000 boys. The educational efforts of Father Zino, Bishop Hughes, Bishops Scandella and Canilla, especially the last two, had certainly borne fruit.

These two Bishops had also done a great deal towards bettering the lot of the average working man. It was on behalf of the latter that they fought the terms of the Aliens Bill of 1873 and the Customs Bill. They had found that often two or three families lived in a flat consisting of just a room and a kitchen; the wages for a man with a big family were inadequate to pay rent for better accommodation. In any case, there was a shortage of reasonably priced, healthy dwellings. When Dr. Canilla, as Bishop's secretary, had written a document in 1876 pointing out this lack of dwellings for low-paid workers, some entrepreneurs had built houses to accommodate such families, but just barely within the laws: the result was a slight alleviation of the conditions of the workers but a great profit for the entrepreneurs. On the other hand, as trade improved, landlords were inclined to convert ground floors of buildings into stores, offices or shops. They profited more by ejecting hundreds of families from their homes. Dr. Canilla's own parents, when at Rodger's Ramp, lived in a house built for twenty persons, which once sheltered a hundred families. People who were put out of houses due for reconversion, were forced to lodge with others already badly housed, which only made the overcrowding worse. In one particular case, one hundred families were expelled from Danino's Ramp to vacate quarters for military personnel and their families. When the Bishop tried to get houses constructed for the poor, the businessman protested that the "conditions the Government and the Sanitary Commission imposed for the erection of such dwellings are too numerous and vexatious."

The overcrowding led to constant squabbling among neighbours, and the police often had to intervene. Sanitary facilities were scarce, and where they did exist, they were very poor. A law was passed, giving access to Sanitary Inspectors and police without prior warning in houses whose landlords paid under 90 duros in rates. To escape such inspection and possible subsequent expense, landlords added to the dwellings whatever was necessary to raise their rate payment above the minimum 90 duros, but, of course, they also raised the rent to the occupiers. When a survey revealed to the Bishop that, of 960 houses in the town itself, only 59 were three storey buildings, 300 two storey buildings and the rest one storey dwellings, he made what proved a fruitless suggestion – to add a storey to some of these in the interest of solving the housing problem.

The Bishop tried in other ways to help the local workers – a class that consisted of boatmen, coal-heavers, porters, stevedors, muleteers, tobacco-choppers, cigar-makers, and such like. There were, of course, other workers such as those who constructed the dockyard – this group consisted of convict labour as well as Maltese, Portuguese, and Spanish labourers. These people had no tradition of forming associations for achieving workers' security. When in dire straits, all they could do was to rely on the St. Vincent de Paul Conferences or the Freemasons' Lodges for relief.

Dr. Canilla started a campaign to enlighten the workers so that they could be brought to confront their problems and take concrete steps to solve them. The encyclical *Rerum novarum* had not as yet been published, but certain other documents were available: Cardinal Gibbons' letters and Cardinal Manning's conferences on the duties and rights of workers. Dr. Canilla translated these works for a *Newsletter* which he published in the Cathedral.[12] The workers thus heard about their right to sell their labour at a proper price; the right to work wherever and for whomsoever they wished; the right to protect their own capital – their ability to work – by associating with their fellow workers. They learnt that it was for the State to legislate against abuses; against low-paid child labour, for example, which deprived children of necessary education, or against exploitation of women, which caused the latter to neglect their homes and their offspring. The workers learnt that the accumulation of more and more wealth by one privileged class at the expense of the moral and social conditions of the majority was wrong. But all this had little effect in the short term.

The employers were quicker off the mark. When the Sanitary Commission decided to put up the rates in order to improve the hygienic conditions prevalent on the Rock and to build reservoirs, the employers sprang into action. They formed the Gibraltar Rate-Payers Defence Association. Five years later, with no workers' unions yet formed, social disorder broke out in the shape of a revolt by coal-heavers against their employers. They complained most of all at being paid in Spanish money, whereas the merchants were paid in sterling. With the variations in the rate of exchange, the workers often lost a large proportion of their hard-earned wages. Other workers were intimidated into joining in the riots. Many were ill-treated in the troubles that followed and put in gaol. The coal merchants also suffered, and troops were called out to help the police maintain order. Those on strike were replaced by Spanish workers. The influx of the latter from across the border greatly affected the position of the inhabitants of Gibraltar and prevented any great social advance. The strike only came to an end with the outbreak of the Boer War, when there was work for all.

Bishop Canilla was in trouble right up to the end of his life, which came early and unexpectedly. In the autumn of 1898, he was involved in a case in the Supreme Court, over a will made by an old lady, Maria Teresa Bonell,

115

who had left her estate to be administered by the Church. Her nephew contested the will on the grounds that it had been made under the undue influence of the Bishop. The dispute was to be cleared up in Court. Meanwhile, on 18 October 1898, the Bishop paid a visit to the Christian Brothers to transfer to them the lease of the Sacred Heart School; from there he went to visit some old friends and finally called in to see his mother. He said the rosary with her and began to recite the Litany of Loreto. At the invocation "Rosa Mystica", he collapsed and died. He was fifty-two years of age. The Bishop's body was taken to the Cathedral and lay in state all night, with many people coming to hold vigil or pay their final respects. At the four o'clock Mass next day, Fr. Jose Sanchez Olmo preached the funeral panegyric. After Mass, the funeral procession, led by a military band and detachments of soliders and sailors, wended its way to Commercial Square and back to the Lourdes Chapel in the Cathedral, where the body was interred. Ten days later the Court case was decided in favour of the dead Bishop.

PART THREE

The Diocese
in Gibraltar

Silver Throne.

The Cathedral of St. Mary the Crowned with a new facade constructed by Bishop Fitzgerald in 1932.

Rapallo's funeral Mass.

CHAPTER ONE

The Right Reverend James Bellord
Vicar Apostolic
Bishop of Milevia 1899–1901

From the death of Dr. Canilla until now there have been seven ecclesial leaders on the Rock. Two of them were Vicars Apostolic each with the title of some old non-existing diocese, and the other five carried more fittingly and proudly the title of Bishop of Gibraltar. It would be presumptuous to expand on the history of these seven personalities at such an early stage. Perhaps someone else in fifty years' time will have access to documents, and the patience to carefully bring to light the development of Christian living during their term of office in Gibraltar. For the benefit of future historians a few notes are appended on each of these men who strove to lead their flock surely and safely in very fast-moving times, and under various delicate pressures.

The Congregation for the Propagation of Faith was embarrassed by the sudden and unexpected death of the young Bishop Gonzalo Canilla. Very little study had been entered into by the Congregation to facilitate smooth episcopal continuity on the Rock. Catholic Bishops in England were immediately approached to assist in the selection of a successor for the Vicariate Apostolic of Gibraltar. A very young priest from Gibraltar, Father Peter Amigo, then working in Westminster diocese, was asked whether, if offered, he would accept such an office. Probably because the recollections of his father's involvement with the late Bishop were all too disagreeable and fresh in his mind, he answered in the negative.

As an alternative, the Congregation of Propaganda Fide was recommended a retired Military Chaplain, Father James Bellord, a Doctor of Theology. Already quite advanced in age he was much given to writing spiritual and dogmatic books. In fact he wrote and published daily prayer books and a highly regarded thesis on the Holy Eucharist. He took possession of the Vicariate after his consecration on 1 May 1899.

Bishop Bellord, seeing that Fr. Luis Calero was administering the Sacred Heart Church competently, elevated it to the status of a Parish on 16 July 1899. Unfortunately this status was short-lived. Fr. Luis Calero became sick and died soon afterwards. There was no-one to take charge of the new parish. Services there were supplied by the priests of the Cathedral Church. The people taking up residence in the new houses there could not be allowed to suffer because of Fr. Calero's demise.

The new Bishop could judge efficiency with great facility, but he was puzzled by the more subtle and idiosyncratic elements in the local ecclesial life. What proved a stumbling-block for him was an admittedly unusual situation permitted by the late Bishop Canilla. In St. Joseph's Parish, Bishop Canilla had granted Magdalena Lugaro, who had founded a religious order, permission to wear the habit of the Third Order of St. Francis. She was to devote herself to the needs of the children in primary schools on the South of the Rock. Many other ladies joined Sor Magdalena to assist her in schools and in the cleaning of St. Joseph's Church. The helpers, however, would not wear Sor Magdalena's religious habit.

People on the whole appreciated and acknowledged the devotion and sterling work done by these ladies for the children of the south district. But Bishop Bellord thought it bizarre that a non-canonical institution with only one member should be allowed to continue. He tried to suppress the "Order" by commanding her to stop behaving as if she belonged to a serious religious order. Unexpectedly the Bishop saw that the faithful of St. Joseph's Parish praised her work and virtues and pleaded in her favour. They suggested to him, as a compromise, that she should be allowed to continue as she was until she died. They argued that she was advanced in years and she could not last much longer. But the Bishop was resolute. He answered them with the following ultimatum. "Either she goes or I leave Gibraltar". Two years after his arrival on the Rock, Bishop Bellord tendered his resignation because Sor Magdalena steadfastly held her position.

CHAPTER TWO

Bishop Guido Remigio Barbieri

Vicar Apostolic
Bishop of Theodosiopolis 1903–1910

The Right Reverend Guido R. Barbieri, O.S.B.
Vicar Apostolic
Episcopus Theodosiopolitanus: 10th November 1903
Died: 15 April 1910.

Two months later, an Italian Benedictine monk from Monte Cassino, Dr. Remegio Barbieri, arrived in Gibraltar already consecrated Bishop. He was small, slightly stout, a priest with great charm and marked simplicity. He soon won the affection of everyone on the Rock. His policy in education could be summed up in his statement, "tell me what Bishop Canilla did so I can continue his good work". Like Canilla, he concerned himself closely with the welfare of children and visited the various schools regularly; thus he acquainted himself intimately with teachers and pupils.

His greatest difficulty was remedying the shortage of priests. He travelled widely through Spain, contacting Bishops and Religious Orders in his endeavours to recruit priests to work in Gibraltar. It was in Cordoba that he received a spark of hope. The Missionaries of the Heart of Mary, better known as Claretians, accepted the invitation to work on the Rock out of respect for the great memory they still held of the late Dr. Gonzalo Canilla. They agreed with Bishop Barbieri to work in Gibraltar for a period of thirty years starting in 1903. The Missionaries were to take over the Sacred Heart of Jesus and the adjacent priests' house. This house was enlarged to take more priests and to include a library. It was at the time Gibraltar was enjoying the news that Father Peter Amigo had been made Bishop of Southwark when the Missionaries took residence in the presbytery at the Sacred Heart.

Dr. Barbieri was far ahead of his time in his relationship with the local Jewish community. He was well known to have befriended the local Chief Rabbi, The Very Reverend Solomon Elmalech, who was a great biblical scholar. Bishop Barbieri would sit at the front bench of the synagogue whenever Dr. Elmalech addressed the community in the Synagogue. They worked together, and with them the two communities.

His efforts at keeping the schools and churches in good order were noticeable to everyone in Gibraltar. Such projects required solid financial backing, which he lacked. Freemasons, aware of the Bishop's predicament, made a collection among their own brotherhood and presented him with a most welcome sum of money. Hardliners in the Church criticized the Bishop for taking such sums of money. The Bishop was heard to answer: "I would accept money for these projects even if it came from the devil himself".

The Bishop died on 15 April, 1910. While it was a short episcopate it was generally agreed that it was a consolidating period and most successfully run. Dr. Barbieri had been in constant communication with the Congregation of Propaganda Fide. He had, therefore, informed the Cardinal of his herculean efforts to recruit priests for the place; his excellent relations with the local teaching Religious Orders and the heads of other religions, including the Jewish. All this encouraged him to recommend to Rome that the Vicariate should be raised to the status of a Diocese. By so doing the dignity of the local Church would be enhanced and its evangelizing mission would acquire a greater impetus. Furthermore, if Rome raised Gibraltar to the status of a diocese and he believed, that if it were placed under the care of the Benedictine Order, the problems of recruiting priests would disappear completely.

CHAPTER THREE

The Right Reverend Gregory Henry Thompson O.S.B.
Bishop of Gibraltar 1910–1927

The Right Reverend Henry Thompson, O.S.B.
First Bishop of Gibraltar
Consecrated Bishop: 12th December 1910
Resigned: 1926. Left Gibraltar 15th October 1927.

The Congregation of Propaganda Fide must have considered these proposals very seriously since they lost no time in setting in motion the process of selection along the lines suggested by Dr. Barbieri. Dom Gregory Thompson, a Benedictine Monk of St. Augustine's Monastery, Ramsgate, then one with the Monte Cassino Community, was nominated the new Diocese's first Bishop on 10 November 1910. A week later, following the late Bishop's recommendation, Pope St. Pius X decreed the elevation of the Vicariate to the status of a Diocese and placed the care of the new ecclesial body in the hands of the Benedictine Order of Monte Cassino.

Gibraltar was at this time affected by the fast-growing unrest in Portugal, as was the case whenever there was a war anywhere in the Iberian Peninsula. The Portuguese royal family took refuge in Gibraltar. King Manuel with his mother, Queen Amelia and the Infante Alfonso arrived in their yacht on 5 October 1910. While Queen Maria Pia left for Italy on the Italian Cruiser "Regina Coeli", the King and other members of the royal family left the Rock ten days later in the British Royal Yacht for an unknown destination.

Two days after their departure, a community of thirty-five Jesuit priests, cruelly treated and expelled from Portugal looked for refuge in Gibraltar. Arrangements were made with the Irish Christian Brothers and the Jesuits were quartered in their residence. One of these priests died soon afterwards from the beating received in Lisbon.

Bishop Thompson arrived in Gibraltar on 7 February 1911. He had missed all the excitement of the influx of Portuguese refugees. It was soon discovered that he did not know any Spanish. When the four monks from Monserrat joined him, he found it next to impossible to communicate with them. There are people still alive who recall the monks with the Bishop praying the liturgical hours on the roof-terrace. This was probably the only one moment of peace in the house. Also living in the same house, there were four local diocesan priests. These objected strongly to the demands made on them by the Benedictines, namely, that they too kept the rules and discipline of the Order while residing in the house. Because of this disagreement there was constant friction and discontent in the house, and as a result of what appeared to be unintelligible discussions, the Bishop would quietly slip away to take refuge among the books of the Garrison Library.

The arguments were intensified and seriously aggravated during the Great War. This war brought about an increase of opportunities for workers in Gibraltar to bring home a handsome income and enjoy a decent living. The local pro-British feeling was greatly consolidated by the presence of the fleet in the harbour. Trouble between Spanish workers and local workers arose over the bunkering of the British ships. The Spanish workers refused to serve British ships. The pro-Kaiser feelings of the Spanish workers, who declared themselves on strike, found an echo among some of the Spanish priests in the Clergy House. The tension in the house was electric, and the antagonism between the two sets of priests, arising now from the anti-British arguments of the Spaniards and their hostile attitude, made the bishop go to the library almost daily. He was unable to bring peace among the priests.

Despite the constant strife in the priests' house, witnesses attest to the uninterrupted pastoral activities of the monks and priests. People alive today still remark that the spiritual growth among the children and people in general in that period bloomed as never before in the history of Gibraltar.

From the outset Bishop Thompson interested himself in the material needs of the people. He directed the charitable Society of St. Vincent de Paul which orientated its activities on the many families affected by the depression and widespread unemployment.

His contacts with the Irish Christian Brothers were nothing but the friendliest and as a consequence there existed harmony between the Brothers and the Bishop and the boys received the best education available at the time. So also were his communications with the teaching sisters of the Institute of the Blessed Virgin Mary, the Loreto Sisters. They were doing solid work with the young ladies of Gibraltar. It was not always easy to obtain everything the nuns required from the Bishop.

The Loreto Nuns once petitioned the Bishop to obtain for them a small area that belonged to the War Department building in Town Range. The open area was exactly behind the Loreto Town Girls' School, it was never used by the Military Authorities, but could be put to good use by the girls as a playground. Bishop Thompson used the first opportunity open to him to bring up the case with His Excellency the Governor. In his turn the Governor approached the War Department which replied with a blunt refusal. When the Bishop reported the negative answer to the Superior of the Loreto Community she considered the matter badly handled and pressed for further force to be used until the site were transferred to the girls. Since the Bishop obtained no favourable results he was not regarded highly by Mother Superior who made her feelings known.

The Bishop extended the procession of Corpus Christi, which had dwindled to a tiny procession around the Commercial Square, to Casemates Square, along Irish Town and then return to the Cathedral. The five candidates for the priesthood were all collared by the Bishop and pressed to train as monks, despite the fact that they had no wish to become monks. In fact they lost their chances of training for the priesthood.

In 1926 Bishop Peter Amigo visited Gibraltar, his birthplace. He never told his sisters or anyone he was going to the Rock. Once in Gibraltar, he moved around swiftly and efficiently, talking to priests, monks and the faithful. Then, like Fr. Weld in Dr. Canilla's time, he revealed himself as the Official Visitor to the Diocese. He had come in the capacity of a delegate, who would later report to Rome on the manner in which the Diocese was being conducted. Amigo met the Bishop before and after he revealed the purpose of his visit. He urged Bishop Thompson to expedite to Rome the report on the Diocese, which was already long overdue, and state there all the difficulties he was experiencing on the Rock. On his return to the U.K., Amigo wrote to Thompson and there again pressed him to make his report to Rome without any delay. When some weeks later Bishop Amigo received notification from Propaganda Fide that nothing had been received from the Bishop of

Gibraltar, he immediately wrote to Bishop Thompson a most forceful, cutting and direct letter. Amigo had to make a report on his findings after visiting the Rock and would wait no longer. Some of the points raised by him in his report were that Thompson lacked the Spanish language and hence could neither endear himself to the masses of his people or to his own monks. He was unable to exercise control over the priests. He was slow and neglectful in writing letters, and vocations to the priesthood had been stifled by his misguided aims. Amigo clearly pointed out that he should resign from office. He would personally ensure that the Abbot of Ramsgate was kept abreast of all the occurrences.

The Congregation of Propaganda Fide lost no time in asking Dr. Thompson to resign, and he did so officially on 15 October 1927. He returned to St. Augustine's, Ramsgate, where he resumed his teaching career, and assisted at some parish or other. He later corresponded regularly with Bishop Amigo telling him how relieved and happy he was working as a simple monk.

Amigo had kept corresponding with Propaganda Fide since he sent off his own report. He recommended that no Benedictine monk be sought to replace Thompson. Ramsgate had no monks with qualifications and Spanish from which to choose a successor. He seriously proposed that for the time being a qualified person with Spanish knowledge should be found other than a Benedictine. The spectrum of selection was thus widened and allowed for a better choice. The English College of Valladolid and the Irish College of Salamanca could well provide the candidates with the proper qualifications sought for the Diocese of Gibraltar.

CHAPTER FOUR

The Right Reverend Richard John Fitzgerald
Bishop of Gibraltar 1927–1956

The Right Reverend Richard J. Fitzgerald, C.B.E., D.D.
Bishop of Gibraltar
Consecrated Bishop: October 1927
Died: 19th February 1956.

Ten days after Dr. Thompson resigned, the new Bishop arrived on the Rock. He was Monsignor Richard John Fitzgerald, an Irishman and a former Vice-Rector of the Irish College of Salamanca in Spain. His term of office proved to be the longest of all the Bishops — twenty-nine years. He was not a Benedictine monk but a diocesan priest with a fluency in the Castillian language that was unparalleled around the Rock. His versatility in cultural matters and world affairs either mesmerized or won the respect of the Spanish Benedictine monks who continued to live in the house. While the friction between the monks and priests persisted, the presence and personality of the new Bishop contributed greatly in softening the tension and bitterness in the house.

It was with the outbreak of the Civil War in Spain that ill-feelings flared once again in the Cathedral House. When Spain was declared a republic in 1936 and civil war commenced, King Alfonso's son, Don Juan and hundreds of families took refuge in Gibraltar. The people of Gibraltar, as usual, generously opened their homes to them and alleviated their sufferings. Tents were set up at Bayside, North Front, Boulevard, and Arengo's Palace. Republicans as well as Nationalists took shelter on the Rock—they were welcomed without distinction. Gibraltarians even helped people escape the Reds by boat from Malaga and Estepona. The vast majority of people arrived by the land frontier. These Spanish refugees of both inclinations took the cue from the Gibraltarians and refrained from squabbling with one another while on the Rock. In this they showed greater prudence than some of the Spanish priests. These openly voiced their anti-British feelings, because a band of local workers, a very small group, favoured the Republicans. The outspokenness of the priests embarrassed the local clergy who prudently refrained from taking sides. In this way their pastoral work among the refugees on one side or the other remained unimpeded. The local priests deprecated the monks, and tension was rekindled. The Bishop resolved there and then not to renew the contract with the Missionaries of the Heart of Mary, the Claretians and also sought an opportunity to relieve the Diocese of the Spanish Benedictine monks.

The Claretians and Benedictines, nevertheless, performed genuine pastoral work in the Diocese of Gibraltar and many people benefitted by their spirituality. The outspokenness of a few priests marred the peaceful continuity of their communities on the Rock. They were also responsible with their political bias for that sector of the population who had turned anti-clerical. It took the better part of 40 years to undo the harm done by priests taking sides in political matters.

When World War II broke out in 1940, the British government had already decided to evacuate Gibraltar. Adolf Hitler's "Operation Felix" was discovered by British spies to mean ".... capturing Gibraltar, march through Spain, force France to capitulate and then invade Great Britain". Repeating the experience of people during the Great Siege in 1778−82, all women, children and men in non-essential jobs were to abandon the Rock. Crammed into the decks or holds of merchant ships the civilian population of Gibraltar was transferred, one and a half days' journey to Casablanca. People were dispersed to Marakesh, Mekness, Rabat, Casablanca and Mogador. People were quartered in most dreadful conditions. It was obvious that nothing had been organized for them once they reached their destination. Thirty days later, things had not improved in any way; it was discovered that France had capitulated to the German forces. Hitler had changed his plans and attacked France first, and then intended to go for Great Britain. Once again, women and children were travelling back to Casablanca port to take the first merchant ship that would return them to Gibraltar. On arrival at the Bay of Gibraltar the ships carrying the people, who, exposed to subhuman conditions, anchored there awaiting orders to move away.

The authorities were undecided as to where the people were to be sent, whether to Jamaica or Great Britain. Meanwhile, the women and children remained out in the harbour. The men ashore would not have it. They rallied together and despite the force exercised by the Military Policemen, Redcaps, to disband them, they demanded and pressed for the immediate landing of their families. Quite a few men were jailed for arousing animosity—a serious offence in wartime. Bishop Fitzgerald represented their strong case and the women and children were brought home again.

By this time all the Benedictine monks, Missionaries of the Heart of Mary, the Sisters of the Poor, the Sisters of the Order of St. Joseph, and Brothers of St. John of God who were Spanish, had returned to Spain. Only Bishop Fitzgerald, Fr. Grech, Fr. Carter, and Fr. Montegriffo remained on the Rock.

The civilian population remained in Gibraltar a mere few weeks. Large sections of people at a time from different districts of Gibraltar were shipped to England, either in Troopers sailing alone or in convoys. Some people reached England in four days, others took as long as thirty, almost touching the West Indian islands to avoid the German U-boats. The Athlone Castle was the liner to take the first lot to Liverpool. The noticeably unhygienic conditions of some Spanish refugee families, who were allowed to join the Evacuation Scheme, preoccupied the authorities. Because of their unacceptable behaviour on the liner everyone landing in Liverpool was forced to take a bath in disinfectant liquids. All types of protests were directed against the Liverpool authorities, but most evacuees did take a bath so as to get away quicker.

Mr. Joseph Patron represented the evacuees in London with Messrs. Huart, Baglietto and Lavagna, and tried to do the best he could in the short time given to accommodate the population from the Rock. In London too the Gibraltarians had Bishop Peter Amigo as their champion and he saw to it that the best was offered to the evacuees. There was a continuous correspondence between Bishop Amigo, Mr. Patron and Mr. Sturdee, the Principal Regional Medical Officer. In London the evacuees were quartered in the following Centres:

Fulham Road Receiving Centre. 3 Blocks.; Empress Hall; Anerley Receiving Centre; Wembley Pool; Dr. Barnardo's Homes; Kensington Palace Mansions; Royal Palace Hotel; National Hotel; Raglan Hotel; Shelbourne Hotel;

5/6 Betford Way; Lancaster Court; 90/92 Lancaster Gate; 55 Lancaster Gate; British Empire Hotel; Broadwalk Hotel; Hyde Park Hotel; Grafton Hotel; Thackery Hotel; Kings College; Campden Hill Hotel; Duchess of Bedford Hotel; Gloucester Court Hotel.

Once in London many of the evacuees experienced the dangers of the Battle of Britain. No-one could leave the Centres without an identity card. Food was pre-cooked and was the cause of the first of the many unpalatable disturbances in those dreadful days. There were times when people dare not cut a cornish pie in two and eat it, for the awful stench emerging from it. It was only through very strong representations that the quality of food was improved.

When people learnt that, while already in London, they were to be re-evacuated to Jamaica, and that people were called to freely register for it, they decided not to go. Mr. Joseph Patron blamed Bishop Amigo for the people's refusal to register. The Bishop had, from the outset, visited the Centres regularly accompanied by Fr. Azzopardi. Dear Fr. Francis Azzopardi was the only Gibraltarian priest accompanying the 11,000 evacuees to England. Bishop Peter Amigo knew that the Colonial Office's intention was to send them to Jamaica, and he did not like it. He had already received a letter from Bishop Fitzgerald requesting him to see to it that the people, who had suffered intensely when repatriated from Casablanca, were treated better if sent to the West Indies. Bishop Amigo proposed to the Colonial Office that the evacuees could surely be placed securely out of London in the country or in Ireland, and even Portugal. But it appeared that the Government's plans to re-evacuate were still unchanged. In Jamaica, meanwhile, the Bishop of Kingston Diocese was caught unawares. He was requested to prepare residences for 11,000 people. There were no lodgings for the evacuees to live in. They had already started constructing the wooden huts when roughly 1,500 evacuees were sent there directly from Gibraltar. More huts were being built for the remaining 11,000 people still in London.

The reason given for this insistence on sending the evacuees to Jamaica was that some medical experts had offered the advice that the people of Gibraltar would be unable to withstand the cold English winters.

It was at this juncture that news broke that a liner carrying a large colony of Italians to Jamaica, had been sunk by a U-boat. Bishop Amigo used this news to his advantage and demanded that, if the Colonial Office persisted in removing the people to Jamaica, they had to reassure him that two destroyers were deployed to escort the evacuees. He was prepared to make a public issue of the whole subject, but out of respect for Cardinal Hinsley he refrained from doing so. He would not rest until he either stopped the evacuees from going to Jamaica, or obtained the appropriate security for them. The Government did not have the destroyers demanded and the people remained in London.

Since the plans made by the Colonial Office were all geared for transferring the evacuees to Jamaica, it was only there that children would receive the appropriate education and practise their religion. It is believed that Brother Dolan held and died with a document granting him permission to look after the education of the boys in Jamaica. So really there was absolutely nothing arranged for the children's education in London. Impromptu arrangements were made under pressure from Bishops Amigo and Fitzgerald. The Irish Christian Brothers hoped they would be brought into the picture and continue the work among Gibraltarian boys, but the Colonial Office never offered them terms inviting them to commence in the U.K. Children were at first accommodated in any schools with vacancies, even if they were Protestant schools. It was only later on that schools with the proper facilities for Catholic children were found nearer the different centres, thus making it easier for children to attend school. Those families who transferred themselves to Tangier were better off in this regard. The Christian Brothers continued their good work among them until the end of the war.

By May 1944 Germany started bombing strategic places in London using the V-Ones. These arrived at such regular intervals day and night that many evacuees took to the tube–stations for shelter. The author's family, like many others, lived in Notting Hill Underground Station for nearly six months, eating fish and chips daily, and not seeing the light of day for that period. Just as the V-Twos were appearing on the scene, the Colonial Office pulled the evacuees away from London and transferred them to Northern Ireland. Repatriation had already begun and some evacuees never stepped into Ireland. Those who did go there, were billetted in nissen huts in seventeen unused military camps. The many sufferings endured in London were to be increased in other ways in Northern Ireland. Men and women who searched for work in Londonderry could not get any because they were Catholics.

Those who were Protestants among the evacuees found no difficulty in getting jobs, but the Catholic majority did. Once again the evacuees were to suffer because of pre-cooked food and lack of it.

The Committees set up in each Camp to voice the people's complaints made the necessary representations to the Government House at Stormont, without avail. Once again the evacuees, now in Northern Ireland, were to suffer continuously because of the pre-cooked meals or lack of them. Supported and led by a very influential local family named MacDonald, the committees were prepared to organize a march of evacuees to Stormont with placards and slogans. Some camps were even surrounded by armed policemen. When the Government saw the evacuees were not bluffing they appealed to the committees not to demonstrate in case the I.R.A. took advantage of the strike. That same week women were employed in the camp kitchens and a fixed amount of pocket money was awarded to each person.

From time to time word that the repatriation was continuing made people resign themselves to the appalling conditions in which they lived. When winter fell covering the camps with snow it brought so many difficulties. Food stores were non-existent in many camps, and when the snow blocked the roads, no provisions would be available for the cooks to prepare and distribute. As if this were not enough, coal or wood for lighting the fire and heating the huts soon ran short and people had to cut down anything that could burn to keep warm. The clothes they wore were inadequate for the severe cold experienced there so some ingenious seamstresses transformed blankets into trousers, jackets, skirts and coats. Some went further using their ingenuity and even dyed these clothes making them look attractive.

The Irish Christian Brothers visited the camps and much was talked about schooling in Northern Ireland, but little was done with them. The Government set up a make-shift classroom, where youngsters could be reminded that there was such a thing as schooling. That same school-room was used by a priest to say his Sunday Masses. That same room was used by Mr. Luis Bruzon who rallied the evacuees around him to support him in his efforts to precipitate the repatriation. He travelled from camp to camp winning the people to his plan of action, thus raising the morale of a people so humiliated by the indignity of the living conditions in which they found themselves. The repatriation did eventually restart and, whereas the vast majority of evacuees did return to the Rock, there were still some Gibraltarians living in Northern Ireland in 1947.

When the civilian population returned to their homeland, it was a very different people that the Bishop and Clergy had to work for. The civilians had been through some extraordinary experiences in various places like Casablanca, North Africa, Madeira, England, Ireland, Tangiers, Portugal and Jamaica. People now returned marked and enriched with experiences that would never have come their way but for the evacuation. The post-war people of God were more mature and deeply aware of basic needs; they had great hopes for the future.

During their absence, the powers-that-be had planned a totally renewed system of education. This concerned the Bishop greatly, but he worked in close liaison with the Government officials. Both the civil and the military authorities esteemed him highly. He was a man of outstanding qualities. He spared no efforts to make it clear to the authorities that as Head of the Roman Catholics he could contribute much to the good government of the colony. When he discovered that a certain group of persons had been at work sub rosa trying to introduce the Jesuits and keep out the Christian Brothers, who had contributed so much to education in the past but had not been to the taste of the ultra-patriotic self-styled elite, he fought the Government's proposals.

He was ready to accept an overall education system run by the Government, but he objected to branding all the Christian Brothers with a characteristic that might be applicable perhaps to the odd members. He brought back the Brothers and the Sisters for the secondary education of the boys and girls.

The "new" Christian Brothers came from the English province of the Order and worked closely with the Bishop and with the secular Governmental authorities, until, irony of ironies, one of their number in due course took over the position of Director of Education for the whole Rock. Once the new system was seen to be developing well, the Bishop made over the leases of the Catholic schools to the Government. He was always a man of wide vision and of generous spirit, gentle and spiritual, unafraid, a scholar and an

132

individualist — when Pope Pius XII consulted the Bishops of the world as to the proclamation of the Assumption of the Virgin as a dogma, Bishop Fitzgerald immortalized himself by being in a minority of one, replying that, in his opinion, the time was not yet ripe for such a proclamation. If he knew of a need he would hasten to satisfy it. He opened up the building of the Little Sisters of the Poor and Gavino's Asylum when difficulties arose over the reabsorption of the "returnees" from the evacuation. Some people have lived in these transit centres for forty years!

Bishop Fitzgerald celebrated his Silver Jubilee as Bishop on 9 October 1952. The crowds that turned out to witness the public ceremony in John Mackintosh Square were proof of the kind of person he was and the impression he left on people. The Queen invested him with the honour of Commander of the Order of the British Empire. He died in 1956, and his burial was the occasion for another remarkable turn-out of dignitaries. It was noted, however, that there were no Spanish Bishops at the funeral — apart from the Archbishop of Tangiers. The Spanish campaigns for the devolution of the Sovereignty of Gibraltar had already begun, and the Bishops were reluctant to come.

BILIGAMUS NOS INVICEM

The Right Reverend John F. Healy, C.B.E., D.D., D.C.L.
Bishop of Gibraltar
Consecrated Bishop: 11th October 1956
Died: 17th February 1973.

134

CHAPTER FIVE

Bishop John Farmer Healy

The Bishop's successor was Dr. John Farmer Healy, who became the Church's leader in Gibraltar eight months later on 11 October 1956. He had been trained at the English College in Valladolid and had worked as secretary to Archbishop Amigo of Southwark for many years. He was not unfamiliar with the idiosyncracies of the latin temperament. His period as Bishop was one of ups and downs. He lived through what might be termed the Golden Age for Gibraltar as regards the number of priests: four young local priests were ordained to work in the diocese. There was a wonderful atmosphere about the work done for the 18,500 Roman Catholics on the Rock. The Church flourished on every side; among the young, in the schools, in clubs, among the sick, the young workers. This was a short-lived period for in the space of four years Gibraltar lost six of its priests.

Bishop Healy, like his predecessor, knew his history. With his lawyer he tackled the thorny question of the transfer of church buildings. Relations between Church and Government were excellent, and by setting up a legal body called the "Registered Trustees of the Roman Catholic Church", consisting of the Bishop, the Vicar General and the Cathedral Administrator, and getting it registered in the Supreme Court, Bishop Healy managed to achieve what Scandella failed to do in the 1870s and Bishop Canilla in the 1880s.

The Bishop showed great concern for the aged people of Gibraltar. He sold the site used by the Little Sisters of the Poor so that John Mackintosh's will could be implemented in favour of the old. The new home for aged Catholics, called Mount Alvernia after St. Francis, is now staffed by the Franciscan Missionaries of the Divine Motherhood. He also had the large Catholic Community Centre built, to cope with the increasing activities of the Young Christian Workers, the Legion of Mary, the Society of St. Vincent de Paul and so on. Some 50,000 persons use the premises every year: it is open to all people of any colour, religion or persuasion. He also started the St. Francis Clinic Service which provides attention for persons who cannot attend hospital for medical treatment. Sister Hyacinth, nicknamed the Flying Angel, does an average of 8,500 visits per year.

Sessions were organized after Vatican Council II to make the laity aware of the revolution proposed in their lives by the fathers of the Council and the

Pope. This was in line with the steps taken by Bishop Scandella after Vatican I. It was unfortunate that not all documents were dealt with as adequately as the one on the Laity in the Church. Not everything in the garden was rosy, however. The Bishop, though a charming person and loved by the children, fell foul of a certain section of the community over his frank presentation of the rickety financial situation he claimed to have found on coming to Gibraltar and his expectation that he would receive great financial support.

There were acute social troubles in all European countries in the late sixties, and Gibraltar was no exception. Spain was tightening the screws and closing off to the Gibraltarians all communication with its territory by land, sea, air, and in the sphere of telecommunications. A new Government came to power − the Integration with Great Britain Party, which saw a need for the restructuring of the whole economic set-up as a result of the non-availability of Spanish labour. There was the merger of the City Council administration with that of the Government. There was anxiety about the Young Christian Workers and the awareness aroused in them by an active, intelligent young priest, Father Bernard Linares; there was the unease on the part of teachers concerning ways of imparting the new orientation of Vatican II: so few things seemed cut and dried, and there was lack of clarity in the field of theology. The Bishop was looked to for guidance, just when he was falling out of touch with his clergy, his people and current affairs. There were men of goodwill who would have been only too willing to help him, and it was the clergy's one desire to assist him in these troubled times, but he kept himself to himself and lived in solitude. The clergy felt somewhat lost without his presence among them. It was a sad time for all who had at heart the interests of the people of God amid a changing world, small though it was. The Bishop died on 19 March 1973. He was buried in the Chapel of Our Lady of Lourdes where he was seen to recite the rosary so regularly in his early days.

CHAPTER SIX

Bishop Edward Rapallo
1973–1984

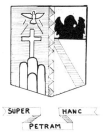

Monsignor Edward Rapallo had been Vicar General to Bishop Healy and was elected unanimously by the Counsellors as Vicar Capitular. The Sacred Congregation of Propaganda Fide was immediately informed of both the death of the Bishop and of the appointment of the Vicar Capitular. It was not an easy time for the Capitular and Counsellors. The Government had decided to pick the interregnum to press for the passing of the new Education Ordinance. This was reminiscent of a similar action on the same subject when Bishop Scandella died in 1880. The Counsellors met and assisted the Vicar Capitular to present to the Government the requisites so that the Christian Education of the Catholic children in Gibraltar be guaranteed and adequate. The appointment of the new Bishop was announced in July and people rejoiced when they learnt that Monsignor Rapallo had been selected. His consecration took place on 7 October 1973. An Ecumenical Committee was formed and the ceremony was held at the Royal Air Force Hangar at North Front. It was once again a splendid occasion manifesting the joy of each and everyone in Gibraltar, regardless of their religious confession. It was also reminiscent of the construction of two chapels at North Front in 1810 by kind permission of the Holy See and the generosity of Mr. James Galleano.

With Bishop Rapallo in office, everyone knew things on the Rock would run differently. And so they did. In ten years Dr. Rapallo livened up the Christian living to an unprecedented degree. First of all, he decentralized activities from the Cathedral and set up three new parishes. Then he pressed for the formation of Christian Renewal by allowing the Cursillo de Cristiandad and the Charismatic Movements to start and develop their activities. In a short while those movements branched off into other associations which took care of the youth and younger children. Other groups concentrated on the enhancement of married life through the Family Social Action and the Catholic Marriage Advisory Council, attending to marital problems and pre-marital talks. As a result of this revitalization of Christian living there has been a noticeable increase in attendance at the services and there are approximately twenty-thousand holy communions administered every month in the whole of the diocese. Confessions have also picked up especially in the Cathedral where people find it easier to obtain a confessor during shopping hours. These activities have inevitably produced vocations to the priesthood as well as to the religious life. Three priests have been ordained in Sacred Orders already with six more in the pipeline, while one young lady entered the Carmelite Convent at Ronda in Spain and another has gone to train with the Sisters of the Institute of the Blessed Virgin Mary (The Loreto Sisters).

Bishop Rapallo was a very hard worker. He did not spare himself but he also expected returns from others....... "feedback, feedback", he would say. He had a long list of projects he wanted to do. Some he had begun to realize, others he kept for the future. Yet there were a few things that marred his years as a Bishop. Firstly there was the Government's decision to make the schools State Schools. The New Ordinance which had made Bishop Healy shed tears was now implemented as law. The comprehensive system was started and, to make everything still more painful, the Christian Brothers also left the Rock.

Seeing the departure of such enthusiastic and dedicated teachers from our midst was no small loss. We do know however, that our loss will undoubtedly be someone else's gain. A monument was erected in their memory at the Boulevard and a Christian Brothers Foundation was set up to help students in need. Ten years have elapsed since many of these things occurred and perhaps there is a need to review the manner in which the "adequate religious education of the children" is being met. Gibraltarians have always adopted English laws and practices to the local needs and by so doing implemented good laws. Methods adopted in other countries, successful though they may be, need not be the right ones or even be tried in this community. Bishop Rapallo was very much a Gibraltarian and he was always very careful not to introduce anything that could in any way curtail the progress of something that was working well, even if it caused disappointment in some people's minds.

The Bishop went through a weak period during the last five years of his life. When on holiday in Singapore he was told by a doctor he had cancer. Examined again in London it was discovered that the Singapore diagnosis has been groundless. The Bishop nevertheless had suffered such a profound shock that he spent many a sleepless night which only helped to sadly weaken him. To aggravate the situation still further another doctor recommended the Bishop to resign his post as bishop. Whether the doctor's suggestion was intended to spur the Bishop out of his entrenched state of fear or really to spare him the suffering of continuing to govern the Diocese in his weak condition is not known. We do know that the Bishop took it only one way. That he was wanted out of the way. He quickly picked up his cases from the hospital he was resting in and went to live with some relatives where he soon showed signs of recovery. But the Bishop, although he worked as always 'till the very early hours of the following day, he worked without any joy'. He constantly asked for reassurance. Such was the effect of the second doctors' remark on his personality. When he died, he passed away not because of the frightening cancer but of a broken heart. He died on 5 February 1984, and was buried in the Cathedral he had decorated only ten years earlier.

CRUX STELLA MEA

140

CHAPTER SEVEN

Bishop Bernard Patrick Devlin
Bishop of Gibraltar 1985

Ten months after Bishop Rapallo died, Rome appointed Monsignor Bernard Devlin, the Diocesan Administrator as the succeeding Bishop of Gibraltar. Bishop Devlin was born in Cork, Ireland, and had arrived in Gibraltar in 1946 newly ordained a priest. The news of his election was pleasantly received since he was already an established member of the local clergy with which he had worked for forty years. His Holiness Pope John Paul II ordained him Bishop of Gibraltar in St Peter's Basilica in Rome on the 6th January 1985.

With the opening of the Spanish frontier in February 1984, the Bishop, even as the Diocesan Administrator, encouraged the development of reconciliatory meetings between the local clergy and the priests of the Camp Area and those of Malaga. These regular communications led to a closer relationship between the priests, and the local clergy was soon invited to attend retreats and in-service training projects on theology, Holy Scripture and Spirituality, organised for their own.

The Bishop himself is invited to attend either the Andalucian Conference of Bishops or that held annually in Madrid at the National Conference of Bishops. This latter one often coincides with the English Conference of Bishops to which the Bishop is also invited. Hence Bishop Devlin availing himself of the generous opening offered to him, he alternates and goes to both on different occasions. In all cases everyone understands that the Bishop of Gibraltar attends these Conferences as mere "observer" since he does not belong to any of the mentioned Conferences of Bishops. It is very gratifying, however, that the Bishops both in the U.K. and in Spain welcome him with open arms.

Only three years after he was ordained Bishop he was reminded that he was nevertheless expected to make his "ad limina" visit to Rome in November 1987. His predecessor had made the visit in the Autumn of 1983 hence it was to be expected that Gibraltar's turn came up five years later. In fact Bishop Devlin went to Rome in November 1987.

Once there he resided at the Pontifical Irish College. He visited the Prefect of the Sacred Congregation of Propaganda Fide, His Eminence Cardinal Josef Tomko, and later on His Holiness Pope John Paul II. This meeting with the Holy Father was most impressive. The Bishop was given a private audience and the Holy Father manifested how well informed he was about

Gibraltar in all its aspects. The Bishop was profoundly impressed by the Holy Father's profound devotion to Our Lady.

Noticing that the exterior structure of the Cathedral was endangering the lives of the faithful as well as the passers by, His Lordship started the delicate but much needed restoration of the Cathedral. The works have now been in progress for three years and it is scheduled that the work will be completed by May 1989. He obtained the handsome sum of £30,000 from the Congregation of Propaganda Fide towards the restoration – a sum equal to the sum already collected at the time by the Fund Raising Committee.

The Bishop also gave permission for a soup-kitchen to be opened for the lower income bracket people. Approximately fifty to sixty take a daily meal at the Catholic Community Centre. It is all run by volunteers and the food is financed by private donations and by Gibmaroc, which provides the kitchen with free vegetables and fruit every day.

At present the Bishop boasts of having four students studying for the priesthood in theological colleges. God willing by September 1989, if these persevere, together with three newcomers the Diocese will be blessed with seven students for the priesthood. In addition a young lady has already taken her simple vows within the Insitute of the Blessed Virgin Mary, alias the Loreto Nuns who are still successfully teaching in Gibraltar.

L.D.S.

EPILOGUE

The Church we can see and study in history is not just a series of successive human events with many imperfections; it is also the mysterious revelation of a redeeming God. The Church of History is also the transcendent Church.

This is why the Church understands herself better by seeing herself in history; discovering in the events God's action and pointers to her mission in the world. And thus, each period − in its lights and shadows − will allow us to know the Church and its mission. That's why, by observing history, we are not to remain on the external surface, but are to endeavour to discover what God has manifested at each moment.

The Church has many aspects. On many occasions it is presented as if the aspects were contradictory and opposites, but they are in reality elements that imprint on her a character that is essentially dynamic. For instance, the Church is both holy and sinner, active and contemplative, spiritual and worldly, it is hierarchical and community, it has juridical structure and living experience.

Five issues emerged frequently in the history unfolded above which deserve certain attention because of their relevance. Firstly, there was the continuous solicitude of the Bishops of Cadiz for the spiritual wellbeing of the Catholic Community of Gilbraltar. While ecclesiastically unconnected to the diocese of Cadiz today we are, nevertheless, grateful to the Bishops for their good intentions then and more so to the present Bishop for his open invitation to us to avail ourselves of their programmed endeavours to strengthen the life of the priests socially, intellectually and spiritually. We would be insensitive to ignore such a generous invitation and miss the wonderful experience of witnessing, at first hand, the new Spiritual Spring among the clergy of Cadiz and Malaga.

Secondly there was the question of succession. A repetition of the sufferings undergone by both the Bishops and people due to the question of succession has been overcome to a great extent. Yet there is still room for improvement. A more generous use of those specially trained priests within the diplomatic service in the Vatican would be welcome. They could easily stay with us periodically just as other visitors do and thus obtain that extra delicate first hand information required beside the facts known from the reports. Such information could well provide the Pro-Nuncio with a more complete set of facts useful for the selection of a candidate.

Thirdly, there is the matter of education of children. The one-and-a-half-century history of successful endeavours must not be allowed to go in vain. There is a deep anxiety among parents that children transferred to the Comprehensive Schools soon lose their sense of religion. It would be strange that communist Russia through glasnost revives their Christian traditions in their Country while we, through the insistence on implementing a rigid academic system, disregard the requisites for a true Christian formation of our children. The change of the Education Ordinance of 1974 was most inopportune and a prompt revision is now overdue. Goodwill on the part of everyone should restore to the children that complete formation of character that will prepare them for the secular as well as for their spiritual life.

Fourthly, there was the issue of lay intervention in Church affairs. There exists today a wonderful healthy interest by lay people who wish to participate in Church affairs. With a clear understanding of their position in the Church since the Second Vatican Council there has not been an instant locally where a lay person has assumed a function proper to a priest. On the contrary there is close liaison between the priest and the laity. The five parishes enjoy a lay person dealing with the finances. They each have a number of Special Ministers of the Holy Eucharist. Priests together with lay persons carry out the delicate task of evangelization in the different movements of Christain Renewal. The formation of the Pastoral Council should assist much in coordinating and orientating the numerous activities of the different groups of lay people.

The relations between the different Christian denominations has progressed solidly from one of tolerance to that of working and praying together. Priests and Ministers meet periodically to plan Radio and Television programmes, to launch an anti-Ads campaign, to organize the Week of Prayer for Christian Unity. Plans are now afoot to deal with British vagrants on the Rock. There exists a sincere, friendly, happy and enthusiastic spirit among the brethren. Occasionally we may have something to discuss with our Jewish neighbours. In fact one can only be optimistic about the manner events are developing on our Rock. We may have lived with a very thick, dark cloud above us all the time in the past. Every cloud, it is said, has a silver lining. One prays the mistakes of the past will not only be seen in their true light and never again repeated but they should also serve to better shape the future.

You do not encounter in the Church a continuous and mechanical evolution, but a marvellous living organism. Hence there are advances and retreats. But we know that the Holy Spirit leads indefectibly towards the fullness of the Kingdom of God. And the Church experiences that tension between now and eternity, aware that it has started the Kingdom but as yet has not received its fullness.

The Son of God at a definite epoch and in a determined culture became man. In the course of time and countries, the Church has incarnated itself in specific cultures. The faith is the same, but it is manifested in distinct manners by an African or an Englishman. With respect and devotion, a man of faith will learn how to discover the mysterious language of God who, through history, reveals to the Church its essence and mission.

APPENDIX ONE

A Diary of Events of the Great Siege 1779–81
by Father Francisco Messa O.F.M.*

"On the 21st June of the same year exit from Spain into this City was stopped. But before that happened, the Governor of San Roque gave orders that all subjects of the King of Great Britain should abandon the 'Campo de Gibraltar', and should withdraw to the City, so that even those young men who were in San Roque recovering from chicken-pox found themselves bound to leave. Since the Governor of the City would not allow the disease to spread into the City, he made provisions for them to remain in the farms outside Landport till they were safely cured.

On the afternoon and evening of the 4th July some English warships captured thirteen or fourteen prize-ships from a convoy loaded with victualling for Spain. After engaging two escorts in battle, and at times immediately under the battery of Europa Point so that these fired at one of them, they were forced to sail with other ships to Ceuta. Nine days later there appeared an Armada of Spanish gun-boats with two heavy armed warships and two frigates which blocked the Bay, thus doing their utmost to prevent the entrance of any provisions to reach us.

On the Feast of St. Ann, 26th July, they started scattering the Campo with military tents and unloaded stores of ammunition which increased daily.

On the 30th August, Mr. Raleigh, the Governor's Secretary, came to see me at my house to tell me that the Governor, General Elliot, had given orders to take over the Catholic Church for storing Naval provisions. I told him that I already knew that but that I thought that the Governor would not deprive us of the place where we performed our sacrifices and the Sacred Sacraments. He replied that it was not exactly like that. . . . It was the Governor's wish that only an area near the entrance of the Church be occupied and that the person in charge of the project was the Commissioner, Mr. Davies. I then respectfully asked him to inform me beforehand when Mr. Davies would visit the Church so that I would point out to him the most appropriate place for that project.

I was notified the following day and as I walked there I met both the Secretary and Mr. Davies in the street. They were coming to me at my house but I asked them whether they wanted to come to the church with me. They agreed and we went there where I showed them "La Capilla de Hierro" (now the Chapel of Our Lady of Lourdes) in case it satisfied him. The Commissioner replied that it was not large enough. I then pointed out the sides of the Chantry and an area behind it but this did not suffice either. Enlarging the area I pointed as far as the first pillars and seeing

*Fr. Francisco Messa recorded the occurrences he witnessed of the Great Siege in the Register of Burials of Children. He wrote in mixed Spanish/Catalan the Menorcans brought with them. The translation attempted here has been done with the intention of maintaining the quaintness of the writing.

that it was still not enough, extended the area as far as the second set of pillars though in vain. The Secretary then remarked to me that it seemed that Mr. Davies would not find the whole Church big enough for his purpose. I, therefore, went as far as to offer the whole area of the Church except the space immediately in front of the three principal altars. At this point we argued for some compromise suitable to the needs of the Church and to those of the King. I suggested that where possible it was better that both myself and himself should be kept happy and thus we parted.

In the afternoon of that same day the Admiral went to have a look at the Church, I was told about it and so I went there to meet him. This gentleman agreed that a partition should be constructed from the door to the column where the pulpit stood and then straight to the wall where the altar of Our Lady of La Soledad was, and thus it was executed. In this manner we were able to enter our Church through one door and they to their store through another. We were happy with the arrangement because we were afraid of losing the whole of it and for less worthy ends as was done in the other Siege when, as the Elders recall, they transformed the whole into a hospital. I was also assured that this was only a temporary measure. On the 3rd September that part of the Church was emptied out putting an end to our use of it and the construction of the partition was begun for the Commissioner's purpose.

On the 12th September 1779 at approximately half past five in the morning the English batteries to the North of the Rock started firing. They continued to do so all through the day to stop the work that the Spaniards were realising along the lines. In fact they were greatly obstructed for on the previous days one could see the loaded carts coming from the Campo to the lines and returning empty, something that was not seen again after that day. It happened to be the day we celebrated the Sweet Name of Mary, and it caused tremendous confusion amongst the families living near Waterport, who thinking that the Spaniards would reciprocate instantly, transferred themselves and their belongings to the South. But the Spaniards did not fire one single shot either on that occasion or the following week. So much so that although the English continued to bomb them, the firing was done at longer intervals. In this same week the cobble-stones were lifted from Main Street and the existon up to the Convent's barrack parade. The belfry of the Convent of Our Lady of Ransom was also demolished together with those Romanesques. That same week the Jews began to build wooden huts next to the Rock near Colonel Green's Gardens, retiring there with their belongings.

On the 26th September 1779 at 10 in the morning on Sunday I was stopped in the street just outside my house. Captain Evelyn was most probably coming to see me at my house. He spoke to me in English and although I understood him I did not trust myself in the English language, so I asked him to come into my house where my brother-in-law Joseph Serra, a teacher who knew English, would make everything clear to me. We went and in my brother-in-law's presence Captain Evelyn passed on the message. My brother-in-law told me that the gentleman was communicating to me that it was Governor Elliot's order that the belfry of the Catholic Church had to be demolished. It was to be lowered to the level where the bells were being rung. I asked whether it was possible to demolish only that part above the windows where the bells hung. But he replied that it was not possible. It was necessary first of all to lower the bells and then they would engineer a way of hanging the bells at a lower level. To this I remarked that since it was necessary I could make no objections but that I expected them to reconstruct everything as it was before once the Siege had ended. He replied that this would certainly be the case. Having agreed on this we parted.

A few days elapsed without seeing any activity so that I began to think that the demolition would not really take place. On the 6th October my brother-in-law came in to tell me that the order for the lowering of the belfry, and to do so as quickly as possible, had been given. When I went to the Church the following morning I met the engineers constructing the scaffolding and by the 7th of that same month as I got out of bed the very first and sad view I had was seeing a soldier removing the first stone from the highest part of the spire. The work was done so efficiently that by the 13th of the same month the belfry and the clock levels were dismantled to just under the top of the lower stage. By December they began to reconstruct the place for the clock, much lower than its original place, and they proceeded to beautify it.

Most inhabitants were suffering a great shortage of firewood for use in the kitchen, but on the feast of St. John, 26th December, there was a mighty storm with a lot of rain. The sea brought with it a great quantity of wood to the very walls from the Spanish coast. We gathered enough to last till the convoy arrived. It was on that same day that the Spaniards fired at the Landport batteries although I do not think they exceeded five shots. Bartholomew Galle, friend of Mr. John Baptist Viale's farmers, brought to my house a shell which fell in his own farm, and which weighed approximately 26lbs.

On the 12th January 1780, the Spaniards fired a few shots at both Waterport and Landport. One of the shots flew over the walls of Waterport and came to hit the roof of Mr. Quartin's house which was then uninhabited. The shell simply made two holes in the roof and then fell into the street near Mr. Boyd's house who was a carpenter.

By the 26th January 1780 food provisions had become extremely expensive. Bacon was bought at 4 reals per pound. Horse-meat at 4 reals per pound. Beef also at 4 reals.

Nobody, however, stopped from buying and in fact did do with great insistence. The cheapest chickens were sold at 2 duros and there was a time when they were sold at 5 duros; eggs at one real each; butter at 4 silver reals and cooking oil at 4 silver reals a quart considering it was not the best kind. Bread was so scarce that only bakery sold it and this with scrupulous rationing. It was on this day that part of the English convoy sailed in, together with Don Juan Langero, Commander of the Armada, and who had received three insignificant wounds.

Prince William, third son of the King of England, of fourteen years of age less a few months, arrived with one of the English warships in the capacity of Naval Commander. He strolled along Main Street accompanied by the two Governors, Elliot and Boyd, two Admirals and other gentlemen. He wanted to see our church, and he went in but no one was inside. I was informed of it and so I went there and met them at the door. I offered to show them around the church but they replied that they had already seen the images. They went away and I accompanied them along Main Street and along Line Wall from Landport to very near the Lieutenant Governor's House. Seeing that they were off to lunch I departed and returned home.

Biscuits and provisions of flour was so abundant with the convoy's arrival that biscuits were sold at the low price of a penny a pound and, alas, we were relieved with great abundance for some time. Since there was a need for storehouses, they petitioned me, on the 1st March, for the use of the Sacristy and the Capilla de Hierro to store the flour. They made use of it the very same day I was asked for them.

On the 26th March, Easter Sunday, the Clock-winder employed by the church proposed to me that the old door to the belfry should be walled up and a new one built outside the cloister of the church. I put it to the Governor that same day but he did not reply then. The following day he sent the Quarter Master General with the message that the door would be constructed and that I would have a key to enable me to go up whenever I pleased. Once the clock was mounted they placed the principal bell to the right of the tower drilling a hole for the rope which would be used to ring the bell from below. We started ringing the bell on the 27th April 1780.

On the 7th June of the same year, between one and two in the morning, the Spaniards very slyly pushed nine ships loaded with fireworks towards the New Mole, judging by the direction they were heading for. But while still some distance away they were sighted by the English launches on guard. They began setting on fire as many as they could. Some were set on fire in the middle of the Bay but others, since the currents were favourable to the New Mole, by-passed it. One of the mentioned ships was about to enter the harbour when, thanks to the efficiency of the English launches, it was diverted to the front of the Wall which is right opposite the Naval Hospital. This vessel was so big that it alone would have sufficed to set the New Mole on fire. It was also so well built with combustible material that despite the great amount of seawater poured over it, it smoked for more than 40 hours. The English soldiers worked relentlessly on this occasion so that four of them scorched their hands and backs and had to be taken to hospital. It is said that the Naval Commander has rewarded the men with whatever was salvaged from those ships. It is also said that one of those fireships which by-passed Europa Point, pushed by a lively wind reached somewhere near Estepona in less than three hours.

In the morning of the 1st October 1780, the feast of Our Lady of the Rosary, one of the farms of the City of Gibraltar was set on fire forming a vast wall of flames. It seemed like the beginning of a barrage of 7 or more cannons. On the night of the same day the huts in the farms and their surroundings were set on fire by the Spaniards. A few contraptions were found near the fence in order to set the farms on fire but they did not succeed to do so.

At the beginning of summer this year the Spaniards succeeded in stopping all communications with Barbary. Only two launches with the Consul's Mail arrived from there. No provisions came to us other than that brought by ships from Menorca and a Danish storeship after the English launches forced a way through the Spanish line of ships. And today the 21st October 1780 a local ship coming from Algiers arrived in port. A few days later two storeships from Menorca and from London arrived with more provisions. They came loaded with butter, cheese, milkstout and other useful articles for the Garrison and the inhabitants.

A few days later there appeared a ship in harbour, en route for England, with the English Consul in Morocco and the Dutch Consul Mr. Francis Butler, together with all British Subjects living in Tangier. They had been forced out of Morocco by order of the Emperor of Morocco because the Spaniards had brought something or other in the Ports of Tangier and Tetuan. Because of this we were deprived of the refreshments that normally came from Barbary thus remaining in dire need for the rest of the year.

It was towards the end of the year that permission was granted to the inhabitants and everybody to construct huts higher up the Rock to the South and Colonel Green's farm. Those more terror-stricken but who proved to be more fortunate, constructed some wooden huts into which they secured most of their possessions. I, for my part, because I was informed and assured by the older people, who had experienced the Last Siege, that the bombs and shells did not go beyond our church, I sought refuge within the church. There I transferred some of the most delicate furniture, like the mirrors and pictures. Thinking that I would be able to transfer the remaining part of my furniture without much difficulty I remained calm, but with very bad consequences.

It happened that a large convoy consisting of a large English Fleet sailed into the Bay on the 12th April 1781, and started unloading great quantities of provisions. When this was happening the Spanish batteries started firing so fiercely that it created a horrible confusion amongst the people, particularly the inhabitants of all nations living in the City. Mothers were seen to take their young ones, some in their arms whilst others almost dragging them, crying and running to some safer ground outside Southport. Fathers did the same forgetting to take anything with them except what they were wearing. And I, who was then celebrating the Last Supper of Our Lord and singing High Mass, was left alone in the Church. Nevertheless, I continued to finish the sacred ceremonies that day with great devotion and calmness in the company of some faithful devotees.

Having finished the solemnity I went home to have my meal, and then, together with those of my house, we went back to take refuge in the church where together with others, although very few devout ones, we sang Matins. Little by little my sacristan, Don Juan Moreno, those of my house and myself were left alone. There, alone, throughout a frightful day and night, we stayed for the remaining part of the ceremony, with His Divine Majesty exposed, till eight o'clock of the following morning which was Good Friday. As I stood very close and under the pillar near St. Anthony's Chapel in the company of my family and the Sacristan, a shell flew in and fell about two yards away from us. We were panic-stricken and two gentlemen who had just come in to find out how we were keeping, seeing the blow of the shell, turned-turtle and ran away without saying goodbye. Taking pity on my sister's tears and the crying of my nieces and nephews, who were so young, considering maturely that it was not fair or prudent to keep His Divine Majesty any longer, I determined to celebrate the ceremonies of Good Friday without solemnity and consumed the Most Blessed Sacrament, which has been our particular refuge throughout the previous day and night. We put this into practice and after the ceremony the Sacristan and I withdrew all the silver objects that we could handle into the sacristy. I decided to run away from the threatening dangers together with those of my house, leaving as keeper in the Church the Sacristan who was a bachelor without relatives and who, furthermore, had volunteered to do so.

The following day, unable to overcome the dangers much longer together with the Sacristan, I hurriedly took away the Globe with the reserved consecrated hosts, the Holy Oils of the Sick and of the Sacrament of Baptism, leaving all the precious silver secured in the Sacristy. Some were locked in the cupboards because the bombing became intolerable, leaving a poor old Genoese, who was ill and could not walk, to take care of the Church. This caused me much distress of mind. I took the Blessed Sacrament and the mentioned sacred articles to Mr. Ambrosio Chichon's hut where my whole family had sheltered on the day of our escapade. With tears in my eyes, which I could not dry, I placed that Sacred container on top of a respectable mahogany table properly dressed up with clean altar cloths. It remained there all the time with a burning light, thus becoming our best companion during the day and during the night, until a hut was constructed on a safer site and I will indicate later on.

On Easter Sunday I visualised that the vast and immense wealth, either in Sacred Images or in so many precious articles, were bound to get destroyed. These things were under the responsibility of the Junta of Elders as the Wardens of the Church, the Confraternities of Our Lady of the Rosary, Our Lady of Europa and that of the Blessed Sacrament. I sent a message to all of them with my Sacristan telling them and advising them to try and save the church properties which were under their responsibility. All of them replied that they could not save their own property let alone that of the church, or that they had had enough in attempting to save their own possessions, and that if anyone wanted to take the trouble of saving the church property to do so. I, therefore, seeing the danger in which the treasure of our church found itself, decided to venture it myself by going there and securing whatever I could.

The following day stimulated by an ardent zeal, and trusting in my Almighty God, having looked for some people of our religion in vain, not even my own assistant, I went to the church with my Sacristan, who insisted on coming, and two soldiers whom I roped in with great difficulty. I carried a stretcher. I entered the sacristy to find that all the silver articles which we placed there on Good Friday, like the Cross, Torches and lamps, were all broken and buried under the rubble which had fallen from the ceiling and roof of the Sacristy.

The soldiers and I, nevertheless, recovered as many bits and pieces as possible from under the rubble and placed them on the stretcher. I noticed that the Tabernacle or what they call here the Monstrance, was still standing on the Altar. We lowered it with tremendous difficulty, and placed it on the same stretcher, which by now could not take any more. I came to the door to look for someone else who could give us a hand with the remaining articles. There I saw a boy who had been sent by my assistant with an ass. Opening the cupboard once more I took away the most valuable things, which I laid on the ass. On our way out of the City I met another soldier who offered to help with some articles if only I stayed behind to collect them for him. I accepted the offer and returned to the Sacristy. I bundled together the most valuable Chasubles and placed them on the soldier's back, doing all this very quickly for the bombing was increasing. As we came out of the Church that same soldier demanded one guinea for his services. Seeing that he was asking too much, I took the bundle, placed it on my shoulder, and with this load followed by shells and bombs, I hurried to the New Gate (Southport). I was concerned with the soldiers carrying the silver and whom I had lost sight of. At the Gate I found the soldiers with the silver and the boy with the burdened donkey. The Guards would not let them pass because the Officer wanted to know who the owner of all the valuables was. I then went to see the Officer who eventually allowed us to go through, but seeing that there was such a great quantity of silver, all piled up, he tried to get me to go to the Palace to get permission from the Governor. Once I explained to him the many risks I had already undergone and which I was sure he did not want me to experience again, he gave me permission to pass. At this I placed the bundle on the stretcher and we went away.

We arrived ever so tired. I left the Monstrance in Father Reymundo's hut because he was my assistant. The rest we took to a tent which I managed to put up with the help of a few Menorcan sailors who gave me a sail, and another sail which I bought from the engineer, Mr. Thomas Skinner. The silver remained quite exposed throughout the whole night and part of the following day but having no chests where I could store them, I availed myself of Mr. Carbone's offer. This Catholic inhabitant lent me two empty barrels with iron rings. Dismantling the articles I packed all the silver into two parts and then filled the rest of the empty space in barrels with all the books which I managed to save thanks to my brother-in-law and the soldiers. That is how the articles were secured while I considered that the bombing from the Campo and the gunboats actually endangered our lives. I then looked for a house or hut where I could stay with my family. Unable to find one, and since everything was too exposed in the shelter we had occupied, as it was crowded by more than 40 persons of all kinds and sexes, I decided to take and transfer my tent to a safer place.

This is how we lived through the rest of the month of April 1781, suffering the destructive visits of the gunboats which arrived nearly every morning at dawn. These visits forced all the families to abandon their huts and tents and run away to the mountain heights or Windmill plains, leaving all their possessions behind. I, however, remained close to my tent and hut so as not to leave the Blessed Sacrament and the other articles unprotected. I used to take shelter behind a flimsy wall and one early morning when I heard of the approaching launches I started dressing quickly with others to take refuge at Windmill plains.

These circumstances prompted me to quicken up the transfer of the tent. Whilst my brother-in-law, Joseph Serra, concerned himself with the saving of some of our jewels and ecclesiastical robes and anything else with the soldiers help and other well paid men, I, with my own hands, levelled a plot under the rock which stands to the right before the entrance to the Windmill plains. With Mr. Ambrosio Chichon's help, who lent me the poles, we constructed a very large tent without a door. There we transferred everything we could salvage. The Blessed Sacrament remained locked in Mr. Chichon's hut. Mr. Chichon had made it his particular duty to look after it, whilst I regularly visited it every day.

When the Spanish batteries had started firing, seeing the whole City dispersed all over the Rock without proper shelter, except in those 13 or 14 wooden huts built by the more cautious people, His Excellency the Governor camped three or four regiments near Hardy Town or Black Town, giving orders that camping tents be given to all the inhabitants who had neither tents nor huts of their own.

I cannot leave unrecorded the fact that, a few days after I had gone to the Church to rescue the more precious articles, fire broke out there and it burnt for three days running. The fire burnt the Chantry, the organ, benches, a new statue of Our Lady of Mount Carmel and the chest in which it was locked. This chest was lent by Mr. Martinez and Philip Montovio precisely to protect the statue in one of the Chapels. Burnt also were the chests and vestments in the Sacristy itself, one of the confessionals, all the wood-work in the Centre Aisle and almost all the aisle of Our Lady of the Rosary. A day or two before this fire, because I was heartily concerned for all the sacred images left exposed in the Church and particularly that of the Virgin, Our Lady of Europa, so old and loved, I sent the Sacristan, who was going to the City and also my brother-in-law, Mr. Serra, who went there every day, to rescue for me all the statues they could and especially that of Our Lady of Europa. Since they could not carry more than one they took away this one, to the exceeding delight of all the Catholics of our community. It was also in those days that the whole of the "Monumento", a beautiful painting, caught fire. It was a vivid reproduction of the Mysteries of the Last Supper and the Holy Passion.

When my very large tent was at last completed on a site quite safe from the bombs, I and my brother-in-law's family moved in. In comparison to the narrowness in which I had spent the previous two weeks this seemed like a palace. But on those calm nights, when people suspected that the gunboats together with the compliment of battery-ships, which the Spaniards had laid on would arrive, the tent became so packed with Catholics who wanted refuge that I found myself worse off then than I was in Mr. Chichon's house. The women who by nature are timid made us all more fearful.

A large convoy was about to leave for Mahon, and His Excellency the Governor offered passage and provisions to all the women who wanted to sail in it. This offer was also made to young people and inhabitants who wanted to go to London, to which another convoy was about to sail. With this opportunity opened to them, many men and women with their boys and girls, Catholics as well as Protestants and Jews sailed away together with all the Anglican Ministers with their own families and also my assistant, Father Pedro Maria Reymundo. Thus I was left here as the only priest, alone with the remaining flock which on all counts numbered about 600 persons. With them went my brother-in-law's family leaving him and myself alone in our tent. We were alone during the day but during the night it was filled by people who took shelter there in their effort to escape danger.

Since a month and a half had elapsed without being able to celebrate Mass because I did not have all the vestments sorted out, also because everyone was more concerned with finding decent accommodation where they could secure the possessions salvaged from their homes, and also because everything was in utter disorder and confusion, when at last an element of tranquility was achieved the people started to cry out and to beg to celebrate at least on Sundays and Feast days. Seeing the people with such holy sentiments I set up a table on the Windmill plain, arranging it as best I could and placing it under a movable tent to protect it from the very strong winds. Availing myself of the freedom that the laws gave me and the privileges of my religion I began celebrating Mass on it. I celebrated Mass there for the first time on the 13th May 1781.

I celebrated Mass in this manner till the month of June of that same year. But during that time I had constructed a small hut next to my tent with a connecting door. I built an altar with the Altar Cards and a Tabernacle which I managed to rescue from the Church. This Tabernacle is very small and had been used, once upon a time, as the container for the ciborium of communion hosts and afterwards for keeping the 'Legnum Crucis' at the altar of the Rosary. Since I arranged it well and properly with yellow silk curtains, I transferred the reserve of the Blessed Sacrament from the improvised altar in Mr. Chichon's house together with the ciborium of hosts, and the vessels of Holy Oils of the Sick, Chrism and Catechumens as also the Lignum Crucis. All these I locked inside the Tabernacle after I had blessed the litle Chapel, assuming to have the power to do so by Epikei. I began to celebrate Mass there every day, and because of its limited capacity on Sundays and Feast days I set up Altar on the Windmill plains and thus pleased all the faithful.

Having settled down in the fashion already described, seeing that the Catholics, in their efforts to attend the Holy Sacrifice of the Mass, were suffering so much inconvenience due to the fierce winds experienced in that place particularly in winter, and since the firing of the Spaniards had already subsided and people were going to the City to gather wood, the Catholics pressed me to build a large hut with the help of my brother-in-law. Connecting it to the cave and small hut it admitted almost the whole of the Catholic community. These bound themselves each to pay a sum to finance it. In this way the hut was built replacing the tent.

What was once a tent became a wooded shelter with tiles, constructed large enough for all and allowing for the celebration under the rock where I placed the Tabernacle and other Sacred vessels safe from the bombs and shells. Once I set up the altar with its proper dressing, I began celebrating in this place. The sails which made the old tent I used to cover the roof of the hut thus protecting it from the rain and winds to the satisfaction of the Catholic community.

In an effort to protect all the sacred articles I filled the barrels containing the silver with earth placing these behind the altar. In this manner I formed a parapet behind which I also sheltered myself with my bed. At first these barrels with the silver stood before the altar but so many people sat on them that they broke the top open. My brother-in-law made a chest suitable enough for the silver articles where they were made more secure. The rest remained in the barrels which, as I say, I filled with earth.

In this new and holy precinct we celebrated all our sacrifices with all the solemnities possible. Exposition of the Blessed Sacrament and Rogations, praying all the time to God, Our Master, to grant us all that was necessary for our own good. For His Great Glory and the good of our souls.

During this period, from the beginning of the Siege and throughout the winter of the first year, I experienced much sadness. Firstly because I was abandoned by the

Sacristan who acquainted himself with a Mr. Francis Carreras and had put up a tent at the New Mole Parade, leaving me alone without coming to assist me at Mass. I often found it very difficult to get someone to help me in the celebration of Mass. Secondly I was saddened by my brother-in-law who was my only consolation. He had become ill and thence he acquired a strong mania against me because he blamed me for the absence of his family. He would never stop pestering me. His illness worsened and finding that place uncomfortable, he decided to go and leave for Black Town. Once he left I then remained alone without company, except for those fears which are customarily experienced by those undergoing great stress".

APPENDIX TWO

Our Greatest Possession, Our Lady of Europe

As the heavy excavations for the construction of St. Christopher's School foundations were in progress, one of the labourers dug out of the earth a bundle wrapped in hexion. Unwrapping the contents he discovered, to his amazement, that it was a wood carving of the crowned Blessed Virgin Mary holding the Child. Keeping silent about his finding he wrapped the image carefully again and took it away into Spain in 1967. The frontier gates were closed to pedestrians in 1969. When the keeper of this statue, now in the Canary Islands, learnt of the increasing devotion to Our Lady of Europe in Gibraltar, he broke the silence and revealed his precious possession to Mr. Joaquim Bensusan, the Curator of the Gibraltar Museum, by sending him a photograph and details of his findings.

This discovery has shed the long awaited light that explains why the devotion to Our Lady of Europe was so widespread so soon after the recovery of Gibraltar in 1462 by the Christians.

The unearthed statue of Our Lady is clearly a carving of the 13th or early 14th Century, coinciding with that period when the Christian Princes captured and occupied the Rock in the years 1309 to 1333. Following the constant practice of the victorious Christian armies, after expelling the Moslem population, the Princes dedicated the Continent of Europe to the Mother of Christ our Saviour, placing it under her motherly protection, and invoked her under the title "Our Lady of Europe".

To mark the consecration and veneration of Our Lady under that new title a shrine was set up. The Princes chose the tiny Mosque built by the Moslems when they first landed on the Rock in 711 at the Southernmost point of Gibraltar and, by common estimation, of the whole European Continent. The Mosque was transformed into a Christian place of worship and a small wooden statue of Our Lady of Europe was carved and placed in it for veneration.

Twenty-four years later in 1333 the Moslem forces returned with overpowering strength to recover the Rock. Realising that any resistance would go for nothing the Christians decided to leave the fortress. Before doing so the hermit in charge of the Shrine, to protect the statue from any possible desecration, enveloped the image in hexion and hid it in the earth near the Shrine where it was found in 1967.

The Moslems ruled over the Rock until 1462, when the Christians came to settle on it permanently. The conquering forces and their families did not all remain on the Rock. King Henry IV, therefore, in an effort to attract people to settle on it, revived the many privileges and prerogatives once decreed by his great-grandfather King Ferdinand in the year 1309.

With these royal concessions was revived also the devotion to Our Lady of Europe. There is no other explanation for the immediate widespread devotion to Our Lady of

Europe so soon after the recovery of Gibraltar in 1462 than that it had existed before. Since there was no statue to be found a new image was carved and set up in the very same tiny mosque at the south tip of the Rock of Gibraltar facing Africa. The revival of this devotion coincided also with the installation of the Shrine of Our Lady of Africa by the Portuguese King across the Straits in Ceuta in Africa.

The devotion to Our Lady of Europe prospered especially after the discovery of the New World in 1492. Generals, merchants and mariners would stop at the beach and climb to the Shrine to pray for protection. Some ancient prints of Gibraltar show that the Shrine and Our Lady were popular to those people sailing to the New World or to fight the Corsairs. They invoked the Mother of Christ as "Our Lady of a Happy Journey" (Notre Dame de Bon Voyage). Many of these captains would even donate large silver oil-lamps with oil provisions to be used while they were fighting, if not the elements, the Turks. People like John Andrea Doria, Martin Blas,. . . . enriched the Shrine with large silver lamps and other precious vessels. The oil-lamps were lit permanently there so that the light of the Shrine acted as a warning beacon to ships sailing near the protruding rocks.

Needless to say the inhabitants of Gibraltar held a profound devotion to Our Lady of Europe and on 15 August the Feast was celebrated with a holiday. People would gather around the Shrine at Europa Point and enjoy picnicking while others would hold games of stick. From Europa Point many people would then hold a pilgrimage to the Shrine at the Almoraima in Spain.

For the priests the Liturgical celebrations were ranked as of Double First-Class, which meant that the feast received maximum solemnity. The devotion and the Shrine became very popular. Some extraordinary cures experienced there made Father Jeronimo de la Concepcion wrote in his *Cadiz Ilustrada* of 1690, that Our Lady of Europe was very miraculous.

A Guild of Our Lady of Europe was founded. This confraternity had the task of looking after the poor people who died and providing for them Christian burial. For this purpose the only crypt for burial that was constructed in the Principal Church of St. Mary the Crowned was to be found at the Altar of Our Lady of Europe, St. Mary the Crowned.

Ever since the Moslems were expelled from the Rock in 1462, the final triumph over the Moslem foothold in Europe at Granada in 1492 was accomplished. It was not surprising that the Turks would attempt to recapture Gibraltar. When the Barbarossa's men landed on the beach below the Shrine pretending to be Christians, the Shrine guards were taken unawares. The Turks, led by a renegade Christian, ransacked the Shrine, stripping it of all its precious possessions. From there they marched north into the town to loot and take people away for ransom. A brave resistance, planned by the nobles of the town, forced the Turks to curtail their stay on the Rock. Fortunately enough the Turkish fleet laden with stolen goods and prisoners, was ambushed by a Christian fleet in the Bay of Gibraltar. Thus much of the treasure stolen was restored.

This traumatic experience revealed to everyone that the Shrine was far too exposed. The hermit in charge of it appealed to King Charles V to take definite measures and give it some protection. It was only later on, when the engineer Calvi built Charles V Wall and the other fortifications in Gibraltar, that the Shrine was enlarged and walled for protection.

It was there to the Shrine that the inhabitants went to take refuge whenever the town was harassed with bombardment from foreign ships. It happened first when the French tried their strength on the fortifications, and women, children and religious marched to the Shrine for protection. On this occasion everyone returned safely home.

155

Another incident was in 1704 when the Allied Forces invaded the south end of the Rock and the inhabitants who had sheltered in the Shrine to avoid being captured returned to the town to fall into the hands of the enemy troops.

The troops, furthermore, entered the Shrine and combed the place of all its precious articles. They even stripped the bejewelled statue of Our Lady of Europe and in the process manhandled it, breaking its head and that of the Child, abandoning it among the rocks. Someone found it and brought the statue to Father Romero de Figueroa who in turn, to protect it from further destruction, smuggled it into Spain. It was taken to Algeciras where many of the Gibraltarian inhabitants settled and continued their devotion to her. The ancient statue was given sanctuary in a tiny church. The news of the desecration of the Shrine and statue was learnt all over Spain, and a great outcry against such sacrilegious action by the British was made public. A replica of the statue was made in Madrid and prayerful processions were publicly held along the streets as acts of reparation.

The feast of Our Lady of Europe and its devotion continued in Gibraltar even after it became British. There was another not so ancient image of Our Lady of Europe in the church of St. Mary the Crowned and the Parish Priest persevered with the devotion. The ancient confraternity of Our Lady of Europe also continued its mission among the poor with the new inhabitants of Gibraltar. It is recorded that on the feast of Our Lady all the members of the confraternity were expected to make a fixed contribution. With the funds raised, the burial of poor people could be financed.

When the Great Siege took place between 1778 and 1782 the Statue of Our Lady of Europe, in the principal church, St. Mary the Crowned, was saved just in time from getting burnt. The statue was already in flames when Fr. Francis Messa pulled it out of the blazing church. When he succeeded in taking the image to Windmill Hill Flats, where the inhabitants had taken shelter, the people applauded and shouted with joy and sang aloud their heartfelt attachment to Our Lady of Europe as she appeared safely among them.*

Once the Shrine at Europa Point was abandoned by the hermit, as with all the houses and churches left without a guardian, the armies took over. The tiny building was turned into a guardroom and then stores. Later on the walled complex was drastically divided by the construction of the road leading to Nun's Well. Thus the tower section of the Shrine was separated from the rest of the building. During the Great Siege the tower was lowered like all the church towers in Gibraltar. In the end there remained what is to be found there now: the ground floor of the tower section of the Mosque. The building, nevertheless, was to remain under military control for over two hundred and fifty seven years.

When Dr. John Baptist Scandella, a native of Gibraltar, became Vicar Apostolic of Gibraltar in 1855, he made the promotion of the devotion one of his main concerns. He wanted to recover the ancient statue that was being venerated in Algeciras. Its true home was Gibraltar where it was first installed. Quite naturally Father Juan Romero, the Parish Priest of La Palma in Algeciras, objected to the withdrawal of the image held by them for 150 years. The people of Algeciras were also devotees of Our Lady of Europe and were not pleased to see the statue taken away from them. Bishop Scandella pursued the matter and after arguing the matter with the Bishop of Cadiz and with the Holy See, he succeeded in persuading the people to part with this treasure after certain promises. He was to have a replica made of the ancient one so that the people in Algeciras would have an image to continue their devotion. The Bishop contracted a Sevillian sculptor who did a most delicate and exacting work in creating another statue similar to the old one. He also restored the old one and carved a new

Child Jesus to complete the Old Statue that had been left childless.

In 1864 Bishop Scandella brought the ancient statue to its place of origin. Unfortunately the Shrine at Europa Point was still in military use so the Bishop and the Junta of Elders organised a fund raising scheme to construct a temporary Chapel to Our Lady of Europa at St. Bernard's Road. Meanwhile the image was placed in the care of the Sisters of the Institute of the Blessed Virgin Mary. These Loreto Sisters had a convent in Town at Gavino's Dwellings and there looked after the statue. It should be noted here that the Child held by Our Lady of Europe had traditionally been known to be naked. The nuns, however, possibly because they considered it irreverent to have the Child naked in their Convent, started to dress up the Child. Since then that Child has been kept dressed like a doll. Alas when the new Chapel was completed (the statue was transferred and enthroned in the new premises in the most solemn fashion), it contained some beautiful and valuable works of craftsmanship worth mentioning. His Holiness Pope Pius IX, who was well acquainted with Bishop Scandella and had donated a most impressive oil painting of the death of St. Joseph for St. Joseph's Church, furthermore donated a Carrara-marble altar frontispiece with his coat-of-arms and that of Bishop Scandella. Above the altar was erected a large white marble baldachino under which the Statue would be enthroned and hold a prominent position in the Chapel.

Bishop Scandella obtained approval from the Sacred Congregation of Rites to transfer the Feast day to 30 May and to continue regarding the Feast as a Double of First Class with a Special Mass and Liturgical Hour.

The nuns of the Institute of the Blessed Virgin Mary had included special prayers in honour of Our Lady of Europe in their official daily prayers from the moment they were asked to look after the image in 1864. The nuns still recite those prayers. And when the Irish Christian Brothers settled at the Sacred Heart Terrace in 1880, they led the boys up to the new Chapel every Sunday to venerate Our Lady of Europe.

It was there in that new Chapel of Our Lady that Bishop Gonzalo Canilla presented the instruments to the Vicar Capitular as the new Vicar Apostolic of Gibraltar and successor to Bishop John Baptist Scandella. The inhabitants frequented the Chapel with such regularity that everyone could see the direct influence of the Irish Christian Brothers and the Loreto Nuns. During all this time people sung a hymn to Our Lady inherited from time immemorial. The hymn in Spanish went something like this:

> *"Virgencita, virgencita de Europa,*
> *Que en nuestro pueblo de Gibraltar"*

This Chapel was cared for by the Little Sisters of the Poor who looked after the senior citizens in a Home in the same complex. When the Second World War was about to break out and the women, children and aged were evacuated from Gibraltar, there remained no further need for the Little Sisters of the Poor and so they too left. Rather than leave the precious ancient statue of Our Lady of Europe in the empty and unused Chapel, Bishop Fitzgerald decided to transfer it to the Cathedral of St. Mary the Crowned. It remained there in the Cathedral throughout the War until 15 August 1954.

In the summer of that same year, a large diocesan pilgrimate to Lourdes experienced a catastrophic train accident which shocked the whole of Gibraltar. The train de-railed at 11 p.m. at Puente Genil near Cordoba in pitch darkness and there were six dead and approximately 30 injured. None of the Gibraltarian pilgrims suffered any injury. They helped the badly injured. Feeling grateful for pulling the people through the accident safe and sound, the inhabitants on the Rock felt like doing something in honour of Our Lady. A group of men approached the Bishop and suggested that the Statue of Our Lady of Europe should be restored to the Parish where it used to belong. Why it was not taken back to the Chapel that Bishop Scandella had erected at St. Bernard's Road may be explained by the fact that the nuns who looked after the Chapel before no longer existed in Gibraltar. Hence in the light of this important consideration they thought it more proper to transfer the Statue instead to St. Joseph's Parish Church, where it would be looked after carefully. A torchlight procession was organised from the Cathedral of St. Mary the Crowned in Main Street, and the statue of Our Lady of Europe was solemnly carried shoulder-high to St. Joseph's Church. The Spiritual character of the event was comparable only to the prayer-filled experience in the annual Corpus Christi procession in Gibraltar.

In 1961 the local government transferred the freehold of all places of worship to a registered legal body of the Church in Gibraltar. Bishop John Farmer Healy saw to it that the transfer also included what remained of the Shrine of Our Lady of Europe. On 17 October, 1961, at a private ceremony, the keys were handed over to the Bishop.

Once it was leased the Shrine became the Church's responsibility, so the Bishop appointed Father Louis Orfila to look after it and promote the devotion.

Fr. Orfila wrote "the work of restoration started in February 1962, and it was undertaken as something to mark the fifth centenary of the commencement of Christianity in Gibraltar. Just before the Bishop left Gibraltar to attend the Second Vatican Council, in September 1962, he celebrated the first Mass there since 1704.

When the political situation between Spain and Gibraltar became so critical and people were so tense, a pilgrimage was organised from the Cathedral to the Shrine. It was on the occasion when Senor Castiella was presenting proposals to the British Government for the future of the people of Gibraltar in May 1966. In an effort to plead that the wishes of the people of Gibraltar should be respected the prayerful march was held and an assembly held at Europa Flats. There must have been over seven thousand people marching in that procession up Europa Road. Half way to the Shrine someone had listened to the late news that the proposals had not been accepted by Great Britain. This inevitably spread quickly along the procession and what started as a prayer of petition ended as a prayer of thanksgiving and rejoicing. On 7 October 1968, the statue was solemnly returned to the remains of the Shrine, and enthroned there by Bishop Healy.

Later on, in 1973, when Great Britain signed the Treaty of Accession into the Common Market, a Mass was celebrated to coincide with the time of Mr. Heath's actual signing of the document. The Shrine was packed with people of all levels of society. That same year, pilgrimages to the Shrine were organised in Great Britain. The significance of the message of the devotion to Our Lady of Europe especially when efforts were being made to create a United Europe began to have an impact in many quarters and so the pilgrimages were widely advertised.

When Bishop Edward Rapallo, another Gibraltarian Bishop, took office, he made the spread of the devotion one of his main concerns. The Shrine was allowed to be enlarged not only in structure, but also in its mission. He decided that the Shrine should have the double function of speaking to the whole of Europe and also to the many needs of the inhabitants of Gibraltar. The Shrine would be the centre for pilgrimage to and from Gibraltar, of ecumenical activities and of family social needs. The Bishop furthermore requested the Holy Father, Pope John Paul II, to officially approve the Most Blessed Virgin Mary as the Principal Patroness of the Diocese of Gibraltar, with the title of Our Lady of Europe. This petition was accepted on 6 August

1979. Soon afterwards, on 5 January 1980, the Holy See replied to the Bishop authorising him to transfer the annual feast of Our Lady of Europe to May 5, "a date which gives the whole 'mystique' of the Shrine the very thing it needed – an accepted relevance to modern times". May 5 happens to be Europe Day.

The following is the translation of the text of the Holy Father's approval of the Blessed Virgin Mary as the Principal Patroness of Gibraltar:

Pope John Paul II

"For permanent record

The reason why successive Popes have always approved, and as far as possible have promoted, devotion to the most Blessed Virgin, our Mother, is clear to anyone who seriously considers her greatness before God, whose Mother she is; her greatness before men, whose Patroness she has become; her sublime holiness, which is an example and an encouragement to us her children; and the power of her intercession with her adorable Son, the Ruler of all.

That is why, on being asked by our reverend Brother, Edward Rapallo, Bishop of Gibraltar, officially to approve Our Blessed Lady as the Principal Patroness of the Diocese of Gibraltar, under the title of Our Lady of Europe, which is the name by which the clergy and faithful of the diocese invoke her there with his approval, I most gladly accede to this request, for I myself am very keen to promote our heavenly Mother's honour.

I therefore approve what the Sacred Congregation for the Evangelisation of Peoples has decided in this connection, and I declare that the Blessed Virgin Mary, the Mother of Christ, be held to be the Principal Patroness of the Diocese of Gibraltar and be invoked with the title 'Our Lady of Europe', towards whom the faithful are drawn with very special devotion.

Her patronage under this title will enjoy all the rights and privileges envisaged by liturgical law, all things to the contrary notwithstanding.

I avail myself of this opportunity to invoke the Divine Mother and ask her kindly to protect the people whose welfare is her very special concern.

Given at Rome, at St. Peter's, under the Ring of the Fisherman, on the 31 May in the year 1979, the first year of my Pontificate.

Authenticated and signed by Cardinal Agostino Casaroli, Prefect of the Council for the Public Affairs of the Church."

Now that final endeavours have been made for the reopening of the frontier gates, the Shrine will become most significantly the one place where people from the different towns of the Campo Area will come together. Contacts with the Clergy in the Campo Area have been made for the realisation of this reconciliation of peoples under the protection of Our Lady of Europe.

The Treaty of Utrecht 1713 and the Jews of Gibraltar*
Sir Joshua Hassan, C.B.E., M.V.O., Q.C.

Sir Joshua Hassan was born in Gibraltar of Jewish family. He became Gibraltar's most prominent son. Although many Jews, even of that same name came from Morocco, Sir Joshua's Sephardic family came from the Balearic Isles early in the eighteenth century. He still boasts and is very proud to have been educated by the Irish Christian Brothers on the Rock.

He is a lawyer by profession and was called to the Bar-Middle Temple in 1939. He was made a Queen's Counsel in 1961. He entered the political arena early in his public life as a founder member of the Association for the Advancement of Civil Rights in Gibraltar in 1942. When the City Council was reconstituted in 1945 he was elected a City Councillor becoming Chairman of the Council. Except for three years he was Chairman of the Council until the Council and the Government merged in 1969. The House of Assembly was created in this same year and he headed the Opposition for three years. He was elected Chief Minister at every election until he retired in the Autumn of 1987 when he saw and felt that the future relationship with Spain was assured to be positively one where the Gibraltarian's interests were to be respected.

Sir Joshua is married and has children with whom he loves spending as much time as possible. He is a practising Jew closely identified with the local Hebrew community. In his many travels he has been requested to talk about the Gibraltar Jewish Community and so he did some research and with the material obtained he addressed the assembly of Jews in the United Kingdom. This address has never been easily accessible to the general public, hence, with Sir Joshua's permission his investigations about the Jews since the Treaty of Utrecht are reprinted here in this book.

The history of the Jews of Gibraltar from the time of the British occupation in 1714 is very much linked up with the development and growth of the civilian population of that city.

However, one aspect of it which is always touched upon when dealing with this matter but which has not been sufficiently investigated is the question of Article X of the Treaty of Utrecht, entered into in 1713, which confirmed the right of Great Britain to keep Gibraltar.

This Treaty dealt with the settlement of the claims and rivalries between the French and the British, one of which, of course, had been the occupation of Gibraltar, which was thereby settled.

Article X of the Treaty, with which we shall be mainly concerned, reads as follows:

The Catholic King does hereby, for himself, his heirs and successors, yield to the Crown of Great Britain the full and entire propriety of the town and Castle of Gibraltar, together with the port, fortifications, and forts thereunto belonging; and he gives up the said propriety to be held and enjoyed absolutely with all manner of right for ever, without any exception or impediment whatsoever. But that abuses and frauds may be avoided by importing any kind of goods, the Catholic King wills, and takes it to be understood, that the above-named propriety be yielded to Great Britain without any territorial jurisdiction, and without any open communication by land with the country round about. Yet whereas the communication by sea with the coast of Spain may not at all times be safe or open, and thereby it may happen that the garrison and other inhabitants of Gibraltar may be brought to great straits; and as it is the intention of the Catholic King, only that fraudulent importations of goods should, as is above said, be hindered by an inland communication, it is therefore provided that in such cases it may be lawful to purchase, for ready money, in the neighbouring territories of Spain, provisions and other things necessary for the use of the garrison, the inhabitants and the ships which lie in the harbour. But if any goods be found imported by Gibraltar, either by way of barter for purchasing provisions, or under any other pretence, the same shall be confiscated, and complaint being made thereof, those persons who have acted contrary to the faith of this treaty, shall be severely punished. And Her Britannic Majesty, at the request of the Catholic King, does consent and agree, that no leave shall be given under any pretence whatsoever, either to Jews or Moors, to reside or have their dwellings in the said town of Gibraltar, and that no refuge or shelter shall be allowed to any Moorish ships of war in the harbour of the said town, whereby the communication between Spain and Ceuta may be obstructed, or the coast be infested by the excursions of the Moors. But whereas treaties of friendship, and a liberty and intercourse of commerce are between the British and certain territories situate on the coast of Africa, it is always to be understood, that the British subjects cannot refuse the Moors and their ships entry into the port of Gibraltar purely upon the account of merchandising, Her Majesty the Queen of Great Britain does further promise, that the free exercise of their religion shall be indulged to the Roman Catholic inhabitants of the aforesaid town. And in case it shall be hereafter seem meet to the Crown of Great Britain to grant, sell, or by any means to alienate therefrom the propriety of the said town of Gibraltar, it is hereby agreed and concluded that the preference of having the same shall always be given to the Crown of Spain before any others.

Despite repeated instructions from London, that part of Article X prohibiting Jews and Moors from residing in Gibraltar was consistently disregarded and disobeyed and the reasons therefore require explanation.

From the very outset of the occupation the religious position of Gibraltar was certainly complicated. The English were hostile to the Catholics. The King of Spain resented the presence of Protestants. And, as the Ambassador, Sir Luke Schaub, wrote to Lord Stanhope on 17 June 1720, "The King of Spain. . . . will never be easy in his Mind, so long as there is a Protestant Garrison on the Continent of Spain". But these

---

*I have to record the considerable help I have received in the Preparation of this lecture for the Jewish Historical Society of England from a first draft by the late Dr. R.R. Kuczynski on the "Development of the Civil Population of Gibraltar" which he wrote while he was Demographic Adviser to the Colonial Office in 1944. [The lecture was given 15 May 1963].

were long-term propositions. Immediate difficulties arose rather from the residence of Moors and Jews. Both these people had been expelled from Gibraltar, but from the first day of British occupation friendly relations had been entered into with the Emperor of Morocco and his Mahometan and Jewish subjects, principally, it seems, because they represented a means whereby provisions could be obtained from the town.

Three days after the capitulation of Gibraltar, the Prince of Hesse wrote to King Charles: "In the meantime I shall see to preserve the good relations with the Moor so that the people here until further arrangements which I expect from your Majesty do not die of hunger."

During both the siege and the blockade Barbary was in fact the main source of food supply for the military and civil population of Gibraltar, and we find on 24 January 1705 Prince George's brother Henry writing to his mother: "The best thing is that we are not lacking good food and drink, which, except the wine, we get all from Barbary from the Moors." Nor did the position change essentially with the termination of the war. Conn summarises the situation as follows:

> "Under the terms of cession in the Treaty of Utrecht, England had agreed to evict the Jews and Moors from Gibraltar; and orders were sent to the Governor to carry out this provision. Since the trade of the town was principally in their hands, such an action would have seriously injured the garrison. And since much of the Governor's private revenue came from these people, naturally he was not enthusiastic about evicting them. Most of the Jews came from Barbary, and were under the protection of the Emperor of Morocco. Spain's refusal to permit communication with the garrison forced England to look across the Straits for supply. When the Emperor agreed to permit the export of lime, timber, bricks, and other materials to rebuild the fortifications, he did so only with the proviso that Gibraltar should be open to his subjects, both Jews and Moors. As time passed, the garrison also came to depend on Morocco for provisions. England was thus placed in a dilemma, for by carrying out her treaty promise with regard to the Jews and Moors she would cut off her own local source of supply".

The situation was solved (at least to the personal satisfaction of successive Governors) by repeated promises to Spain that these people would be evicted, and by a corresponding non-compliance with order to that effect sent from England.

The three main factors in a complicated situation were therefore:
(i) the inclination of the British Government to fulfil the obligations towards Spain,
(ii) the corruption of the local authorities at Gibraltar,
(iii) the need to receive provisions from Morocco, in view of the Spanish refusal to supply them.

(i) The inclination of the British Government to fulfil the obligations towards Spain.
On 28 November 1713 Lord Lexington informed Congreve that the Queen wanted Article X of the Treaty to be scrupulously observed. On 5 January 1714 Governor Congreve reported to Lord Bolingbroke that he "had some discourse" with the Commanding Spanish Lieutenant Colonel "how we were to have Provisions from the Country, and Conserning the Moors & Jews. . . ."

To the latter, he said "that they should all be gon Immediately, and upon this subject, I begg leave to give yr Lrdship this short Account of them, of the Moors, seldom, or ever any have bin here, and then, only just come, and goe, and of the Jews there are about one hundred and ffifty, two thirds of which are Natives of Barbary and the rest some from England, and Holland, but most from Italy, and as they have dealings in all parts, yor Lrdship will soon judge the Loss their Correspondents must have, if they are sent away without settleing their Accounts, and paying what they owe, for want of a reasonable time, allow'd them for this purpose".

On 25 February 1714 Lord Bolingbroke replied:

> "It is. . . . the Queen's pleasure, that you do not suffer under any pretence whatsoever, any Jews or Moors to inhabit at Gibraltar, and that you take care, that such as are at present settled there, do within the space of a Month, from the receipt of these Orders, make up their accounts, remove or otherwise dispose of their Effects, & Transport their Persons and Familys from thence. They will have no reason to complain that the Term Limited for their removal is too short, when it shall be considered, that they have had several Months already knowledge of what is stipulated relating to them."

On 13 May Lord Portmore reported to Lord Bolingbroke that all Jews "Except Six principal Jews of Barbary" had been removed. But they were actually not the only Jews to stay on, and two years later they were apparently again quite numerous in the town. Governor Congreve, on 18 November 1714, wrote: "That I had received her Majties Commands for remoueing the jews and the Moores from hence, which has bin put in Execution Accordingly, Except Six jews of Barbary and as Many European jews that are Detained here, till they sattisfie the English Marchants, for what they owe them, which Sir James Wishart who was then in the Bay approved of, the Marchants haueing represent'd to him that they should be intirely ruined if these jews should be Suffer'd to goe before they had paid their Debts, and for want of their being able to doe it, they are Still detailed here."

This excuse that the Jews could not be allowed to leave before they had settled their accounts and paid their debts was a favourite one with all Governors explaining to the Government at home why instructions had not been carried out. It will be met with again and again.

On 28 March 1717, "the Spanish Ambassador in London having represented that contrary to the 10. Art of the Treaty, there were then more than 300 Jews established at Gibraltar, Mr. Secretary Methuen signified the King's Commands to Colonel Cotton that he should cause the stipulations of the Treaty to be strictly observed". Colonel Cotton replied that "the Spanish Ambassador's complaint was unfounded. No synagogue had been opened there: and the number of Jews did not exceed one hundred". He reported furthermore on 9 June to Secretary Addison:

> "I Have the Honour to acquaint you that I have already removed many of the Jews, and the rest are daily going hence so that there remains but few, who have applyed to me for time to adjust their affairs, and I hope my complying with their request will meet with your approbation since some English Merchants have represented to me that many of His Majesty's Trading Subjects will suffer much if they have not a sufficient time allowed to dispose of their effects, and to settle their accounts with those they have had very considerable dealings with."

In consequence of the renewed instances made by the Spanish Ambassador for the removal of all Jews from Gibraltar, Secretary Addison on 26 September 1717 repeated the orders already given upon this subject, sending at the same time a list of those Jews who were known to be still resident there. Cotton replied on 2 November:

> "Before I Received your Commands of the 26 September in relation to the removal of

the remaining Jews in this place, I had given positive orders for their immediate departure, as you will find by the letter I had the Honour to write you of the 19 October and I have removed them accordingly, Except two of the Barbary Jews, who I have been obliged to detain as prisoners for a small time, at the request of some English Merchants, to whom they are greatly indebted.

I have the Honour to inclose your a Memor'l of one of the Europeans, he being a man of mighty good character, and assures me that many considerable Merchants will address themselves to you in his favour, but I have obliged him to leave this & go to Barbary, till I shall know what weight His friends' solicitations will have with you.

I Cannot avoid taking Notice of the Ambassador's representing my having removed only the poorest sort and suffered the richer to continue. The former were people of no consequence in Trade being such as but barely earned their livelyhood, and cou'd at a few hours warning adjust their small affairs; and I have often very hearyly wish't that those more concerned in Commerce had met with no greater difficulty. I should then have had the pleasure, & satisfaction, of putting His Majesty's orders in Execution without the least delay, but their dealings have been so large & general both with British Merchants, and some of other Nations, that some months cou'd hardly be judged sufficient for them to settle their accounts to the satisfaction of all their correspondents. I therefore humbly submit it to you, if these were not the properest persons to be detailed. . . .

I am extremely sorry you have had the trouble of writing to me concerning the Jews, but when I assure you that my permitting them to remain here was purely out of regard to His Majesty's Trading Subjects who must otherwise have been great sufferers, it will I hope in some measure plead my Excuse."

The memorial referred to in this dispatch was from a Jew, Manuel Diaz Arias, to Cotton, dated 28 October and began as follows:

"Upon The Incouragment That her Latte Majesty Queen Ann Was Pleased to Grantt To all The March'tts And Traders Thatt would Come to Satle in Gibraltar I Came from London In ye year 1713 with a Considerable Cargoe of English Manifature Recommended To Colonel Congrave, Then Leautenant Govr. who was Pleased To Incourag me to Carey on my Trade As Usuall To all English Marchts. As yr Honr has been Pleased To Doe The Same To all In Generall.

And upon The ordr. That yr Honr Gave That all ye Jews should Inmidly Leave This Place I Humble Represent To yr Honr That my affairs Are In Such A Condition That it will be Imposible To obey So soon without a Considerable Lostt To my Selfe and sever'l Marchantts in London haveing Gratte Summs of Money to Receive from Severall Inhabitants of This City Grate Many accountts to Satle and Considerable Efects and Marchandises, In my Hands That I do not Know how to dispose of with out Their owners orders.

And Not with standing That yr Honr was Pleased to give me Notice About The Begueenin of May to Leave This City My afairs haveing Been so Backwards That I Could not Posible obey without a Totall Ruinn of my Selfe And Severall Marchtts.

Therefore I Humble Desire yr Honr will be Pleased To take Intto Consideration My Circumstancys, and Distinguis me from all The Restt Being an English Man and freeman of London. . . ."

On 25 November "The orders for the removal of the Jews" were renewed.
On 5 January 1718 Cotton wrote to Addison:

"I flatter myself that my conduct in relation to the News will meet with the same success, having strictly complied with what is stipulated in the 10th Article of the Treaty of Utrecht, By removing both from the Towne and Bay the Jews of all Nations one only excepted, whom at the request of some English Merchants his Creditors, is still detailed as a prisoner for a few day's longer he expecting by one of our Men of War goods sufficient to discharge his debts as this Ship is hourly expected he shall on her arrival instantly depart."

This statement appears not to have been true. However, before leaving Gibraltar, Cotton, in his Instructions to Colonel Peter Godbey, dated 8 February 1718, said: "I must recommend to you, that upon no account whatsoever you suffer Jews of any Nation to reside here."

(ii) The corruption of the local authorities at Gibraltar.
It is evident that high British officials extorted bribes from the Jews who wished to stay, though some accusations to this effect may have been caused by dislike of the Jews rather than by knowledge of facts.

On 1 June 1717, Vice-Admiral Cornwall complained about the equivocal attitude of Governor Cotton.

"There was an Order of this kind from her late Majesty to ye late Lt Governour, wch was so far from being observed yt, from several frivolous pretences, great Numbers of Jews were suffer'd to remain here; & wch I am inform'd by ye Merchants, & other Traders His Majesty's Subjects here, has proved very injurious to ym. And therefore I cannot so much as Suppose yt ye Gentleman who at present commands here will suffer any one to remain upon any pretence whatsoever, & more especially since ye same is a direct violation of ye 10th Article of ye Treaty with Spain, whereby ye cession of this Place is made to Gr. Br. & upon wch ye Spaniards make pretence of treating His Mjty's Ships, when they come into some of their Ports, very Scurvily; & particularly at Cartagena & Alicant. . . .,,

On 7 September, in discussing the differences with the Emperor of Morocco, he said:

". . . . I resolv'd to endeavour to trace out the secret Spring from whence their violent proceedings against us arose; And from the best Information I could get, find that they were occasion'd by a combination of the French Merchants & Jews at Sally, in conjunction with the Jews that are Inhabitants of this Place. . . .

As ye Jews yt are permitted to reside in this Place have been greatly instrumental in occasioning our present Rupture with the Moores; & who continue from time to time to give them such Advices as may prove very injurious to us, wch I have not been able intirely to prevent; And not only so but I further humbly take leave to represent, that any of them being allow'd to remain here is very detrimental to ye Nation, for that as long as they do so there is no encouragement for any English Merchants to come and reside here, since all the Trade will pass thro' ye Jews Hands, & ye vast Sums they get thereby are all sent to Barbary ? other Country's. But if ye Jews of all Nations were sent hence, the Trade would naturally fall into His Majesty's Subjects hands & be a means to draw greater Numbers of Traders hither, & the advantages reap'd thereby sent to Gr. Br.

I need not further urge ye many complaints the Spaniards make for the Jews remaining here, wch they say is a violation of ye 10th Article of their Treaty wth us;

And therefore, I humbly submit it to your consideration, if this be not soon remedy'd, Whether, or no, ye Spaniards may not form pretensions from thence for violating such other Article of the Treaty that may prove advantageous to them?

Indeed it is my humble opinion that ye Trade to this Place very much wants a thorough regulation & encouragement, whereby it might become very beneficial to ye Nation, & I dare take upon me to say, in time, more than wo'd compensate for ye charge Gr. Br. is at in ye maintaining of it. . . ."

On 15 November he reported:

". . . . ye Jews have not only remain'd here till a very few days past (contrary to His Majty expres command) but there has been encouragement given them for Trading also, as will appear by the Extract of a Letter from Mr. Hatfield, His Majtys Consul at Tetuan (dated 23 October) wch I herewith send you."

In this letter Hatfield said that "the Governor of Gibraltar, this day fortnight, sent for some of them [Jews], or messages to them that the Trade was open betwixt Gibraltar and Barbary, & for his trouble in procuring it they were to make Him a purse of Two thousand Dollars".

Admiral Cornwall continued:

"But I must at ye same time humbly begg leave to note, That if Collonel Cotton did take upon Him to give encouragement to the Jews, by declaring that ye Trade was again laid open betwixt Gibraltar & Barbary, without having any authority for so doing; it is my humble opinion He cannot well justify such a proceeding. . . .

I begg leave here to observe, That, on ye 9th of June 1714, The House of Commons address'd her late Majesty to have apply'd towards the Support of this Place the Rents & Profits of ye Houses in it: And on ye 22d of ye same Month Mr. Bromley inform'd the House, That Her Majesty had commanded Him to acquaint them, that ye said Rents & Profits of ye Houses of Gibraltar should be apply'd towards ye support of yt Garrison as they had desired; but notwithstanding wch, if I am rightly inform'd, they are at present otherways employ'd."

On 3 January 1718 he wrote to Addison:

"The following is a Paragraph of a Letter I rec'd from Collonel Cotton, dated ye 16th of October last. vizt, I have told ye Jews of all Nations that none are to expect to remain in this Place beyond ye Time you have named to me, so convenient for your present Negotiation, this you may depend (if you believe I have any honour) shall be put in execution.

From hence I concluded that all the Jews had been remov'd as I wrote you in my Letter of ye 15th of November; but to my great surprise I am inform'd, that there are not only some remain yet within the Town, but many yt only lye on board a vessell in the Mold, who are allow'd to Trade notwithstanding His Majtys express commds to ye contrary; And therefore whether His Majesty will think such an evasion a full observance of His Orders for their being remov'd, is humbly submitted.

And whatever pretences yt Gentleman may have made for suffering ye Jews to remain here, I hope in due time to make it appear to His Majesty, that ye real one was no other than from ye great Sums He had at several times drawn from them. . . . And I will take upon me to say, that, by the Governors frequently drawing Sums of Money from ye Trading People here, it has proved a greater prejudice to ye Trade of this Place than trebly any Duty yt is laid in other Places and had been certain."

(iii) *The need of receiving provisions from Morocco in view of the Spanish refusal to supply them.* Until 1712 the relations between the authorities in Gibraltar and the Emperor of Morocco seem to have been on the whole friendly, but in that year it proved difficult to renew the truce, and the Peace Treaty with Spain (2 July 1713) by which England had pledged herself to expel the Jews and Moors from Gibraltar, of course, aggravated the situation. On 14 March 1713 Stanwix had already asked in a dispatch:

"And there being several Jew's Subjects of Barbary who have resided here a long time, what is to be done with them, and whether they are to have any Correspondence with their Country."

On 22 July 1714 a new "Treaty of Peace, Friendship & Commerce" was made with the Emperor, but soon difficulties again arose about the purchase of provisions in Morocco. Congreve's dispatch 18 November 1714 states:

"I begg leave. . . . to Acquaint you, that the Basshaw at Tituan refused to allow of any Article whereby he should be obliged to permit our buying Cattle in Barbary for the use of this Garrison, in the Treaty of Peace Signed by him and Captn Paddon, which is to be look'd upon as the Sense of that Signed at Maqueness by the Emperor."

Moreover, the question of the residence of Jews caused constant trouble. The negotiations for a new treaty dragged on, drafts were prepared, agreed, altered, and then abandoned, but finally peace was concluded by a treaty signed on 13 January 1721. Article VII provided:

". . . . And that the subjects of the emperor of Fez and Morocco, whether Moors or Jews, residing in the dominions of the king of Great Britain, shall entirely enjoy the same privileges that are granted to the English residing in Barbary."

This agreement, which plainly contradicted the Treaty of Utrecht, offered, of course, no satisfactory solution of the vexed problem. On 18 August 1725 Lieutenant-Governor Kane, who had just arrived in Gibraltar, wrote to Lord Townshend:

"I shall obey His Majty's Commands in using my best endeavours for keeping a good Corrispondence with the Spaniards; & to the best of my understanding shall observe such treaties stipulated with that Crown as have come to my Knowledge, but am greatly apprehensive of some difficulties if they should strictly insist upon one part of the 10th Article of the Utrecht Treaty in 1713, for there it says in these words, (viz) 'That no leave shall be given under any pretence whatsoever either to Jew or Moor to reside or have their dwelling in the sd town of Gibraltar'; & in the 7th Article of the Treaty concluded with the Emperour of Morocco in the Year 1720 is it Expres'd (viz) 'And that the Subjects of Fez & Morocco, whether Moors or Jews residing in the Dominions of the King of Great-Britain Shall entirely Enjoy the same priviledge that is granted to the English residing in Barbary'.

  Now My Lord, as these two Articles are directly oppostie one to the other I humbly submit the Consideration of them to your Ldsp; and again as the Port is to be free to Moors by Treatys, upon some Occasions it gives Offence to Spain."

On 25 September, Kane wrote again to Townshend:

> *"I was so particular in my letter of the 18th of August touching the Treaties of Peace which respect the Jews, that I shall say no more of them than to hint that they are in number 111 Males & 26 Females, and that they have been allowed a Synagogue.*
>
> *Whether the Spaniards Shall Call this a breach of Treaty or not, may be a Quere, but hitherto the Majr Genll, who Commands the Cantoonment before this Place, has not made any mention of the Jews to me, and hope he will not; This Gentleman is very Courteous, and has the Character of a good disposition, and not Subject to Cavill at Trifles."*

In his "Representations & Proposals touching the present State of the Garrison of Gibraltar", sent in the same month to Townshend, Kane said:

> *"It is not to be doubted but that most of the Princes in Europe would rejoice to see his Majesty dispossess'd of Minorca and Gibraltar, for the Peace which they preserve with the Government in Barbary does greatly advance the British trade."*

On 13 October Kane, in a letter to Delafaye, again pointed out the contradictions between the treaties with Spain and with Morocco. He added:

> *"Ever since my being here I have had a very good Corrispondence with the Majr Genll that Commands the Cantoonment before this Place, from whom I had a visit of Compliment, and having returned it the other Day was received with great Marks of respect; and hitherto no mention made by him of the Jews: Nevertheless I have been told that some in Town, have dropped expressions as if their dwelling here is ill taken at Court; from whence, and from the Silence of the Court upon that head, it may be conjectured that if ever they intend a breach with us, they may make this their pretence, and these things I shall humbly beg leave to offer to the Consideration of their Excelcys the Lords Justices, and with them the following observation, vizt The Article which permits the Jews to reside in the King's Dominions is the 7th, and that by which the Treaty acknowledge's the King to be the Sovereign of Gibraltar is the 13th, then the Question is whether Gibraltar was understood in the Dominions mentioned in the 7th Article."*

Concerning this query, there does not appear to be the slightest doubt that "Gibraltar was understood in the Dominions mentioned in the 7th Article". Article XIII began: "and as it has pleased Almighty God, that by his majesty's arms, the island of Minorca and city of Gibraltar are now in his majesty's possession, and are become part of his Britannic majesty's dominions. . . ." Kane's letter continued:

> *"I know that the Jews here explain this in their own Favour, and seem to rely much upon the Bacha of Tetuan, (with whom I have hitherto had a good Corrispondence) but it is not improbable but the Jews of London might oblige them to decline the thing, rather than they should Occasion a breach with either Spain or Morocco, and here I shall take the Liberty to Send you the Copy of a Letter I writ to Mr. Secretary Craggs from hence, when I came to Command here in the Year 1720, at the time that the Peace with Morocco above mentioned was in agitation by Commodore Stewart."*

In a letter of the same day to Newcastle, Kane said:

"Mr. Delafaye haveing signified it to be the pleasure of theyr Exls the Lords Justices that I should have due regard to the Treaties with Spain, I have thereupon represented to him some things touching the Treaty of Utrecht, and the last Treaty with the Emperour of Morocco which may Merit theyr Exls Consideration."

On 10 November Kane wrote to the British Consul Hatfield in Tetuan:

"Every Vessell that has lately come from Tetuan has brought Some Jews, and none but one Mention'd by you, but Since they make this a practice, not only from Your Coast, but from all other parts, I am resolv'd to put a Stop to that Current and think to begin with Some that Hugh Bromige has Brought over, for there are now 160 here Males and females.

These people fancy that the last Clause in the 7th Article of the late Treaty with Moroco gives a right to all jews in Barbary to Setle in Gibraltar, who Shall Call themselves Subjects of Moroco, So that by their way of Explaining that treaty we are not to refuse any Jew of Barbary that Shall demand the priviledge of recideing here; But as Gibraltar is not Mention'd untill ye 13th Article of that treaty, I understood the Dominions Mention's there to be only the Dominions at home, nor is it Possible it Should be meant otherwise, Considering what is Said against admitting these people into this town in the 10th Article of the treaty of Utrecht: nor is it to be Supposed that Crouds of any Strangers whatsoever Should be admitted to dwell in a frontier Garrison, that lyes So Lyable to Surprize, for under Such Circumstances we are not to trust any Sett of people but the Kings protestant Subjects.

I have writ to the Kings Ministers upon the direct opposition there is in the two Articles above Mention'd, to which I daily expect an answer, in the Mean time I Should be glad to know how your Bacha (who was one of the Plenipotentiaries in that treaty) understands the Dominion Mention'd in the 7th Article (Since Gibraltar is not mention'd till ye 13th) if it Could be moved to him as accidentally, and without giveing Umbrage: But Should he understand Gibraltar to be meant in that treaty then the above reasoning's Might not be improper to Move to him, and again that if this place is to be incisted on, then to have it Explain'd thus, Number for Number; a More or a Jew for a Britten, Man for Man; a Woman for a Woman; a Protestant Minister for a Jewish Rabby a Church for a Synagoge, and under Such Limitations this Garrison would be Eased of this Sett which in my oppinion would be an advantage to the British traders, and give great satisfaction to Spain.

I shall order the Jews that are here to give Notice to their Correspondence in all Parts not to come hither with a view of Inhabiting here; and Shall acquaint all Jews who have families that they are to prepare to retier from hence with their famalys, and that none are to be admitted here but as travelers."

On 25 October 1726 he wrote to Newcastle:

"I shall have due Regard to the King's Commands in Conniveing at the Jews Staying here who are Subjects to the Emperour of Morocco."

The only reference to such instructions which can be traced in an undated "Draft to Kane", later marked "after July 1725". which said:

"And therefore tho' the permitting of Jews to reside in that Town is not strictly comformable to ye Treaty of Utrecht, yet upon the Applications that have been made to

> *the King in behalf of those who are now at Gibraltar, whom ye Empr of Morocco asserts to be his Subjects His Maty, considering the present circumstances of our Affairs, thinks that without allowing this claim of ye Empr of Morocco, those Jews being at Gibraltar may for ye present be connived at, & would accordingly have you suspend ye Execution of any Orders that may have been formerly sent for removing them from thence."*

Kane continued his letter:

> *"I find that friends at that Court can get any Letters of Recomendation from the Emperour that they incline to have. I have lately had a Letter from him in favour of a particular Jew in this Town:*
>
> *I shall have beg leave to observe to your Grace that haveing found vast numbers of Jews comeing to this place, Not only from Barbary but from other parts, (as mention'd to your Grace in former Letters) I thought it necessary to write upon it to the Basha of Tetuan, who was for limitting their Numbers &ca, Such Numbers haveing settled here with their wives and famillies, and haveing a Sinnagoge where they performe their worship & Circumsisions, publiquly, gives offence to the Spaniards; and as the Court of Madrid have not Made any representation upon it, it has given me reason to think they may have Some obscure Views, touching the treaty of Utrecht."*

If the Court of Madrid had "Some obscure Views, touching the Treaty of Utrecht" they were not long to remain so. On 21 December 1726 the Spanish Ambassador in London, Marquis de Pozobueno, told the Duke of Newcastle that "the cession which His Catholic Majesty had previously made at the peace of Utrecht had become null and void, because of the infraction made in the conditions on which the English garrison was permitted to remain in possession of Gibraltar; seeing that, contrary to all the protestations made, they had not only extended their fortifications by exceeding the limits prescribed and stipulated, but had also, contrary to the express literal tenor of the treaties, permitted Jews and Moors, enemies to the Catholic religion, to reside in the city". When four weeks later (17 January 1727) Parliament met, the King announced that "His Catholic Majesty is now making preparations to attack and besiege Gibraltar". But the friendly relations with Barbary were now to bear fruit. On 12 January 1727 Kane wrote to Newcastle:

> *"When it was heard in Barbary that this place was to be besieged the Basha of Tetuan wrote me a handsome Letter offering Supply's of provisions &ca. And protection to all who should come thether under English Collours, with offers of other Services, and at this time Admirall Hobson has sent over his tender for Catle &c."*

The question of provisions was all-important, for although the Dutch troops had been entirely withdrawn in March 1713, and during the whole of the period from 1713 to 1726 the British garrison was small, there had from the beginning been difficulty in obtaining fresh food from Spain. In 1713 Stanwix complained repeatedly of the scarcity of food. About 20 July he mentioned "an order signed at Madrid, above 20 daies ago, that all [&] Spaniards were prohibited to bring any thing to sell to us on pain of being sent to the Galleys, or their Garison's in Barbary".

Lord Portmore, in a letter of 21 March 1714, said:

> *"What ever ye method be, it is certain this garrison must be victuall'd by the queen, and that ye least deminution of ye present allowance without changing ye guarison,*

would occasion a mutiny, as it is, ye soldiers are so harrasd since ye late reduction, by being upon continual duty, and under a necessity of eating ye salt provisions almost raw for want of coals, that they desert dayly. . . . You are now my lord so fully instructed of ye true state of this affaire, that I am apt to think your Lp. will not be surpris'd to know, I am under a very great aprehension, that if a speedy supply is not sent and solid setlement made for this guarison it is a great question if ye town of Gibraltar will be long in Her Majestys possion."

There were in 1713 and for a long time to come three British regiments in Gibraltar, with an establishment of 1,500 men. On 27 August 1715 the strength of the garrison was 1,349, of whom 1,059 were "Centinels" (privates). In 1718 the garrison was temporarily reinforced, but when England towards the end of the year declared war upon Spain, the garrison again was weak. Colonel Cotton asked for reinforcements but there cannot be found any evidence that his demand was fulfilled. In August 1720 the garrison had only "a force of 1,150 men". But now the British Government considered the position to be critical and on 8 September ordered the Governor of Minorca, Colonel Kane, to embark as great a part as possible of his garrison and repair to Gibraltar, where he was to act as Chief Commander during the absence of the Governor. Kane on 20 October landed 500 men. The Governor, Lord Portmore, who arrived on 10 November, asked on 18 November for further reinforcements in the following terms:

". . . . it may be depended upon, they [the Spaniards] se well know ye consequence of this place, that if it can't be had on other termes, they will, whenever they have a good opportunity, endeauour to recouer it with all ye force of Spain, which you are sensible, is uery different from what it was when this town was last besieged. This, Sir, leads me to offer it, not only as mine, but ye opinion of all good and impartial judges, that this guarison, considering ye many posts that are to be mentained and ye great extent of them, can't be defended, as it ought, with less than three thousand men, and prouisions in proportion an article, I find has hitherto been too much neglected."

Lord Portmore rejected Kane's proposals to return his troops to Minorca, and Kane left on 15 December without his men; he got them back, however, in February 1721. This means the garrison of Gibraltar was again reduced to three regiments, for no notice was taken of the request for 3,000 men.

In the summer of 1725 the position again became serious, and on 10 July Kane was appointed Lieutenant-Governor of Gibraltar and was authorised to retain there two regiments from Ireland which were on their way to relieve the two regiments stationed at Minorca. Kane arrived on 16 August and reported two days later that the garrison, consisting of only 1,361 men (including 291 officers and non-commissioned officers), was not sufficient, and that in his view at least four regiments were necessary.

When two regiments from Ireland arrived on 6 September he retained one regiment and "Compleated it out of the other to the Irish Establishment, which is 10 Comps. making 340 private men".

He now had four regiments, and this number, he maintained, should always be stationed at Gibraltar. The strength of the garrison remained unaltered all through 1726, but owing "to the Low Establishment of the Regiment", as Kane put it, the private soldiers seldom exceeded 1,400 during the year.

As regards the civil population of Gibraltar in the period from the Treaty of Utrecht until the siege of 1727, I shall first submit the available statistical evidence. On 17

February 1721 the civilians able to bear arms consisted of 45 English, 96 Spaniards, and 169 Genoese. It is impossible, of course, to draw therefrom any conclusions concerning the total civil population, and "a Gentleman of the Navy", in his pamphlet published in 1725, submitted a plan for obtaining the lacking data. He proposed "That some creditable Person, well experienced in our Trade that way, may have a Commission from His Majesty" and that this Commissioner, among other things

> *"Should frame a Book, or Register, wherein should be set down, in the most compendious manner, every Person's Name in the Garrison, his Nation, and Employment, and how long He has been an Inhabitant?*
>
> *The Register, or General Muster-Roll, proposed to be framed by this Magistrate, should not be taken from any Pattern, or copied from old Books and Papers, since to build on a corrupt Foundation might be destructive of the Design.*
>
> *I allow, that the Method here proposed for this Enquiry may at first View appear some thing harsh; but when the true Design shall be considered, vis. That it is to set Matters on a new footing, to correct what is defective, and to give the Government a new, and more wholesome Constitution, surely it will not appear strange."*

It was, to be sure, a mere coincidence that Lieutenant-Governor Kane actually included in his "Representations & Proposals touching the present State of the Garrison of Gibraltar", which he sent in September 1725 to Lord Townshend, a table showing in detail the composition of the inhabitants of the town on 20 August. "The Number of Inhabitants in Gibraltar Spaniards and others Exclusive of those belonging to the Troops & Navy. August 20 1725."

Nations	Number of Souls		Males from 16 to 60	Spaniards that have born arms since ye siege
	Males	Females		
British	57	56	55	
Spaniards	233	167	100	52
Genoese	301	113	190	
French	17	6	14	
Dutch with Spanish wives	8	13	7	
Algerines & Moors	5			
Jews	111	26		
Totals	732	381	366	52

Spanish Clergy   4
   2 Seculars
   2 Franciscans
Males, Jews & from what Nations:
England   4
Holland   3
Leghorn   17
Barbary   86
Turky   1
    ───
    111

The total number of (civil) inhabitants on 20 August 1725 was therefore 1,113, of whom 414 were Genoese, 400 Spaniards, 137 Jews, 113 British, and 49 of other nationalities. The garrison consisted at the same time (18 August) of 1,361 men. Including the families of military persons and officers' servants, the total population probably was not much less than 3,000.

Though the Genoese were more numerous than any other group of civilians they are seldom mentioned in official documents. The authorities evidently were not interested in them as such, from either a national or an international point of view. The position of the Jews has already been discussed at some length. Here it may suffice to point out that seven-ninths of the male Jews had come from Barbary. It seems likely that ten years earlier not only the number but also the proportion of Jews from other countries was larger.

In August 1725 Kane arrived in Gibraltar to defend the fortress against an unexpected attack. Towards the end of the following year vast numbers of Spanish troops were concentrated in the neighbourhood of Gibraltar. Kane reported:

> *"These things has so Terrified the old Spanish Inhabitants that many of them have desierd to quit the town with their Families & Effects those who had old grants of houses have Sold them to English Officers: both which I have Encouraged, for by that means we Shall get rid of a people who are not in the Kings Interest."*

Some of the houses were also sold to British civilians; the number of British inhabitants was small all the time. On 20 August 1725 there were 57 males and 56 females. The fact that of the males all but two were between 16 and 60 years old indicates that there were hardly any children among the British civil population. This makes it the more difficult to believe that there were as many female as male adults in the town.

"A Petition of the Inhabitants of Gibraltar against Colonel Congreve" signed by four British women who had returned to England shows that the Government discouraged ex-Servicemen and their families from staying on in Gibraltar, and also reveals the autocratic power of the Governor at that time:

> *"That the said Serjt and the husbands of the sd Women having served during the late war and being reduced out of the severall Regiments they respectively belonged to did in the year 1713 settle in Gibraltar upon the encouragement of a Proclamation or Order from her late Majestie read by Brigadier Stanwix then Governour at the head of each Regiment declaring that all such Subjects of the Crown of Great Brittain as would build or repair any houses at their own charges should enjoy the same without paying any rent or taxes.*
>
> *That upon this encouragement the above named Persons took old houses which were falling down and rebuilt or repaired them at their own cost which was a very great expense to each of them for such houses were very ruinous the better houses being given to the Jewes and Genoeses.*
>
> *That notwithstanding they were oblidged to an excessive charge to put such houses in a little order to live in they were nevertheless compelled by Collonel Congreve the Lievtent Governor to pay great fines and a monthly rent contrary to her Majesties declaration and altho' to enable them to pay such duties they had no other means than by selling such goods and necessaries as were brought by the Spaniards to the Markett without the Gates or by Ships into the Harbour yet they could not have leave to go on board such Merchant Ships without a spesciall order or to go out of the Gates to the Markett till 9 aclock in the morning. Whereas the Genoeses Spaniards & Jews had leave to go on board such Ships or the the Markett as soon as the Gates were open by which method such Jews and Genoeses engrossed the whole trade & the poor English were in a starving circumstance.*

That whereas by the Articles of Peace the Jews were all to be expelled the Towne and in compliance therewith many Jews were sent away yet Colonel Congreve soon received others in their room and when they wanted houses he found pretences to turn out the poor English and sold such houses which they had repaired at their own cost to such Jews and other Forreigners for great sumes of money particularly the said Patrick Murphy for no other reason but petitioning Colonel Congreve to be himself and Wife protected from the insults of a Person in the Garrison was turned out of his house and it was given to another Person for the Premium of thirty five pounds and the said Mary Brandon was likewise without any cause turned out of her house which was given to a Genoese for the summe of twenty five pounds and not only the abovenamed Persons are unjustly dispossesst of their houses but ten or twelve poor English Families more are since turned out of the place which by this method will be in a little time wholly inhabited by forreigners who are or may be more numerous than the Garrison which in consequence of such proceedings may be in danger to be lost.

That it has been the usage of former Governours to permitt any of the Souldiers in the Garrison skilled in Butchery to kill Cattle for the use of the Place but Collonell Congreve was pleased to retain that liberty to four Persons whereof the above named Patrick Murphy was one who were compelled for that priviledge actually to pay before hand as a gratuity to Colonel Congreme 100 Pistoles and to give him some choice parts of each Bullock besides. Yet notwithstanding those four Persons were soon after they had paid their fine removed from that employmt and the business of providing the Garrison with meat was given entirely to a Spaniard who paid him a larger gratuity and who by reqson thereof sold his meat at a very extravagant price so that the Inferiour Officers and the poor Inhabitants could very seldom afford to provide fresh meat at such rates.

That when they would have addresst to Colonel Congreve for relief he ordered the Centinells to suffer no persons to come to him with Petitions so that no redress could be had but on the contrary he turned the above named Persons their Wives and children out of the gates where there was no Shelter or any relief to be had but they remained in a starving condition 'till some Masters of Ships in pity to their distress took them on board and gave them a passage to England whither they are come to implore Justice and to be relieved for such oppressions.

Elizabeth Murphy
Mary Brandon
Elzbath Asly
Katherin Crompton"

Colonel Cotton, in 1716, on the other hand, made some efforts to persuade English merchants living in Spanish ports to transfer their residence to Gibraltar.

"Since my coming to this place it has been my Chiefest Care, to remove after the best manner that I possible cou'd some Grievances that has without doubt been most justly complain off, and my publishing the paper that I have the Honour to Enclose to you has I think given perfect satisfaction to the whole Garrison. I at the same time writt to the Merchants at Cadiz & Malaga acquainting them of my having taken of the Imposition laid on provisions, and have also assured them that any English protestants that were included to setle here, should meet with all the encouragement I cou'd possible show them, I further added that they shou'd on all occasions find me ready to joyne with them in all things for the advantage of Trade, and making this Garrison vsefull to His Majesty's Subjects, without having the least regard to my own private Intrest, which is I think all I can do at present but I hope to receive you Comands which shall ever be obeyed most punctually."

The question of consuls also came up, and although he reported the local objection to them, he did not put forward any reason for this attitude.

"The trading people seem to think it hard there shou'd be any Consuls allowed in this Towne, there is at present one from France, others from Holland & Genova I beg you will send me your directions about them."

Later, on 23 March 1717, he wrote in favour of keeping the consuls from Genoa and Holland but against keeping the French consul or admitting a Spanish consul. However, on 2 November 1717 he wrote to Addison:

"Pursuant to His Majesty's pleasure, I have admitt'd Dn Francisco Garcia to act as Consul here:. . . . He having produced to me His Majesty's confirmation of the King of Spain's Commission to him for that Employment."

The possibilities of attracting British traders were discussed repeatedly. On 8 February 1718 Cornwall wrote to Addison:

"Indeed it is my most humble opinion, that there wants a thorough regulation of ye Affairs of this Place, & particularly as to ye encouragement of Trade; & of wch I think there cannot be one till such time as there is a Civil Power established; & wch I think would be ye chiefest motive to induce numbers of His Matys Subjects to resort hither. But as it at present stands ye advantages of its being a Free Port are chiefly reap'd by Foreigners; there being very few, but the Garrison, but what are so."

In 1725 Philaletes, referring to the proposal of "a Turkey Merchant" (1720) "that the King might, by Act of Parliament, be empowered to grant Leases of Houses and Lands at Gibraltar for a certain Term of Years", said that this scheme "will be so far from being prejudicial to the Place, that it will much encourage Families to go and settle there, which would not only soon restore the Towne to its primitive Beauty but make it populous, and thereby add to its Trade and Security".

On 30 September 1726 Kane wrote to Newcastle:

"Should the Barracks & Pavilions be built that are proposed, it would not only be for the Security of the Place and a good to the Troopes, but would Likewise be an Ease to the Inhabitants, and a great Incouragement to Commerce; For the officers & men being removed into Pavilions & barracks, the houses where they now quarter would be Convenient for British Subjects who should Incline to come and Inhabit here, for at present there are no houses for them to come to; And it is Certain that the Greater Number of British Protestants Shall be here, and the fewer fforraigne papists, the Greater Security it would be to the Garrison, and the greater would be the traffick for English goods; which at this time bear no proportion with the traffick in fforraigne Goods."

The housing question, both of the military and the civilians, continued to cause endless trouble. The officers of the garrison, in a petition, complained of the actions of Governor Congreve:

"That during the time Gibraltar was besieged by the French and Spaniards all or the greatest part of the houses were reduced to ruins and greatly damaged and for want of

due repairs many are since fallen downe so that few are in any condition for quartering the Officers of the Garrison. Yet nevertheless those few which are in any tolerable repair are disposed of by Colonel Congreve to Sutlers for great premiums and monthly rents and the Officers are putt into such old ruinous houses that they are under a necessity to be at the expence to put them into a tenantable condition and in case any Officer removes from such house which at a great charge he has so repaired yet the same is never given to another Officer who had worse quarters, but is imediatly let by Colonel Congreve for the aforementioned considerations to the Sutlers."

On 30 September 1726 Kane wrote to Newcastle:

"As it may be Necessary to apprise your Grace of the Nature of the present Quaters, I Shall further Leave to observe that the Men of the three old Regiments have had old houses fitted for them by the directors of the Fortifications, and perpetually in want of Some Repairs, but the officers of these Regiments have been oblidged from time to time to repair old houses for their Owne Quarters; and There being No Such Quarters for the Regiment I deteyn'd Last year to reinforce the Garrison, Nor for Many of the officers who have come to their Post's upon the King's Late order, there was no other way Left for Quartering them but upon the Inhabitants, and their houses being only old Ruins, Ill Repaired, the officers & men are Miserably Quarterd, and the Inhabitants greated Incommoded, which occasions a vast deal of uneasiness in the Garrison."

A year earlier Philaletes had given the following description of the town:

"It wears at present a dismal Aspect, and still shews the Face of War: Those who have Houses only repair them for the Time they may continue in them; so that if Care be not taken, they will soon fall into a Heap of Rubbish, and lie like those which were batter'd down at our taking the Place, which none have yet thought proper to reer from the Chaos they are in; which no doubt, would have been done, had a Civil Power been established there so early as it were to be wish'd."

Throughout this period – *i.e.*, from 1715 to 1727, there were secret negotiations for the surrender of Gibraltar to Spain. King Philip V had an absolute obsession about the return of Gibraltar to Spain and in order to bring this to a head Spain was refusing to renew the "asientos", or trading facilities, with the Spanish Indies, mainly in the slave trade.

In order to improve his relations with Spain and continue enjoying trading facilities, George I, supported by some of his Ministers, promised the Spanish Monarch in 1721 the restoration of Gibraltar "on the first favourable opportunity", subject to the approval of Parliament. No such "favourable opportunity" arose for seven years, and the continued hostile attitude of Spain to the British made it seem unlikely that any such opportunity would arise.

Indeed, while these secret negotiations were going on, Spain made a determined effort to recapture Gibraltar at the end of 1726. She was unsuccessful despite heavy bombardments and superior numbers of troops. Hostilities came to an end in May 1727 but negotiations for peace were not concluded until 1728 by the Treaty of El Pardo. Two years were spent in bickerings and disreputable and shifty diplomacy before the articles of settlement were fully agreed at the Treaty of Seville in 1729.

The Jews, who by then had well settled in Gibraltar, continued to its defence, as is clearly shown in an interesting contemporaneous pamphlet entitled "An Impartial

Account of the late famous Siege of Gibraltar. . . . by an Officer who was at the Taking and Defence of Gibraltar by the Prince Hesse of Glorious Memory and served in the town during the last siege, 1728". It states:

> The Jews were not a little serviceable; they wrought in the most indefatigable manner, and spared no pains when they could be of any advantage, either in the siege or after it.

I would say that the siege of 1726–1727 set the seal on the settlement and subsequent growth of the Jewish community of Gibraltar.

With their substantial participation on Britain's side during the siege they showed that they were an integral part of the population of the garrison, thereby consolidating their position as such.

Spain naturally continued to refer to that part of Article X of the Treaty of Utrecht which prohibited the Jews from settling in Gibraltar but the frequency and strength of her representations commanded less and less respect.

Moreover, her own actions in other matters continued to make the presence and the increase in the number of Jews the more necessary.

In 1728 the Spaniards issued an edict which prohibited all dealings between the Barbary States and Spain on the ground that there was danger from the plague. By the same edict Spain had forbidden all intercourse with Gibraltar, which had to obtain her supplies of provisions from the Barbary States. It is clear that the 1728 edict was aimed at isolating the Rock.

At this very time the British Ministry made an effort to please Spain by sending orders, via the Minister Keene, for the eviction of all Jews and Moors from Gibraltar in accordance with the 1713 Treaty. This was, of course, well received by the Spaniards, but when they showed no signs of allowing supplies to reach Gibraltar or of withdrawing from the advanced lines as they had promised to do when hostilities ceased after the siege, Keene withheld the execution of these orders. When Keene conveyed to the Governor of Gibraltar the instructions to evict the Jews the Governor advised that the continuance of communications with Barbary for obtaining supplies was essential and more preferable than to have to rely on Spanish sources even if supplies were available from these sources.

The eviction of the Moors and Jews would no doubt have disrupted relations with the Barbary States and cut off the only reliable source of supply.

The policy of quarantining Gibraltar continued and was, as Conn states, "a standing pretext of the Spanish throughout the century for not permitting the intercourse between the Fortress and Spain provided for by the Treaty of Utrecht".

In 1729 a further Treaty was entered into between Britain and Morocco.

The first article provided:

> *That all Moors and Jews subject to the Emperor of Morocco, shall be allowed a free Traffick to buy or sell for Thirty days, in the City of Gibraltar, or Island of Minorca, but not to reside in either Place and to depart with their effects without let or hindrance to any part of the said Emperor of Morocco's Dominions.*

This article gave some specific legal basis for the presence of Moroccan Jews in Gibraltar and the 30-days' limit was never, of course, enforced.

I have dealt in some detail with what I consider was the most crucial period in the

177

history of the settlement of the Jews in Gibraltar – *i.e.*, up to just after the end of the 1726–1727 siege.

Thereafter the right to the British possession of Gibraltar was confirmed by various treaties.

The Jews continued to work and carry on their business, building a considerable number of houses and generally prospering at the same time as the rest of the population.

Owing to the way in which the civilian population grew, sharing common difficulties and living closely in a small garrison town, comparative tolerance for the non-Christian faiths was developed on the Rock at an early date.

The number of Jewish residents continued to increase and by the time of the Great Siege there were already about 1,000. When the Great Siege started, civilians were first encouraged and later ordered to leave. However, those who had property and were ready to defend it were allowed to remain in the town. A number of Jews went to Minorca, which was then British, and from where some had come to Gibraltar a few years before. Others went to England and other places. A great number of them appear to have been evacuated by the fleet and details of the sufferings of some of them are clearly gathered from the correspondence of the Mahamad of the Spanish and Portuguese congregation in London during the eighteenth century, which has been so ably analysed in an article by the Society's former President, Mr. Richard Barnett.

Many Jews remained in Gibraltar and shared in the sufferings and privations of the siege, which lasted from June 1779 to February 1783. Their contribution to the defence of Gibraltar was very important and it is well exemplified by the concession to one of them, Abraham Hassan, who was rewarded by General Elliot with a house and premises situated in an important part of the city for the term of 21 years in consideration of his service during the last siege, "he having voluntarily offered himself to do the duty of a private soldier in which character he behaved in a very spirited and exemplary manner".

Early in the nineteenth century the community continued to prosper and the Jews, together with other residents, were instrumental in obtaining more respect and status for the civilian inhabitants. Several Charters of the Justice had curtailed the control of the military, and Jews took a prominent part in establishing beyond doubt their right to own property, which, though initially allowed, was later questioned. By an Order in Council of 1819 all elements of religious discrimination in the holding of land by either Jews or Catholics were removed.

During all this time the community got highly organised, providing for all social, religious, and welfare needs of the Jews, both residents and those who continuously visited Gibraltar on business or for another reason. Indeed, among non-Jews our community always enjoyed and continues to enjoy the highest reputation for looking after the needs of its coreligionists. Prominent men like Mr. Aaron Cardozo and Mr. Judah Benoliel gave valuable services to Gibraltar and Britain. Mr. Cardozo was Consul in Gibraltar for the States of Tunis, Algiers, and Tripoli early in the nineteenth century and was entrusted with many delicate and important diplomatic missions, particularly with the Sultan of Morocco and the Bey of Tunis. He was also entrusted by the Governor, Sir Robert Boyd, with taking upon himself the management of various important branches of the Police Department of the town as well as the representation of the Jewish community, the latter being no doubt the most difficult of his assignments. He discharged these responsibilities "not only without the slightest view to emolument or benefit but with considerable expense and trouble to himself". He was also the moving spirit in getting the Order in Council giving Jews and Catholics the right to hold land freely which I have mentioned.

Mr. Judah Benoliel was Moroccan and Austrian Consul and was also entrusted with the negotiations of treaties with the Sultan of Morocco. He also intervened in a dispute between Morocco and Sardinia and was instrumental in settling the conflict. His services were recognised by the King of Sardinia, who presented him with a gold box with brilliants bearing the royal cipher.

The Board of Sanitary Commissioners, which exercised the functions of a local authority and was the predecessor of the City Council, had a number of Jews as its members from time to time during the nineteenth century, one of them, Mr. Moses Serfaty, also a prominent public man, being once elected as its Chairman.

During the present century the Jews have continued to live in an atmosphere of complete freedom and equality, completely integrated with and taking an active part in every aspect of the life of the city, while at the same time preserving their own identity as a religious community and developing their religious and communal institutions.

Gibraltar has always been notable for the internal peace and friendliness in which people of different religions, customs, and interests exist. This has continued and improved and both Christians and Jews in Gibraltar are proud of the harmony and amity in which all live, each maintaining their own religious observances. It can certainly stand as an example of tolerance and partnership to communities which claim to be more enlightened.

Jews naturally made their contribution during the two world wars and since the end of the Second World War they have played a prominent part in the constitutional development which has taken place and which has given Gibraltar virtual autonomy in internal matters.

The prominence, importance, and prosperity that the Jewish community enjoys today are due first to those officials who for about 15 years after the signing of the Treaty of Utrecht, be it for self-interest or for the benefit of Gibraltar and the importance of keeping its troops well supplied at a crucial time in its history, dared with cunning, ability, and perhaps foresight to challenge the orders repeatedly issued from London that Article X of the Treaty prohibiting the Jews from settling in Gibraltar should be strictly observed and secondly to those enterprising Jews who during the first quarter of a century of the British occupation of Gibraltar underwent all kinds of hardships, difficulties, and privations, firm in their faith that British rule and justice would protect them and their descendants – a faith which has been amply justified.

APPENDIX FOUR

CHART OF APPOINTMENT OF VICARS FOR GIBRALTAR AND THE CONTEMPORARY PERSONALITIES

Date of Appointments of Parish Priest	Parish Priests	Bishop of Cadiz	Governors and Acting Governors of Gibraltar	Popes	Kings of England	Kings of Spain
1704	Juan Romero de Figueroa	Juan Alonzo de Talavera	Prince Goerge Hesse	Clement XI	Queen Anne	King Philip V
1720	Fco. Roman Trujillo	Don Lorenzo Armengual De La Mota	Lord Portmore	Clement XI	George I	King Philip V
			Brig. General Kane			
1726	Gregorio Antonio Savanda	Don Lorenzo Armengual De La Mota	General Hargrave	Innocent XIII	George I	King Philip V
1734	Ignacio Ximenez	Tomas del Valle, O. Pr.	Lt. Gen. T. Sabine	Clement XII	George II	King Philip V
1743	Domingo Finocchio	Tomas del Valle, O. Pr.	Lt. Gen. T. Sabine	Clement XII	George II	King Philip V
1747	Antonio Fontcubierta	Tomas del Valle, O. Pr.	Lt. Gen. Colombine	Benedict XIV	George II	Ferdinand VI
1748	Juan Freber	Tomas del Valle, O. Pr.	Lt. Gen. Colombine	Benedict XIV	George II	Charles III
1750	Francisco Hinojosa	Tomas Del Valle, O. Pr.	Lt. Gen. Sir H. Bland	Benefict XIV	George II	Charles III
1768	Rafael Messa	Tomas del Valle, O. Pr.	Major Gen. Irwine	Clement XIII	George III	Charles III
1773	Francisco Mess	Tomas del Valle, O. Pr.	Major Gen. R. Boyd	Clement XIV	George III	Charles III
		1777 – Bautista de Juan Cervera				
1792	Pedro Raymundo	Antonio Martiniezi de la Plaza	Lt. Gen. Sir. R. Boyd	Pius VI	George III	Charles III
1804	George Staunton	Fco. Javier de Utrera	Lt. Gen. Henry Ed. Fox	Pius VI	George III	Charles III
1806	Isidoro Dominguez	Fco. Javier de Utrera	Lt. Gen. Sir H. Darlymple	Piux VII	George III	Charles IV
1816	Juan Bp. Zino	Armo. Juan de Vera y Delgado	Major Gen. Smith	Pius VII	George III	Charles IV
1840	Bishop Henry Hughes	Domingo de Silos Moreno OSB	Major Gen. Sir A. Woodford	Gregory XVI	Queen Victoria	Charles IV
1857	Bishop John Bp. Scandella	Juan Jose Arboili y Acaso	Lt. Gen. Sir J. Ferguson	Pius IX	Queen Victoria	Isabella II
1881	Bishop Gonzalo Canilla	Don Jaime Catalia y Albosa	Gen. Lord Napier of Magdala	Leo XIII	Queen Victoria	Isabella II
1899	Bp. James Bellord	Jose Maria Rances y Villanueva	Gen. Sir. R. Biddulph	Leo XIII	Queen Victoria	Alfonso XII
1902	Bp. Remegio Barbieri	Jose Maria Rances y Villanueva	Fd. Mar. Sir G.S. White	Leo XIII	Edward VII	Alfonso XII
1910	Bp. Henry Thompson	Jose Maria Rances y Villanueva	Gen. Sir A. Hunter	Pius X	George V	Alfonso XIII
1927	Bp. Richard Fitzgerald	Marcial Lopez Criado	Gen. Sir Charles Monro	Pius XI	George V	Alfonso XIII
1956	Bp. John F. Healey	Tomas Gutierrez Diez	Gen. Sir Charles Monro	Pius XII	Elizabeth II	Gen. Franco
		1964 – Ant. Anoveros				
1973	Bp. Edward Rapallo	Ant. Dorado Soto	Air Commodore Sir J. Grandy	Paul VI	Elizabeth II	Gen. Franco
1985	Bp. Bernard Devlin	Ant. Dorado Soto	Admiral Sir David William	John Paul II	Elizabeth II	King Juan Carlos

BIBLIOGRAPHY

ARCHIVES:

Sacred Congregation of Propaganda Fide
Scritturae Riferati nei Congressi, Spagna, Gibilterra, Portogallo, vols 1−5
Udienza 1780−1816
Att. Sac. Congr. 1774−1816
Lett. Sac. Congr. 1815−1820

Gibraltar Cathedral Archives
Junta Files, Cols 1−3; XX−XXII
Olla Podrida (Compiled documents on various topics)
Official Report to the House of Commons 1882 on Bishop Canilla
The Blue Book
The Aliens Ordinance Counter Report
Vindication (by Monsignor Tom MacAuliffe)
Return to Judgement (by Monsignor MacAuliffe)
Correspondence with Anglicans (by Monsignor Tom MacAuliffe)
Garrison Schools Report 1885

Government Secretariat Archives
Spanish Church File
Account of General Bland's Conduct when Governor (1750−1751)

Public Records Office. CO 91−92 files

British Museum Add. Mss.
23, 637; 29, 267; 23,659−23, 666; 20, 926; 36, 137; 35, 883; 35, 870; 35, 590

Cathedral Registers of Baptisms, Marriages & Burials (1692−1783)

PERIODICALS:
Gibraltar Chronicle (1876−1883)
El Calpense (1880−1883)
Mons Calpe (1880−1883)

BOOKS:
Bethencourt, Antonio *El Catolicismo en Gibratar durante el siglo XVIII* 1967
Lopez, Rafael Caldelas *La Parroquia de Gibraltar en San Roque* Jerez, 1976.
Francis, David *The First Peninsular War 1702−1713.* London, 1975
Bacon, Chief Justice Roger *A History of the Courts of Gibraltar* 1704−1951
Rule, Dr. W. *Memoirs of a mission to Gibraltar and Spain.* London, 1854.
Ayala *Gibraltar* Madrid, 1778
Montero *Gibraltar* 1880
Fray Jeronimo de la Concepcion *Cadiz Ilustrada.* 1695 *History of the Christian Brothers'
Institute* vol.1−2

ANNOTATIONS

The following can be described as a combination of bibliography, footnotes and commentary on the points mentioned in the body of the work. They are intended to indicate to the reader the sources of the information there recorded and, on occasion, enlarge upon the incident or person referred to.

CHAPTER ONE

page 3
[1]Whatever has been used here on the Peninsular War, the attack on Cadiz and mess-up in Port Santa Maria has been obtained from the work by David Francis: **The Peninsular War 1702–1713**. London, 1976.

page 3
[2]**This was the fourth occasion.** . . . "Fray Jeronimo de la Concepcion": His book **Cadiz Ilustrada**, Amsterdam, 1690, is a most enjoyable work. Once the reader perceives the old prejudices against the Jews and the Moors who were reckoned as infidels, he will discover that the author endeavours to trace the origins of famous Old Testament personalities to some Spanish or Sephardic family or other. Also he will discover the detailed descriptions of the number of invasions made by the British on Cadiz Port making havoc of so many of the churches and treasures.

He names the churches and chapels to be found then in Gibraltar:

> "Habitanla 2500 vecinos. Una Parroquia de la advocacion de S. Maria la Coronada, con 5 Beneficios. Un Convento de S. Francisco de la Observancia. Otro de la Merced Calzada, fundacion de el Rey d. Enrique IV. Otro de S. Juan de Dios. Otro de Monjas de Santa Clara, sugetas a su Religion. En la cual ubo en tiempo de los Reyes Catolicos una religiosa de conocido espiritu de Profecia, que predijo a D. Fr. Jim enez de Cisneros, que N.Sor. le tenia guardado para grandes cosas.
>
>   Ay en la ciudad muchas Hermitas. La de N. Senora de el Rosario. La Misericordia con sasa de ninos expositos. La Vera Cruz. S. Sebastian. Las Angustias. N.Sra. de la Cabeza. N. Senora de Europa muy milagrosa. N. Senora de los Remedios. S. Juan Bautista. Y Extramuros S. Roque. En el muella una Capilla Real de titulo de N. Senora de la Piedad. Y dentro de la Ciudad la Iglesia de S. Juan Lateran, exempta con los Privilegios de S. Juan Laterano de Roma, con Sacramento, y esta consagrada la Iglesia".

page 5
[3]**Bishop of Cadiz** The letter Father Romero de Figueroa received from the Bishop is not available either in the archives in Gibraltar or in those of Cadiz. The parish priest, however, refers to it and its contents in the remarks he left behind in the Register of Matrimony. He remarks on it because it appears that there was a question among the clergy that remained behind. These doubted whether Father Romero continued to have the faculties, given by the Bishop in 1702, once the Siege of 1704 ended and communication with the Bishop was resumed in 1708.

page 5
[4]**40 Priests** Marriage Register, Bk.1
The foundation of this city of Gibraltar, my beloved native place although abandoned and laid low by the bombardment of war.

In this present year 1707, 2948 years have elapsed since this city was founded. The first part to be established was the Villa Vieja which lies beneath the Castle, and as years went by, and the city increased, it was extended to the Barcina, and for this reason both of these quarters are walled and have their own gates. The castle is the work of the Moors, who constructed it during the time of their occupation of Spain.

The most ancient foundation of all in Gibraltar, is the "White Tower" of the Castle, where the Watch Bell is.

There is a tradition that it was built by Tubal, the grandson of Noe, whence at first the city was called Tubaltar, and this name was afterwards corrupted into Gibraltar.

Such was the condition of the town of Gibraltar when it was taken by the Moors a little more than 700 years after the birth of Christ, and they possessed it until King Fernando IV took it from the Moors in the year 1295.

About 1330 it was lost through the treachery of Vasco Perez de Reina, Governor of Castile, who sold it to the Moors and passed over into Africa.

King Alonso XI, son of the aforesaid King Fernando, came and besieged it twice in different years. On the second occasion while his army was encamped in the Pradelto, King Alonzo was stricken with pestilence and died after having gained the glorious and miraculous victory over the Moors in the "Salado del Tarifa", and taken Algeciras after a siege of 22 months.

After the death of King Alonso the siege was raised, and the Moors were established in this place for about 120 years until it was captured by the Christians in the year 1463. This was on the 20th of August, the Feast Day of St. Bernard, the patron of the city, and from that time until today it has been possessed by the Christians.

After the Christians had conquered this place, the families increased in number, and as there was not sufficient room for them in the old city of Villa Vieja and Barcina, they spread themselves up in this direction, and houses were built on the territory where the Moors had their gardens and orchards. To this day one sees in many of the houses draw-wells, like the one attached to this Church.

Having seen this arched courtyard of the oranges, designed and constructed by the Moors, the door of which is now hidden, in the outlying premises they arranged to build this church adjacent to this court-yard; and it is a point worthy of note that these very orange trees that exist today are the same as were to be found in this courtyard in the year 1463. Thus care has been taken to preserve them, by watering them in the Summer, as I have done during this anxious and troublous time of siege, which, at the time I am writing, is in its fourth year. I have watered them many times with my own hands.

They built the church, the chancel of which was the arched portion that is adjacent to the pulpit; afterwards, round about the year 1550, the church was enlarged; they built what is now the chancel, the two side aisles, the two arches of the gate, and the tower; and the Knights, Piñas by name, built the chapel of the iron in the courtyard.

At that time the walling of the quarter which extended from the Barcina as far as the Alameda still remained to be carried out, and Moorish or Turkish galleys were wont to come and plunder the church and the houses; the people used to withdraw to the Castle with their clothing and money.

I have ascertained from authentic sources that in the year 1540, 16 Turkish galleys landed their forces by the ladderway behind the "Tarfes"*; they got into the town and pillaged it, they reached the gate of the Barcina and were repulsed by the Christians; the alarm was given to the countryside; assistance was rendered, and they pursued the Turks so vigorously up to the landing place, that they compelled them to reship the force they had brought, and to re-embark against their will.

The Governor of this town sent off by posting messenger despatches to Cartagena in the East, where the Galleys of Spain were based, and these on receipt of this information put out to sea in such quick time that they had the good fortune to encounter the Turks in such manner that of the 16 galleys, only one escaped.

This is the reason that in the archives of this Parish the registers of baptisms and marriages are missing for a period of more than 90 years, because these raids of the Moors were very frequent; they used to plunder the houses, enter the church, and open the archives, and finding nothing but papers, they tore them up or burnt them and so I insert here this notice in order to inform the parish priests, my bretheren and successors, that if at any time account is taken of this defiency by the Bishops and visiting inspectors, they may know and ascertain the cause of this notable deficiency.

The oldest register of baptisms, which is in quarto, commences in the year 1556, the date of the taking of the town from the Moors being 1463.

At this time the magistrates of this city wrote to His Royal Majesty Charles V, then Emperor of Germany and King of Spain, informing him of what the town was suffering from the continuous raids of the Moors, and then His Majesty commanded that the city should be walled and that gates and moats should be made. At this time, i.e. about the year 1540, the city was enclosed with walls, and the landport was constructed with its moat and bastion, and also the New Gate (South Port) with its moat and bastion. Also was built the wall which runs from the New Gate up to the mountain, and the reason for there being over one of the portals of the New Gate the Imperial coat of arms is evidently that this was built in the time of the Emperor Charles V.

In this reign were constructed the walls which protect the lower part of Europa and those which protect the "Tarfes"*; the New Mole with its castle was built in the year 1620, and it was extended in the year 1676.

Marriage Register, Bk.1 (Gibraltar)

"De trabajos y miserias. . . . esta a miserable ciudad de Gibraltar patria mia en cuia parroquia y fuente bautismal recibi Santo Sacramento de baptismo 1 setiembre de 1646 anos y en esta consideracion viendo que de quarenta eclesiasticos que avia ninguno queria quedarse, me resolvi a quedarme en mi parroquia y a dejar la amada compana de mis hermanos y sobrinos que a todos lo remiti a Ronda, y a imitacion mia seguia conmigo Don Juan Ascencio Roman teniente de Cura mirando atentamente que no fuese esta iglesia profanada y robada estando de continua guardia muchos dias y noches en los cuales he

pasado bastantes horas catalogando los Matrimonios esta. . . . en los siglos
venideros. . . . esta nota mia de Setiembre de 1704. Figueroa".

The historian Montero in his history of Gibraltar (1880), says that Romero gives the
impression that he had written a more complete history of Gibraltar besides the notes
he made on the Registers. He remarks that the historian Ayala used many precious
documents kept in San Roque in Spain but were lost during the French occupation of
Southern Spain 1810–1811.

* The Tarfes was identified as Windmill Hill

page 5
⁵**Prince Abdul Malik**: Most of the information on the Moorish occupation of
Gibraltar has been obtained either from Montero's history or the earlier Ayala, (1782).

page 6
⁶**Fatality. . . .**
(Fatalidad)
"El dia uno de Agosto entro la Armada Inglesa.

(Confusion y horror)
El sabado 2 echaron bombas a media noche, no es decible los llantos y gritos,
angustias y tristezas.

(Bateria de balas de artilleria)
Domingo 3 de Agosto fue la Bateria de la Balas desde las cinco de la manana
hasta la una del dia.

Dispararon veinte y ocho mil balas y tambien bombas y este dia capitula la
plaza y se rindio, y el dia 4 por la mañana estando en las capitulaciones y
habiendo tomado el muelle nuevo los Ingleses fueron a Nuestra Señora de
Europa y robaron su santuario, quitaron doce lamparas de plata, candeleros,
atriles, coronas, joyas y vasos consagrados, todo el vestuario de muchas familias
que alli se habian retirado y cuando no hubo que robar quitaron la cabeza a
la imagen, que es oraculo de España y el niño Jesus y la echaron al campo
entre las piedras.

!O patria mia! yo no te dejare y mis cenizas se confundiran con las tuyas.

De dia oraba a Dios y de noche me aprovechaba de sus tinieblas para llorar.
Salia a recorrer las puertas de mi templo, llevando por companeros el miedo y
el dolor. Muchas veces barriendo los ladrillos de esta Santa Iglesia, regue el
suelo con el sudor de mis ojos".

Baptismal Register, Bk. 18, p.1
Father Romero de Figueroa bursts out in classical Latin putting into words his
innermost feelings:

Epigram
Shed tears in abundance, citizens of Calpe, your city, for so long time famous, is
enveloped in sudden ruin.

The day of bitterness came filled with misfortunes, in which our walls were to fall
before the destroying fire of the enemy.

Fiery bombs, horrible to tell, resound through the air day and night.

Women, the aged, and children lament disconsolately, and their cries ascend the skies.

Towers collapse under the fierce assault, and death on all sides threatens those who are overpowered.

Lamentations grow louder like the waves of a stormy sea', and the soul already stricken with sorrow grows pale with horror.

Some seek the churches, others worn out with fear flee in haste to the mountain, while others more nimble depart to hide their perishing bodies in the dark and ancient cavern.

Suddenly rapine invades the houses, and the best houses stand deserted.

Already the inhabitants of Calpe look with eyes red with weeping upon their beloved homes and fly in confusion; but behold! the fury of the flames takes complete possession of them, and few are the houses that escape devouring fire.

We are chastised for our sins; when iniquity is multiplied the anger of God waxes strong.

When the inhabitants decided to leave the Rock, after the Terms of Capitulation had been agreed upon, Father Romero Figueroa wrote in the Register:

Marriage Register. Book 9, last page:

"Fatal suceso. El dia seis de Agosto de 1704 anos haviendo sido esta pobre ciudad poseida de las Armas Inglesas segun las Capitulaciones echas en que se daba permiso para que el vecino que se quiera quedar en la Ciudad con sus vienes se quedase y el que se quiese ir se llevase sus vienes mas fue tanto el horror que habia causado las bombas y valas que de mil vecinos que tenia esta Ciudad quedaron tan solamente hasta = doce abandonando su Patria sus casas y vienes y frutos; fue ese dia un miserable espectaculo de llantos y lagrimas de mugeres y criaturas viendose salir perdidos por esos campos en el rigor de la canicula este dia asi que salio la gente robaron los Ingleses todas las casas y no se escapo la mia y de mi companero porque mientras estabamos en la Iglesia los asaltaron los mas de ellos, y robaron y para que quede noticia de esta fatal ruina puse aqui esta nota. Romero.

page 8

[7]**Henry Nugent.** . . . While Irish by birth and only 36 years of age, he won the title of "Conde de Valde Soto" from the late king of Spain. He was killed in this first Siege put on by the Marquis of Villadarias. He was buried within the Franciscan Convent Chapel (now known as King's Chapel). Father Romero buried him there without knowing his name, such must have been the confusion, and did so during the night. He simply knew him to be the English Garrison Commander.

page 8

[8]**supplies of food:** Colonel Joseph Bennet, appointed to keep the accounts and number of people who left and remained on the Rock, left this excellent report of events. **British Museum, Additional Manuscripts 10, 034.**

page 9
[9]Marriage Register, Book 1.
Father Romero records incidents and observations he makes during the Siege put on by Marquis of Villadarias.

> "El dia 4 de octubre una escuadra de navios franceses, hasta veinte con chicos y grandes, y estos dieron fondo hasia el lanse nuevo. Echaron en tierra artilleros, valas y bombas para la gentre del campo que hicieron sus ataques entre los molinos y la alcantarilla con los quales pusieron diferentes baterias con 28 canones de abatir y quatro morteros de bombas, y el dia 26 de octubre comenzo la bateria de parte del campo con lo qual desmontaron casi toda la artilleria del baluarte y cortina de la puerta de tierra y algunos canones caieron al foso, – – la bateria de la plaza al campo era de cinco morteros y toda la artilleria que vi desde el fuerte de San Juan hasta el salto del lobo donde avia ocho canones ubo dias que pasaron de mil canonazos del campo y otros tantos de la plaza y bombas sin cesar de dia ni de noche –"

> "El dia 9 de noviembre entro la armada inglesa y los navios franceses que estaban en lanse nuevo assi que los vieron se quemaron y (uno) que quiso salir, lo apresaron los ingleses no se quemo toda la esquadra porque algunas se avian ido. Romero."

> "El dia 11 de noviembre asaltaron gente de guerra del campo el Monte Calpe con escalas porcima de la er. . . . hasia los tarfes. Amanecieron en el lomo de la montana mas de doscientos hombres que desde la ciudad se veian al viso llegaron hasta la silleta de adonde desalojaron seis ingleses que estaban de sentinela, acudio la gente de la plaza por diferentes partes y los cortaron aunque Pelearon mas de ora, los que Pudieron huieron Por silleta y algunos se despenaron, en la batalla que tubieron en la montana murieron algunos de una y otra parte, finalmente trajeron prisioneros a la plaza mas de cien hombres en los quales avia un coronel, su teniente y un capitan a los quales desarmaron y desnudaron los ingleses y se les dio buen quartel."

Burial Register. Book 1. Pages 94–95

> "Conde de Valde Soto gobernador que fue de esta plaza por el Sr Principe de Onestar en el tiempo de la guerra de edad como de 36 anos Irlandes de nacion fue herido de una bala de artillerio recibio los Sacramentos y murio a 1 3 de noviembre 1704 y fue enterrado en el Convento de San Francisco de esta ciudad, yo testo y firmo – en sabiendo como se llamaba le pondre el nombre".

Marriage Register, Book 1

> "La bomba de arriba de mas de la fosas mato un ingles en la casa inmediata y poco despues en el mismo dia domenica in albis echaron otra del campo que revento sobre los tejados de esta iglesia en el aire y un casco pego junto al tejado del arco que da luz a la Capilla de hierro en el patio y dejo alli la senal para memoria y de rechazo dio en los ladrillos del claustro en lo cubierto junto a la puerta baja de la Torre donde rompio dos ladrillos cerca de mi".

"El dia 15 de noviembre se volo en el campo uno de los tres molinos de viento en que estaba la polvora y justamente dos o tres carretas que llegaban cargadas de polvora. Dicen que fue la casera estava tomando tabaco de humo, el molino salio de raiz. Se dijo avian perecido hasta 200 hombres y lastimado otros tantos y fue tal violencia del guego y viento que temblo toda esta ciudad como yo lo experimente en esta iglesia que toda se movio y muchas puertas que estaban cerradas se abrieron y otras se rompieron. Romero".

Burial Register Book 1, Page 1 51.

VALAS Y BOMBAS

"El dia 21 de noviembre de 1704 tiraron del campo a la plaza 1566 valas de artilleria de los cuales e tercio caio en el mar y en el monte y las bombas pasaron de ciento y toda la noche de este dia 21 no calleron dichas bombas de campo con quatro morteros, y oi dia 22 se continua lo mismo Dios aya misericordia de nosotros. Amen. −"

"El dia 22 en la noche despues de la bateria de todo el dia echaron del campo ciento y sesenta bombas y de la plaza se le correspondia con otras tantas y todas las noches sucede lo mismo con poca diferencia y hasta oy que somos 25 de noviembre no ha tocado esta iglesia vala ni bomba, si algunos cascos en las paredes. gracias a dios por todo".

It must have been the affliction and torment that he was suffering that made him write the following Epigrams in classical Latin:

Baptismal Register Book 18, Page 1 San Roque

Mars, et mors pariter regnant in tempore nostro,
hos duplices reges quis tolerare potest?
Nomine quam similes gentes consumit uterque,
Dissimiles illos syllaba sola facit.
Mars vocat ad pugnas homines, mors devorat illos,
Est actus Martis funebre mortis opus.
Mars socios eius sine febri mittit ad umbras,
Sanguine mars vivit, funere mors et ovat.
in tota Europa vastans dominatur uterque
vulnera mars affert, morsque sepulchra parat.
Tu, Deus Omnipotens, iubes dirumpere coelos,
et pacis nobis munera mitte tuae.
Fundite corde preces, ad coelos mittite voces,
Non aliunde potest nostra venire quies.

Baptismal Register, Book 15, page 2 San Roque

Vita quid est aliud nisi quaedam vespera mortis,
quae extremam nobis mostrat adesse diem,
est fumus volitans, nimio est cum pondere puppis
nam fraga per fluctus, quam grave mergit onus.

Est labor assiduus, dolor est, et pugna frequenter,
et mors irrupens terminat ista mala,
ergo timenda magis vita est, quam terminus eius
hic quoniam tanit meta laboris erit.
Parce mihi, Domine, nihil enim sunt dies mei =
Job, Cap, 7
Cras nihil est nobis, hodie nihil esse putatur,
Dum vita est nobis, quid sumus ergo? nihil.
Cras non venit adhuc, hodie iam praeterit, unde
est magis ad nostram proxima meta viam.
Sit semper vigilater homo, nam quaelibet hora
mors inopina venit vespere, nocte die,
ne dicas veniet, sed dicto, iam venit hora,
nam tempus praesens terminus esse potest,
culpaque nom tantum, sed culpae causa recedat,
nam dum causa viget, culpa revivit adhuc.

Qui seminant in lacrymis, in exultatione metent.
Psal−125
Quilbet aeger homo lacrymarum fonte lavetur,
nam fletus morbis est medicina suis
quem pupilla facit, lacrymetur palpebra culpam.
haec undis purget, quod tulit illa, scelus.
Sunt lacrymae gem mae pro nostro criminae fusae,
Quae in oculis madidis fit diadema suum.
Felices oculi lacrymoso fonte fluentes
post culpas, undis germinat omnis ager.
Ploremus, fratres, contrito corde reatum.
Sint lacrymae nostra victima grata Deo.
Sit lacrymosa dies, lacrymosus mensis, et annus,
Sint oculi fontes purificantis aquae.

Burial Register, Book 1, Page 96

"El dia 2 de maio de 1705 se retiro el campo y abandono los ataques, queda
alguna caballeria de aquel cabo de los molinos, y quedamos libres de bombas
y balas que no cezaron de dia y noche desde el dia 26 de octubre de 1704 y
todavia sitiados."

page 10
[10]. . . . **traitor to the nation.** Ayala p.309

"i le culpaban muchos, porque decian obro mal en quedarse en su iglesia,
debiendo seguir el ejemplo de los hombres grandes que le abandonaron; otros
que obro temerariamente exponiendose a los riesgos de los incendios; otros que
obro como vasallo infiel, i otros que se quedo por su propia conveniencia. . . ."

page 10

[11]**Philip V to cede Gibraltar.** Stenton Cox, **Gibraltar in British Diplomacy in the 18th Century.** Yale University Press, 1942.

> "The French king did not suggest specifically that Spain give up Gibraltar; but soon after the receipt of this letter, Vendome wrote his master that the Spanish king would grant Gibraltar and port Mahon to England if the rest of Spain were left to him. On May 31 Torcy informed the English through Gaultier that Spain would cede Gibraltar as a security for English commerce in Spain and in the Mediterranean. . . ."

Bolingbroke Correspondence, 1 pp. 178–179. Louis XIV to Vendome, 31 May 1711, Cor.Pol. Espagne, Vol.207 fols. 113–114. A copy of the Spanish king's authorization to France to cede Gibraltar and Port Mahon to England was sent to the French king on June 11; the original, in King Philip's own hand, was retained by Vendome (Cor.Pol. Espagne, Vol. 207, fol.219).

page 11

[12]**Bishop of Cadiz:** Don Lorenzo Armengual de la Mota suceeded Don Alonso de Talavera. He is recorded in the Marriage Register as making his visitation:
"Estando haciendo visita general en esta ciudad visitamos este libro, donde se escriben las partidas de los que se casan. . . . (fol.39).

page 12

[13]**particular districts** Portuguese Town was centred in what we now call Crutchett's Ramp.

Black Town was to be found at Rosia Parade.

Hardy Town has been difficult to trace. These two last towns were especially important during the sieges among the English families who stayed together.

Irish Town is still called that.

Jewish Town is not clearly marked. Spanish people have earmarked the area around Lynch's Lane and Turnbull's Lane. But there is a strong indication that the community did spread along Engineer Lane near the Synagogue SHAAR ASHA-MAIM.

Genoese Town. No such town existed in the city of Gibraltar. We do know that the people at Catalan Bay were mainly of Genoese stock. The present author came across a most interesting document belonging to Mrs. Cecilia Hankey, in which it was revealed that accompanying Admiral Sir George Rooke was the auxiliary fleet, part of which belonged to the shipbuilder Mr. Francis Francia. He followed Rooke wherever the British Fleet sailed into battle. When ships required repairs, caulking, sails, etc. Francia's men would ground the ships on the nearest beach and work there.

Rooke's ships were repaired in the secluded beach of Sandy Bay (Caletilla Vieja as the Caleteños call the beach). When the assault was made by the Spanish forces from the eastern side of the Rock a guardroom was set up at Catalan Bay manned mainly by the Catalan Troops. The presence of the permanent guardroom to which regular food provisions were to be found influenced the Genoese on the other beach, where they had set up a camp, to move to Catalan Bay.

Colonel James points out that there were times when it was difficult to know who was standing guard at Catalan Bay since both the Genoese and Catalans wore similar red gear.

CHAPTER TWO

page 14
[1]**Francisco Feroci:** British Museum, Jure Emptionis: 23, 637

page 14
[2]**General Orders.** . . . ibid., pp.38 ff.
"General Orders for the Troops and Inhabitants in the Garrison of Gibraltar. (1725)
1. Duty to read and obey General Orders.
2. All manner of vice to be stopped.
3. One regiment to march to church every Sunday armed and the armes to be left ledged under the low gallery of the Convent in any weather.
4. The clergy of the Romish Church not to act in anything lending to the Inquisition; not to give Sanctuary to any person flying from justice, or conceale any persons, arms, ammunition or contraband goods; nor marry or Baptize any British Subject or visit their sick without the liberty from the Governor or Commander in Chief.
5. No offence to be given to any Clergyman of the Romish Church, neither in they're performance or worship; no soldiers to go into their churches in the time of they're service, and no offence to be given to the inhabitants on account of their worship.
6. If any dispute shall happen between a soldier and an inhabitant neither to offer to redress themselves, or take their own satisfaction, but to make their complaint.
   The notice for church times to be given to inhabitants will be by a Drums beating to the landport and return to the church at which the service is held.
   All disputes in Civil causes among the maritime people, trader, inhabitant or others to be handed by the Judge Advocate, and to him application must be made for process in his manner.
   All persons coming from the Campe to be stopped at the Mills till the Governor be acquainted with it. At noon the outer barrier of the Couvert Way to be shut and nobody to go out or in without orders till 2 o'clock.
   No snuff to be passed out' of landport on any account. No goods to pass in or out whatsoever without the governors leave.

page 14
[3]**Bayonet point.** . . . The expulsion is described by Avala even though he seems to have been ignorant of the reasons for Fr. Lopez's departure from the Rock. He seems to attribute the expulsion to the smuggling of the jewels into Spain.

page 15
[4]**Precious articles.** . . . It appears from the reading of those early writings that when the Terms of Capitulation were signed and the majority of people decided to leave the Rock and churches and chapels they followed a Plan. They appear to have gathered all the treasures and jewels from the different chapels and churches in the Parish Church of St. Mary the Crowned. Much was taken away by the religious themselves when they marched out but a lot was left behind with Father Romero de Figueroa. He was followed by Father Lopez Pena in gradually transferring the precious objects to Spain. They used visitors to the Rock to make the courvert transfer of goods to the specific chapels. Father Rafael Calde as Lopez, Parish Priest of San Roque has compiled a list of the different objects and the various chapels where they were expected to have been deposited.

Father Caldelas has done an excellent piece of work there and his book is a most useful production. It is called **"La Paroquia de Gibraltar en San Roque"**.

Father Sabanda, who left Gibraltar to fetch the Holy Oils from the Bishop just before the Siege of 1727 started never returned. Clandestinely he took with him the Baptismal and Matrimonial Book he could carry together with the four solid silver angels belonging to the Monstrance. He did all, like his predecessors, after the command by Bishop Armengual when he visited Gibraltar in 1717. (Cadiz Diocesan Archives: Books. Ms. "Mandatos given in them by my lord bishop", Vol.23.

Paradoxically most of these treasures were either destroyed or appropriated by the French troops when they occupied the south of Spain in 1809/1810.

page 15

[5]**as in Menorca.** . . . Sacred Congregation of Propaganda Fide Archives. Scritt. Ref. nei Congressi. Vol 1, page 43. MAHON.

". . . . that you no longer permit the supremacy of the Archbishop of Valencia, but submit all spiritual transactions, which require reference, or superior sanctions through His Majesty's representative to the See of Rome. . . . that you relinquish all pensions held of the Court of Madrid, and abstain from correspondence and communication with the Peninsula of Spain, leaving it for his Britannick Majesty's Government to claim such sums as may from time to time be due out of the money taken from Menorca by His M.C.M., and appropriated to the increase of the revenue of your Bishoprick. Charles Stuart.

page 16

[6]**Marguillers.** . . . This was the nickname given to the "Vestrymen" of New Orleans in the United States of America in 1780. They looked after the temporalities of the church to enable the priests to travel widely and thus administer the sacraments to all and sundry. They tried to influence the appointment of the successor to the See of New Orleans.

page 16

[7]**satisfactory solutions.** . . . It is difficult to attribute such an absolute denial of the exercise of any ecclesiastical jurisdiction to one or other of the Governors. In view of the fact that four acting Governors were of the same mind, it is fair to assume, failing the appearance of some illuminating document, that orders had been received from the Court of St. James.

page 17

[8]**Bishop of Cadiz:** Bishop Don Lorenzo Armengual de la Mota was succeeded by Dom Tomas del Valle, O.P. in 1730. Like his predecessor he left no stone unturned to uphold his true canonical right over the Parish of Gibraltar. The letters he wrote to the Spanish Court to press the British Government to allow him access to the people of the parish that was his by ecclesiastical right were innumerable and reveal his keen and sincere interest in the spiritual welfare of the inhabitants of the Rock. He was very much aware that if he did not grant the priests nominated by the Governors the required spiritual powers, then the interest he had shown for the spiritual welfare of the people would have been meaningless. He was really placed in an awkward situation by the chosen priests whenever they went to him and not to the Bishop of Malaga for spiritual faculties.

page 17
[9]**Count Marsillac:** Cadiz Diocesan Archives on Gibraltar: Mss. 63 Series 1°

page 17
[10]**padre vicario de la parroquia:** idem Mss.73 Series 1°

page 18
[11]**this petition:** idem Mss.76 Series 1°

page 18
[12]**ordinary jurisdiction:** idem Mss.83 Series 1°

page 18
[13]**the Junta of Elders:** idem. Mss.88 Series 1°

page 19
[14]**extra masses:** idem. Mss 89/90 Series 1°
This document manifests ever so clearly that because families were so large, with so many children, and houses were so small the doors had to be kept wide open. Also we discover that many houses necessarily had to keep the doors open to allow the soldiers or officers quartered there free access to them. There was a need for taking turns in keeping guard over the houses if people were to attend Holy Mass. There were too many burglaries going on at the time.

page 20
[15]**Mr. Gavino:** idem. Mss 100−122 Series 1°

CHAPTER THREE

page 21
[1]**Port Mahon.** . . . Tyrawleys Papers: Br. Mu. Jure Emptionis 23,637, pp 170 ff.

"It was an Article of the Capitulation that the Garrison should be conveyed here by the fastest passage at the French King's expense. Among them were some Greeks and other natives of the Island, who had retired into the Castle and assisted in the defence of it. . . . 31 transports were placed at our disposal. . . . It was difficult to lodge all. . . . so they were quartered with the inhabitants. A survey of the houses was already available when the troops arrived here. Tents at Windmill Hill were difficult so the homes of the inhabitants were used as quarters."

"There is no distinction made either in English, Jew, Genoese or other inhabitants, only the better part of the people and the Civil Officials of the Army and Navy. . . . were allowed to take what officers they chose and their homes could conveniently contain. All were accommodated by the night of the 30th July 1756".

page 22
²**to inspect the works.** . . . Gibraltar Secretariat's Archives. The Spanish Church File, P. 4.

Muy Senor Mio,

The Vicar of San Roque Don Pedro Joseph de Ribera being commissioned by the Bishop of Cadiz to inspect the works the Catholic Church of Gibraltar stands in need of and other matters pertaining to the same, and it being necessary that the said Don Pedro and another person who is to accompany him should remain in the Garrison a few days for that effect, I shall esteem it a favour that your Excellency grants your permit for that purpose advising me whether they can go in, that I may give my permit for their passing the Lines. I renew to your Excellency my sincere desires obliging you and that God may preserve you many years etc.

Camp of Gibraltar. 6 March 1768.
Signed: Diego Tabares.

REPLY

Exmo Sor..
Muy Senor Mio,

I am honoured with your Excellency's Letter of the 6th inst. I shall always be very sorry when it is not in my power to comply with your desires. The commission 'coming from the Bishop of Cadiz, to the Vicar of San Roque, makes a difficulty in my admitting him into the Garrison; I cannot allow that any Jurisdiction of the Bishop should take place here, but if anything is amiss, or that your Excellency thinks it necessary, for any person authorized by your Excellency to inspect the church, be so good as to advise me of the matter, and I flatter myself that what I shall do will answer the end of your Excellency's desires, as I shall ever have a singular pleasure in obeying your Commands, with attention to which, I remain sincerely praying God to preserve the life of your Excellency many years. etc.

Gibraltar 8 March 1768.
Signed: Edward Cornwallis.

REPLY

Dr. Sr.

I received your Excellency's letter of the 8th inst. in which you are pleased to answer mine of the 6th and I cannot help telling your Excellency that it has caused me much surprise, that your Excellency should have a difficulty in permitting the Vicar Ecclesiastic of San Roque Don Pedro Joseph de Ribera's going to the Garrison, to execute the orders of the Bishop of Cadiz, touching the works which the Catholic Church stand in need of, and other concerns of the same Church, for I do not find that, in any manner, this is opponent to the Sovereign Dominion of His Britannic Majesty, to the rules of his Government, nor to the authority of your Excellency when it is expressly convened between the two Crowns of Spain and England by the 10th Article of the Treaty of Utrecht. That the Inhabitants of Gibraltar are permitted the free use of the

Roman Catholick Religion, for which reason no objection can be made thereto without falling into an infraction of the said Treaty, as in the present case, your willing (desirous) to hinder the Bishop of Cadiz (to whose Diocese the Church, and Roman Catholick Inhabitants of Gibraltar belong) to take cognizance of the matters peculiar to the said Church, and of the Consciences of said Catholics, being as he truly is, their legitimate Ecclesiastical Prelate, and as such exercising his function in matters of religion. The two Divines who act as Vicar and Curate in the same Church, being dependant on the said Bishop, in virtue of the Powers substituted to them in some Points, and the power of separating them, or putting in others, and of making any other Disposition in the said Church residing in the said Bishop, without your Excellency being able to hinder it, while it does not interfere with matters of Government, and Civil Laws, nor distrust the fidelity which said Catholicks should preserve to His Britannick Majesty.

The proposal that your Excellency makes me, that if there is any irregularity, and that I will inform you of it, your Excellency will remedy it, in the same manner that I can desire, I cannot, for my part, admit, for though it is certain that the Bishop of Cadiz has communicated to me his concerted intentions, in consequence of which I wrote to your Excellency begging your permit for the Vicar of San Roque to go in, yet I cannot myself determine anything, this matter being in the power of the Bishop and not mine, though this does not prevent my supporting the measures of the Bishop as I ought to do, being founded on reason and Justice, and in any case where your Excellency's authority might be requisite I would require it, being correspondent to the Equity of your Excellency to grant it, preserving the good faith of the said Treaty, and the reciprocal good harmony in our commands as I should do in any like occasion where your Excellency should stand in need of my assistance for I wish all promptitude do your Excellency all the Justice which should be due to you and pay your Excellency all the attention in my power.

I hope that your Excellency in your Justice admitting the above reasons do not find a difficulty in the Vicar of San Roque going on his Commission to the Church of the Garrison and will grant the Permit I required for his staying the few days in it that are necessary, assuring your Excellency that I should be exceeding sorry that notwithstanding the Justice of my request you should not agree to it, because I shall find myself obliged to give an account to my Court of the matter that the King may take the measures he shall think proper.

I renew my desires of serving your Excellency etc.

8 March 1768.
Signed: Diego Tabares.

Exmo. Sor.
Muy Senor mio,

Yesterday I received your Excellency's letter of the 8th inst. It is with concern and surprise that I find you insist on a point which if I complied with, I think would be contrary to my duty, you insist on defending the right which you say the Bishop of Cadiz has of an extended Ecclesiastic Jurisdiction over the Roman Catholick Inhabitants of this place, and found that Claim on the 10th Article, which is short, clear and explicit, to wit "That the Inhabitants of Gibraltar shall be permitted the free exercise of their Religion". This grants them the free use and exercise of their religion, allowed, and have they not had it? Have they not it now? Then where is the Infraction of Treaty? Or is it to be inferred from that, that the Bishop of Cadiz has or may claim the Jurisdiction? No, Sir, he never had it, nor never claimed it that I know of; and if he has, it has been constantly refused him, nor did he ever appoint the Vicar or Curate. So long ago as when General Sabine was Governor the Vicar died, the Governor sent to Minorca for a Priest, he was established and died; then there were two candidates, and the Governor permitted the Catholic Inhabitants to chuse one of them; this is confirmed by the most ancient and reputable Roman Catholic Inhabitants of the Garrison. In a word, in sixty-four years that Gibraltar has been possessed by the Sovereigns of Great Britain, no such claim if ever made has been allowed, nor can I possibly submit to any Jurisdiction of the Bishop of Cadiz over the Roman Catholic Inhabitants have been interrupted in the free and open exercise of their religion? When their Church wanted repairs have they ever been refused, or debarred sending for materials for that work? I hope your Excellency will allow the Governor a right to be acquainted with every thing pertaining to the Garrison under his command, and its Inhabitants. I, to avoid any alteration informed your Excellency that if the church wanted repairs, and your Excellency thought it was necessary (acquainting me of the matter) I would allow Don Pedro Joseph de Ribera to come in, to examine the church. This I thought would have answered the purpose you wished for, and opinion merely ideal, had my good intention been received by your Excellency in the manner I hoped, there would have been no occasion of troubling the two Courts, but if, after what I have said your Excellency thinks it necessary to apply to your Court, I also must apply to mine. Governors may explain, and give their own opinions of Treaty, but the Sovereigns can only decide on them. Our difference in opinion shall not prevent me at all times from continuing to do everything in my power to preserve and promote the good Faith of both Courts, nor interrupt the Harmony which has hitherto subsisted between our commands. Dios que etc.

11th March 1768
Signed: Ed. Cornwallis.

page 23
[3]**San Roque**. . . . According to Father Caldelas's book the Registers were sent to San Roque and there the Head Sacristan Don Manuel Tangar tore out the opportune pages. The tearing out of the records was something unpardonable for the authorities and Father Hinojosa was made responsible for the occurrence. He was not reclaimed.

page 23
[4]**forestalling**. . . Government Secretariat Archives, Spanish Ch. Files, Page unnumbered.

St. James' Court writes to the Governor on 3rd May 1773.

Sir,

The death of the late Vicar at Gibraltar having given occasion to the Court of Spain to renew their instances on the behalf of the inhabitants of Gibraltar, professing the Roman Catholic Religion, the Marquis de Grimaldi has spoke to Lord Grantham on that subject and I have also received a Letter thereon from Monsieur de Escarano, Secretary to the Spanish Embassy. The Court of Spain appears to be much more moderate on the occasion than they were some years ago, as they acknowledge now, that they do not mean or desire to exercise any jurisdiction over the Roman Catholics, who are under the Government of Great Britain, and pretend only to attend to the observance of what was stipulated in their favour by the Tenth Article of the Treaty of Utrecht, and with regard to a new Vicar, the Court of Spain have proposed an expedient that the Bishop of Cadiz should give the names of several Priests, in order that the Governor of Gibraltar might chuse one of them, to reside there during his pleasure, and, if not agreeable to the Governor, to be replaced by another.

My answer to Mr. D'Escarano was, that the King was determined that the said Article 10 should, on his part, be strictly observed, and that His Majesty, in case any complaints had been made in a proper manner, by the Roman Catholic Inhabitants of Gibraltar (which has never once been the case) of their being in the least restrained in the free exercise of their Religion, would have carefully attended to them,. and concerning the nomination of the new Vicar, that the Governor would be instructed to take a particular care in naming one of the King's Subjects to be Vicar, (who should have all the proper qualifications for the Functions of his Office) and to act in concert with the Bishop of Cadiz in those points where there was no question of Jurisdiction, and only for what regards the proper qualifications necessary for the due discharge of that Employment, and that you may be more particularly appraised of the contents of Mons. D'Escarano's Letter, and of my answer, I send inclosed Copy's thereof.

I have had several conversations with General Boyd on this subject, the particulars of which he will soon relate to you. He is of opinion, in which I very much agree with him, that provided you name for Vicar, a Subject of the King, which Rule, for the Future, His Majesty will never suffer to be departed from, it will make it much easier to avoid disputes with the Bishop of Cadiz about Ecclesiastical matters, and therefore if the Bishop will give up all pretensions to Jurisdiction (which can never be allowed and confined himself to those usages in the Roman Catholick Church, whereby Priests must in certain cases keep up a correspondence with a Bishop, it does not appear that any prejudice is likely to happen, when due precautions are taken by the Governor, that neither the Bishop nor the Vicar exceed the proper Limits, and that care is taken that their whole correspondence may pass under the Governor's inspection.

The King therefore leaves to your prudence and discretion to adjust and settle this point according to His Majesty's sentiments, and that you endeavour, if possible, to prevent any occasion of discussions between the two Courts.

I send you inclosed for your information an extract of a letter from Sir John Goodricke, His Majesty's Envoy in Sweden, which it is needless for me to comment upon.

I am, etc.
Rochford.

P.S. Since writing the above I have received from Lord Grantham a Copy of Your Letter to His Excellency dated the 15th of March, by which I find that you had actually appointed the new Vicar, and that he happens to be the very Person objected to by the Court of Spain. It was impossible you could have known their sentiments about him, and I am persuaded, from the character you give of him, and by the ready concurrence of the inhabitants of Gibraltar that there ought to be no objection to him. But as the Court of Spain, for some

197

reasons not known, point him as an improper person, it is rather to be wished to facilitate the matter by your appointing the other priest, proposed by General Johnston, as fully qualified for the Office. And if it may be necessary to allow some reasonable gratification to the Vicar now at Gibraltar, for his trouble in coming from Minorca, and his return thither, you are at liberty to give it, and, on your notice, it shall be reimbursed you.

(To Lieut. Genl. Cornwallis)

page 24
[5]**Mr. De La Rosa.** . . . Gib. Govt. Sec. Archives, Spanish Ch. Files, page unnumbered.

page 25
[6]**Superior of the Augustinians.** . . . Gib. Gov. Sec. Archives, Spanish Ch. Files, P.9

6 de agosto 1773

R.P. y Hermano,

Recivida la V.P. hize los oficios correspondientes con Su Illustrisimo quien me dixo, que por el nombramiento que ya havia remitido a V.P. veria ese Governador la distincion que hacia de Su persona: Que esas eran imposturas de un clerigo Genoves de esa plaza, emulo de V.P. Que la carta del Senor Grimaldi en respuesta la conserva su Illustrisima y ella hace fe de ser impostura que le aigan dicho a ese cavallero Governador.

N.Sr. que V.P. mag. etc.

Signed: Fr. Antonio Martinez (Prior del Convento de San Agustin.
To: R.P. Francisco Messa del Orden de San Agustin, Gibraltar.

page 25
[7]**cooling of friendship.** . . . Government Secretariat Archives, Spanish Ch Files, PP20−21

page 26
[8]**Inquisition.** . . . Government Secretariat Archives, Spanish Church Files, P.7

Muy Sor. mio y de mayor veneracion.

Los Illustrisimos Senores Inquisidores Apostolicos de la fe, tienen comisionado entregue a Vuestra Reverencia en mano propia ciertos documentos, y sobre los quales, le instruye y practique alguna breve y formal diligencia, y siendo a mi de grave reparo el transito a esa plaza, he de merecer a Va. Ra. asi por mi suplica, como por la orden de dichos Senores se tome el chasco de pasar a la Linea o abansada el dia que guste, senalandomelo, y la hora, para que yo le remite la correspondiente Licencia de este Cavalleroso Comandante y este en el sitio que se sirva asignarme para que de este modo no se nos siga extravio. Este motivo me ha sido de la mayor complacencia por franquearme ocasion de ofrecerme ingenuo a la obediencia de Va. Ra. quien asegurado de que soi su seguro servidor y Afectisimo Cap ellan podra insinuarme los preceptos de su agdo. para exercitarme gustoso en su obsequio, pues hace diass deseava ofrecerme a su obediencia y que Dios le Gde. M.A.

Don Joseph de Rossas.

Reply by Fr. Messa after he had asked the Governor for advice.

Muy Sor. Mio,

Para fielmente tratarme en el Sagrado Ministerio que su Divina Majestad se ha dignado encargarme, para cumplir cabalmente las ordenes inviolables del Rey mi Senor (que Dios guarde) y para poder dar publicamente al Cesar lo que es del Cesar y a Dios lo que es de Dios como antes de ayer nos intimo en su sagrado Evangelio, Cristo Nuestro Bien, me dicto mi prudencia serme indespensable el comunicar la que recibi de Vuestra Merced el Viernes pasado, al Exmo. Sr. Governador de esta ciudad, y asi se la comunique por conducta del Senor Su Seccretario, y en consequencia Su Excelencia se digno responderme con una carta que es el sequitur:−

Revdo. Padre Vicario,

Habiendo usted Padre como Subdito fiel del Rey nuestro Amo, y en consequencia de sus reales ordenes, comunicandome una carta dirigida a usted Padre, firmada "El Comisario del Santo Oficio de la Ciudad y Puerto de Gibraltar Don Joseph de Rossas", citando "Ordenes de los Ilmos. Senores Inquisidores Apostolicos de la fe".

Devo informar a usted Padre, que el Tribunal de la Inquisicion, por Gracias del Omnipotente, es cosa no conocida en el dominio Britanico, siendo totalmente opuesto a nuestras leyes y por consequencia inadmisible en qualquier Territorio del Rey mi Amo, como Usted Padre siendo natural de Menorca, deve muy bien saver; Por lo que, no solamente, prohibo a usted Padre la salida al encuentro de Don Joseph sobre lo propuesto en dicha carta, pero le advierto que si acaso forastero alguno, por distinguido que sea, presum iera venir a esta plaza para atentar a exercer qualquier funcion de orden el expresado Tribunal, sera tratado de Espia; y si qualesquiera de los subditos Catolicos de S.M.B en esta Plaza, sea Eclesiastico o secular se atreve a asistir a el que se llamase Ministro de inquisicion o a obedecer la orden de tal Tribunal, en la Ciudad y Teritorio de Gibraltar, sera tratado como Traydor de su Rey y Patria.

Luego, enterado Don Joseph de Rossas (quien se intitula Comisario de un Tribunal que no existe en esta Plaza) de mis Resoluciones, en quanto a las ordenes de dicho Tribunal, si tuviere gusto de venir a esta Plaza sin otra pretencion, ni distincion que ese de cavallero para ver sus Amigos, seria yo el primero para manifestarle mi atencion (sin embargo del Lance que paso entre nosotros) y tendre especial gusto en tal ocasion de reconocer las grandes urbanidades que en varias ocasiones ha usado con los Oficiales de esta Plaza".

Al Revedo Padre Fr. Francisco Messa,
Vicario de la Iglesia Romana
Gibraltar.
24 Octubre 1774.

B.L.M. de V md.
su mayor Servidor

Signed: R. Boyd.

199

Esta es, Senor la verdadera Copia de la que como original me he retenido en mi poder para mi govierno, con ella podra ver usted serme imposible el poner en practica, ni aun intentar, lo que me pide, lo que siento por el deseo que tengo de ver y tratar su notoriamente urbana y politica persona, pero espero lograrlo si vuestra merced quiere no despreciar el noble Brindis que le dispensa magnanimo el dicho Senor, y en este caso espero no quedarme privado del honor de tener en mi casa tan noble Huesped por ultimo devo decirle que podra vuestra merced informar a los Senores Inquisidores del presente sistema y podra asegurarlos de mi parte que en la Isla de Menorca no exercitan Los Inquisidores su Oficio ni embian circunstancias que se halla esta Plaza, si que el Illmo. Senor Obispo de Mallorca por medio de su Vicario General que reside en Menorca obra lo que se puede obrar en materias de Fe y Religion con la vigilante atencion a las circunstancias del Lugar y no teniendo cosa mas particular que comunicar a vuestra merced ceso rogando a Dios le guarde muchos anos.

Al Sr. Don Joseph de Rossas, Comisario del Santo Oficio en los Barrios.

B.L.M. de Vmd.
Su seguro Servidor y Capellan.

Signed: Fr. Francico Mesa
Vicario.

The Bishop of Cadiz after reading all the documents and being unwilling to force anyone to do anything that would convert him into a spy, writes to Fr. Messa on the subject. He was not to dwell on the matter ever again.

R. Padre Vicario

He visto copias de las cartas, que V.R. me remite, y su respuesta a Don Joseph de Rosas comisario del Santo Oficio de la Poblacion de los Barrios, sobre los pasages ocurridos, y trato el don con V.R.en virtud de las ordines que tuvo del tribunal de Sevilla, a fin de facilitar en esa plaza cierta informacion. Tambien he leido la copia del papel que el cavallero Governador de ella escrivio a V.R. prohibiendo le la salida de esa ciudad a verse en la Linea con don Rosas, inti mando, que si alguna otra persona entrare en ella para tratar, o ofrecer qualquiera function de orden del Santo Tribunal sera tratado como a espia.

En inteligencia de todo, debo decir a V.R. que atento a lo critico de esa Plaza y a que por ningun motivo se debe nadie exponer a los rigores que amenaza al cavallero Gobernador, es presiso no tocar mas en semejantes materias, pues me persuado que los Sres. Inquisidores de Sevilla considerando discretamente esos acaesimientos, bien sea por informe que Don Joseph de Rosas o V.R. les dieren seran del mismo sentir.

Cadiz 20 diciembre 1774.

Signed: Thomas, Obispo de Cadiz.

page 26
[9]**Catholic Burials**. . . . Government Secretariat Archives, Spanish Ch. Files, PP23−25
  The surgeons appointed to do the enquiry were: Arthur Baynes, Moses Chisholm and D.McNaier.

The Junta made up of Fr. Messa, Bartholomew Dagnino, Mathias Adams, Alberto Biales and Nicholas Quartin drew up a memorial and sent it to the Governor accepting the decision made by the Governor after the advice of the surgeons.

"TO HIS EXCELLENCY ROBERT BOYD ESQUIRE, MAJOR GENERAL OF HIS MAJESTY'S FORCES, COLONEL OF THE 39TH REGIMENT OF FOOT, LIEUTENANT GOVERNOR AND COMMANDER IN–CHIEF OF THE TOWN AND GARRISON OF GIBRALTAR."

The memorial of the Vicar, members (and major part) of the Congress of the Roman Catholic Inhabitants, duly assembled by the said Vicar, in the Church of the Blessed Virgin of the Crown, in this Garrison, whose Names are hereunto, subscribed, on behalf of themselves and of that Communion.

Humbly Showeth

That They your Excellency's Memorialists, who are faithful and loyal Subjects of His Britannic Majesty: with all humility beg leave to represent to your Excellency; that the said Vicar having signified to them that it was your Excellency's Pleasure, they should discontinue the Practice which they have had, time immemorial, of burying their dead, (as well Parishioners as Strangers) within the Walls of the Spanish Church: And that such a Prohibition on the part of your Excellency, had arisen from the report of the three Gentlemen Surgeons, who by your Excellency's Order, and at the request of the said Vicar, had examined the Carnel House, the place and manner of burying; and have given it as their opinion that tho' the present method of internment may be attended with Inconveniency, yet that every evil Consequence may be effectually remedied or prevented, by filling up the Carnel House with Earth, making the Graves for the future of the Depth of five feet, which should not be opened again for four years, and lastly by throwing Lime over the dead Bodies when burried.

That they your Excellency's Memorialists are ready to oblige themselves and they, do hereby severally promise and become bound to your Excellency that they will henceforth punctually and inviolably adhere to keep and perform and cause to be kept and put in practice, the aforesaid four Articles, recommended by the Gentlemen Surgeons, together with any conditions your Excellency may judge proper.

Consideration of the Premisses, and that your Excellency will be graciously pleased to continue to them generally the practice of burying their dead in the Spanish Church as formerly, but under the above mentioned Restrictions.

And they your Excellency's Memorialists as in Duty bound will ever pray etc.

page 28

[10]**Ordinary powers.** ... Government Secretariat Archives Spanish Church Files, P.19

El Exmo. Sr. Don. . . . . Expone

Que desde que esta plaza y Ciudad de Gibraltar pertenece a Nuestra Nacion Britanica, siempre en ella se ha conservado una Iglesia de Catolicos Romanos, y esta governanda por medio de un Sacerdote Romano ya Secular ya, y la mayor parte del tiempo, Regular, con el titulo de Vicario, y Cura de la parroquia de Santa Maria la Coronada, y su Patron San Bernado: Que todos los dichos vicarios siempre, y en todo tiempo han sido puestos y nombrados por los Governadores de esta Guarnicion, y Confirmados por los Senores Obispos de Cadiz como Diocesanos mas proximos, y los quales en tiempo, que esta Plaza pertenecia a la nacion Espanola, eran Obispos propios de ella: Que dichos Vicarios por faltarlos una llena y Ordinaria Jurisdiccion Espiritual se ven presisados en muchos casos a tener, y mantener cierta correspondencia secretas de Confesion, las quales no dejan perfectamente seguros los Governadores de esta Guarnicion de la fidelidad que deben tener dichos Vicarios al Rey Nuestro Senor, que deseando que se quiten todo genero de sosopechas en dichas Personas, y que sean Miradas de todos los Britanicos con ojos seguros de su entera fidelidad, y sin el menor reselo de infieles por alguna correspondencia con la nacion Espanola: Suplico a Su Santidad se digne poner en el Rdo. Padre Sr. Jurado Fr. Francisco Messa de la Orden de San Agustin, que al presente regenta el Vicariato y Curato de dicha Iglesia, una llena y Ordinaria potestad como la que acostumbran tener los Vicarios Generales Provisores en sus Diocesis, y aun en todo lo que sea possible, toda la que usa los mismos Senores Obispos, poniendole a el, y a todos Sus Sucesores, fuera de toda sujecion y dependencia de la nacion Espanola y sujetandoles immediatamente a la Santa Sede Apostolica de Su Santidad; dandoles y concediendoles para este fin, la dignidad y titulo de Protonotarios Apostolicos y Vicarios Generales de esta Ciudad de Gibraltar y Monte Caspio. O elevando esta Vicaria, al titulo de Abadia, creando al Superior que es Vicario de ella Abbate de dicha Iglesia de esta Ciudad de Gibraltar y Monte Caspio, habilitandole en todo lo que sea necesarios para dicho efecto y consediendole a el y a todos sus succesores todos los honores, privilegios regalias et alias, que suelen y acostumbran tener los sujetos condecorados con semejantes dignidades. Y por ultimo que su nominacion y presentacion sea en adelante, asi como antes, hecha por el Excmo.Governador de esta Plaza que es, o que sera, quien debera proponer como candidatos tres Sacerdotes Catholicos Romanos, y Su Santidad elegir y confirmar uno de ellos.

page 29
[11]**Needs of a fortress:** vide APPENDIX ONE. THE GREAT SIEGE.

CHAPTER FOUR

page 32
[1]**Genoese Patricians.** . . . Government Secretariat Archives, Diary of Occurrences: 1782–86.

Information is given there of the dates when the inhabitants evacuated to Genoa, Tangier, Portugal, Menorca, England and even Malaga. The first group returned on 1st July 1783 from Genoa. The 2nd July states that Jews from Tangier returned. On 11th July those who went to England landed. On 31st July arrived 41 evacuees from Nice. Jews who had sailed to England were the first to be repatriated arriving on the Rock on 8th May 1783.

It appears that a new influx of Genoese arrived on the Rock under very different circumstances. Don Baccio Garassino has made a particular study of some of the Genoese immigrants to Gibraltar. He states that soon after the Great Siege the British authorities appealed to the Government of Genoa, then friendly with Great Britain, to send 70 families to assist in the reconstruction and livening up civilian life here in Gibraltar.

He goes on to say that in response to the appeal went many of the Patrician families to Gibraltar. Eventually what was the aristocracy of Genoa became the aristocracy of Gibraltar. Among the names mentioned are The Marquis Recagno, the Gustavinos, Garbarinos and Raggios who belonged to the Great Council. Then there were the Counts Galliano, the Corsi, the Celesia, Spotorno, Bassadone, Pittaluga. Genoese Seafaring Captains who decided to settle in Gibraltar when married to local girls were the Possos, the Cassolas, the Lavarellos, the del Pino, the Celesia, the Fabres, the Dassoy, the Chiozza, the Bagliettos, the Sanguinettis. Some of these preferred to stay in Tangier.

The report states that in the Republic of Genoa only noble families were allowed to build battleships, trade in cereals, wines, oil and keep windmills and butcher shops.

page 32
[2]**Proposition in 1800**. Gib. Cathedral Archives, Junta Files, vol. 2, pp 8–10.

General Boyd when Governor proposed to fulfill the promise made by General Elliott during the Great Siege, namely, that of building the Tower as it was before it was lowered. It was proposed that the authorities were prepared to grant £1000 towards the reconstruction of the tower and church but that a section be sacrificed for the construction of the one straight street.

The plans were drawn by a Mr. Joaquin Valerio and approved by the Governor. It appears that little progress was visible so the Governor requested for three men to be appointed to supervise the construction:

Sir,

His Majesty having been graciously pleased to grant one thousand pounds sterling towards the rebuilding of the Spanish Church, and a considerable progress having been made in that work by Joaquin Valerio, who had entered into contract with Government, for building the Western Front and Belfry to the same; but the work having been of late suspended in consequence of some difficulties which had occurred in its execution, being desirous however that every advantage should be taken at this favourable season of the year, for completing the work agreeably to his Majesty's gracious intentions.

I have to desire for his Majesty's Service, that you will forthwith select from the Roman Catholic Congregation, three persons to be invested by the community with full power for entering into an agreement with a builder: – giving the preference to Mr. Valerio for the completion of the whole edifice, with as little delay as possible, according to the plan already determined upon, by the commanding engineer.

Charles Barnett. M.G. Acting Commander in Chief.

page 38
[3]**Father Joyera.** . . . ibid. pp 4–6.

7th January 1802.

In consequence of the annexed request, the Governor permits the Reverend Francis Joyera to reside in the Garrison, and officiate in the Roman Church, as a Lent preacher for twelve weeks.

He must be fully apprised that no foreign Ecclesiastical Jurisdiction is admissible in any part of the British Empire, being incompatible with the King's sovereignty, and he consequently will be aware of inculcating submission to a foreign authority ecclesiastical or temporal, in this Garrison, or performing any act himself in virtue of such foreign power, while in the Garrison, either of which would be considered as Treason.

The Vicar and Elders are also to hold in constant remembrance, that the Roman Catholic Inhabitants are indulgent by His Britannic Majesty with the Free exercise of their Religion on the foregoing conditions.

Chas O'Hara. Governor.

Sirs,

The Vicars and Elders of the Roman Catholic Church having represented to me that on account of the debilitate nature of the Vicar's health, and the dismissal of the Curate by the late Governor, for infamous behaviour, that congregation are in great want of a person to assist in the Sacramental Offices, give instruction from the pulpit, and train up their youth with principles of Religion and morals; and having represented to me that the Reverend Francis Joyera, admitted into the Garrison by the late Governor in character of a Lent preacher, is a person, whose erudition, talents, and piety render him eligible to perform the duties above mentioned.

I do therefore in virtue of the authority vested in me, as Commander in Chief of this Garrison, hereby nominate and appoint the said Reverend Franc. Joyera to fill the office of Curate to the Roman Catholic Church here, he having taken an oath of allegiance and fidelity to His Britannic Majesty, and of submission to the laws of the Realm, and the Order and regulations of the Fortress.

1st April 1802.
Charles Barnet, M.G.
Commander in Chief.

page 38
+**Regulars in Rome.** . . . ibid., p.21.

In an audience held with the Holy Father on 16th July 1802, I the undersigned Secretary of the Sacred Congregation for the Bishops and Religious, His Holiness kindly gave his consent and by so doing ordered the Vicar General the appellant, that given the reason presented to be true, he should grant the named religious the faculty to exercise his office as Curate, even when he has to live outside the Cloister, for as long as it is laid down, according to his judgment and conscience. Nevertheless, he should retain his religious habit and lead a life worthy of a religious. This indult should in no way be understood as a relaxation of the discipline of the Religious Order. Meanwhile he is to live by force of his religious vows under obedience to the same Vicar.

Signed: Cardinal Carasa.

page 39
[5]**General Henry Ed. Fox** Gibraltar Cathedral Archives, Junta Files. Vol.1 (G.C.A./ J.F.Vol.1)

The Elders of the R.C. Congregation with the highest respect beg leave to approach Your Excellency upon a most serious importance for the whole Community, and in their names, to state their grievances on the subject, with the most submissive reliance to obtain such an efficacious remedy, as they may expect from Your wise and generous Patronage.

In the first place they humbly beg leave to refer to the Secretary's official letter dated 18th February last directed to the few members of the committee then existing after the fatal havoc of the epidemic sickness, wherein after acquainting them of their request for a Lenten preacher being granted by Your Excellency and Gentleman, by Your Excellency's desire expressed himself in the following words. "It may however be necessary to add that His Excellency expects the arrival of a Catholic Priest, who has been strongly recommended as a fit person to succeed to the vacant vicarage in this Garrison" in compliance to which intimation said members readily desisted from their intention of providing a proper person to fill that station in hopes that the proposed Priest would fully answer the whole community's expectations though they had at some time sufficient reason to apprehend that such an election would soon prove as unpleasant, as a former appointment made by the late Governor Charles O'Hara of another Irish Priest to the Curateship who tho' strongly recommended as a fit person, fully turned at the end as unfit as at first represented by the Elders and was on that account expelled from the Garrison by the same Governor, which circumstance convinced him, that the Elders were the proper persons to provide their own priests, in consequence whereof they were left at liberty to fill that vacancy and had the satisfaction to appoint thereto, the worthy and for ever lamented the late Reverend Francisco Joyera, who fell a victim of his charitable zeal, and unremitted assistance to the poor and sick catholics at the above melancholy period.

That on the first appearance and introduction in the Catholic Church of this new Vicar, said members could as well perceive his unfitness, and that of the above mentioned Curate, they forbore venturing any premature judgement on his talents and capacity, but thought it their duty to wait for both the results of his behaviour, and the return of their absent fellow brethren, but how their diffidence has been justified, and their hopes frustrated, they can hardly express, for ever since his installation to the Vicarship, he has endeavoured to overturn the old fundamental rites of the Catholic church, by substituting to the Spanish (the sole language therein adopted since its existence) the English and Italian never heard and made use of in the pulpit, and usual ceremonies, by neglecting the most essential duties of his Station, and suppressing the explaining of the gospel, and the children's instruction in the Catholic Doctrine, by which irregular conduct, and his particular disregard to the long established rules of this Catholic Congregation, they find, that all his study is bent on the overthrow of the worthy and respectable constitution from time immemorial existing in the Catholic Church, and ever generously supported by your predecessors:

The absent fellow brethren but one being since returned in this Garrison, the Elders humbly beg leave, to state, that all the preceding Governors fully depending on the honest and loyal character of the Committee, as the representatives of the whole community and depositories of their moral and religious sentiments, have ever been graciously pleased to leave to said Committee the sole direction and management of their church concerns, with the free enjoyment of its ancient privileges; that agreeable to such a kind condescension from Government, which the Elders have ever studied to deserve, (the benefits whereof the hebrew nation in particular have ever unboundedly enjoyed) their Committee or assembly acknowledged by the Lieut. Governor Lord Cornwallis, and confirmed since by his successors, has ever since been at liberty to choose their own Pastors, being themselves considered as the best judges to find out what kind of Priests would better suit the whole Community for their Church with the required dignity and submissive deference to British Government; in which their compliance has ever deserved the Governor's approbation, as it was with the appointment of the late worthy curate aforesaid, who by his edifying conduct, evangelical capacity, christian and social morals has so clearly promoted the instruction and honest principles of all the congregation, and has ever with his efficacious persuasions good example, and indefatigable attendance contributed towards the final re-edification of the Catholic Temple. The Elders being thus the conveyors of the whole humble complaints, and bound in honour and conscience and thro' due regard and duty to their expectation, to implore from Your Excellency's benignity the most efficacious redress, and to prevent the decline of their religion so well calculated for the Christian and social virtues, and the danger to which their children are exposed to loose the fundamental principles of their duty to God and their Sovereign, they beg leave to represent that the enjoyment of their former rights and privileges so graciously confirmed to them by all Your predecessors can never give room to the least difficulty or apprehension on their conduct, if Your Excellency is pleased to consider, that their own interest, their honour, their religion, the preservation of their properties and the safety of their families are so closely linked with their duty and loyalty to their king and country, as to put out of their power the least idea of acting in any wise to the prejudice of Government.

They humbly apprehend that considering the valuable esteem and regard so generously bestowed upon them by the former Governors, as well as their hard pains and troubles, heavy contributions and most valuable sacrifices made to Government for the re-edification of their temple, it would be very hard upon them to be deprived of the liberty of choosing their own ministers, and obliged to suffer a person, whose culture and arbitrary disregard of the long established rites and statutes of the Catholic Church, endangers the moral and Christian education of their children, and causes a general discontent and uneasiness in their congregation.

They therefore respectfully hope that their submissive representations after a mature and impartial consideration will be found worthy of your Excellency's gracious attention, or consistent with truth, honour and faithful obedience to Government Regulations and most Humbly Pray, that the appointment of a proper person for the Vicarial dignity may be trusted to their own care and knowledge of the required capacity and qualification for that situation, which they flatter themselves will fully deserve Your Excellency's approbation.

To: His Excellency the Rt. Hon. The Honourable General Henry Edward Fox.
The Junta.
Gibraltar, 24−12−1805

Reply
Gibraltar Cathedral Archives, Junta Files Vol.2

Sirs,

Having considered your Memorial in which you present reasons for desiring the expulsion of the Rev. Mr. Staunton, and petitioning the nomination of another ecclesiastic for the Spanish Church, I am obliged to make clear, that I do not consider myself authorized to renounce on behalf of the Government the right to appoint 'alone and name the Vicar of the Roman Catholics, if at such times the existing circumstances require it.

However, since it is my desire to please and express my support to such a distinguished Body such as the Elders of the Roman Catholic Church established in Gibraltar, I am inclined in the present instance to accede to the petition of the Memorial, and given that the subject proposed to replace Mr. Staunton is recommended for his piety, and good conduct, and adjust to the Oaths of loyalty, and is enacting in his fulfilment of the Laws of the Place and with the Government, just as the late Father Reverend Francis Joyera, there should be no difficulty in approving his nomination.

Fox.
January 1806.

page 40
[6]**He felt in conscience.** . . . ibid., p.X
Father Dominguez writes to the Junta.

. . . . Yo creí no debia apuntar unas causas que presumi no ignoraria esa respetable Junta. Esta es verdad puede tener como tiene la facultad de proponer Ministro Idoneo para el desempeño de la Vicaria. El Govierno, baxo cuya protecion y cuyas leyes se halla, puede aprobar la eleccion que se hace del sujeto que ha de proponerse; circunstancias indispensables que pide el buen orden y las reglas establecidas en el derecho para estos casos. Pero este no es un nombramiento lexitimo, y aunque podamos darle el nombre de indirecto, no puede facultar a un Ministro para que exerza funciones Pastoales y de jurisdiccion. Jamas este ha podido instalarse con sola la eleccion para pesentarlo, ebe pues pra ello esperarse el nombramiento por la potestad lexitima que puede darlo. Tal es el orden y economia que debe observrse en los Superiores eclesiasticos segun el establecimiento de los Sagrados Canones, de aqui es, que aun quando El Oispo sa elegido y presentado por el Soberano, segun el Concordato, no puede aquel tomar posesion de su obispao sin que antes se ostenga el nombramiento y Mision de la Silla Appca. a quien corresponde. Lo mismo sucede con los Canonigos, Beneficiados, y Parrocos, respecto de los Obispos, quando estos los proponen a las Camaras o Consejos de la Nacion, de donde les viene por dereho establecido la Confirmacion, sin la que jamas pueden posesionarse en sus empleos. El Vicario de Gibraltar, como que se halla independiente de los Obispos, puede por concesion y Concordato con la Silla Appca. elegirse por la Junta Catolica de Ancianos: esto, puede determinarse por ella el sugeto que se ha de presentar a aquella, para que lo nombre y autorize. Sin este nombramiento, y mision no hai Vicario, ni puede licitamente alguno tomar posesion de este empleo ni directa, ni indirectamente so pena de ser un intruso, un prevaricador, de hacerse reo la paz de la Iglesia y el Orbe Católico, y de quedar invalidos y nulos todos los actos relativos a su ministerio, desde su posesin en adelante.

page 40
[7]**Mr. Breciano pleaded.** . . . ibid., pp XI–Xii

.... Si le sirve V.ª Paternidad considerar algo despacio lo sucedido con el mismo Padre Joyera en la aceptacion del ministerio que se le confirió durante su mansion en esta como Predicador Quaresmal, no dexaré V.ª Paternidad, de mirarnos en algun modo, como escusables pues no sera natural de inferir en el Estado en que nos hallamos de que si dho Religioso admitió anticipadamente el nombramiento y se revistió de la authoridad Pastoral, sin haver precedido la nominacion de la Potestad legítima, no podia haver embarazo en solicitar la inmediata presentacion de su actual sucessor, atendiendo a tan urgente necesidad, como la de no tener Pastor alguno al presente, otra consideracion que tambien concurrió en aumentar nuestras inquietudes y apprehensiones fué la sospecha de no haver nuestro comisionado tal vez empleado todos los esfuerzos y persuasiones para determinar a V.ª Paternidad en acompañarlo de buelta, pero queda del todo desvanecida aquella duda por el elogio que se sirve hazernos de la eficacia con que desempeño su encargo, sin embargo todo ello nunca nos dió lugar a la menor desconfianza en la Religiosa Palabra de que tenemos las mas evidentes pruebas, sino al natural sentimiento de una ponible y larga privacion; quedando pues estos sus humildes siervos plenamente convencidos de que sin el previo nombramiento y mission del Summo Pontifice no puede haver Vicario, ni puede este legitimamente tomar posesion de aquel Empleo reconocemos que por aquel aspecto su presentacion en esta seria infructuosa por las razones que se sirve explicar, pero nos permitirá V.ª Paternidad representarle que pudiendo facilmente allanarse aquellos obstaculos, con tomar el camino derecho que menciona, y considerando que para obviar las fatales consequencias que pueden resultar de la independencia absoluta de esta Iglesia, de qualquiera Obispo, el Santo Padre actuado de aquel Espiritu de Paz, Caridad y Mansedumbre de Jesu Christo, se dignó en igual ocurrencia, no solamente aprobar la eleccion del Padre Joyera al Curato, pero aun anteriormente confirmar a nuestro difunto Vicario en la posesion de la Vicaria, de la que sin requisito a guno, se havia anticipadamente posesionado, absolviendole por lo pasado, y autorizandole por lo futuro (como havra reconocido V.ª Paternidad por los documentos remitidole en 6 del corriente en carta particular de nuestro Secretario) tan benigna condescendencia del Subdelegado de Dios en la tierra, no puede menos de avivar nuestras esperanzas de lograr con la misma facilidad igual y tan amplia concesion, y de consiguiente podemos libremente prometernos la especial satisfaccion de ver a V.ª Paternidad presentarse en esta, antes del largo termino annunciandonos en su primera apreciable Carta, pues a la verdad de otro modo, seria una privacion muy dura y nada proporcionada al general afecto que le profesa de corazon toda esta Católica Congrecacion.

page 40
[8]**Canonical rights.** . . . ibid., pp.XIII
The Parish Priest of Algeciras D. Geronimo Caballero solicitous for the consciences of the Vicar taking on the office in Gibraltar as well as for the people insists that it was necessary to grant the necessary faculties. 10 February 1806.

".... Insta la habilitacion p.ᵃ el Pe. Isidoro Dominguez, Vic.º electo de los Catolicos de Gibr., u otro qe. provisionalmte. se encargue del Minist.º p.ᵃ seguridad de su conciencia de aquellos fieles. Dho. Pe. Isidoro les ha escrito una Carta erudita, haziendoles demostrable, qe. sin mision de ligítima autoridad no puede exercitar su Minist.º, ni exponerse a incurrir en algun exceso.

El Gobierno da al Vicario desde la conquista dos raciones de oficial, qe. cada una es de libra y med.ᵃ de pan, una lib.ᵃ de manteca, otra de carne y otra de tocino, qe. reducidas a moneda importan mas de 40 rs. diarios y cien ps. fuertes annuales. Los feligreses le ofrecen mil duros pr. las obenciones del Parrocato, quedandole la Misa, cuyo estipendio es de veinte rrs. cantada y rezada diez; los juramtos. de contratos y de toda prueba, que tienen fuerza de ley en el Gobierno con el sello Vicarial, y es renglon de mucho ingreso; p.º es tal el tezon del Gobierno en estorvar qe. V. S. I. intervenga en los casos de autoridad, qe. con el nombre de Dn. Jaime lo cito, p.ᵃ consolar a los Catolicos, quando les anuncio su consesion de indulgencias, o de Jurisdn. p.ᵃ sus Patores, haviendolos concertado en esta cifra."

page 41
[9]**British interests.** . . . Sacred Congregation of Propaganda Fide Archives (SCPFA), Litt. Script. p.172.

page 42
[10]**General Don requested.** . . . ibid., p.174

page 42
[11]**On Sunday 29th October.** . . . ibid., p.184

PART II CHAPTER ONE

page 45
[1]**Monsignor Esteban.** . . . ibid., p.186
The Bishop's name was Andres Esteban Gomez. Chosen to discreetly investigate the occurrences on the Rock he not only makes the mentioned recommendations but reveals something else. It appears that a Fr. Ferguson had suddenly appeared on the scene claiming to be the successor. He was sent by Bishop Hay, Vicar Apostolic of Scotland and that Rome knew about it all because of their own representative living there. The Junta rejected Ferguson and concentrated on seeing that Fr. Zino and not Fr. Panizza was made Vicar.

page 45
²senza titolo. . . . ibid, Lettere, 1817, p.247.

page 46
³guidelines for the Junta. . . . ibid., Lettere, Maggio 1817, p.247.

DECRETO

DE LA SACRADA CONGREGACION DE PROPAGANDA FIDE

Habiéndose notado que de algun tiempo a esta parte se habian introducido algunos abusos en el régimen espiritual de los Catolicos de Gibraltar, con gran detrimento tanto de la paz como de la administracion Eclesiastica; la Sagrada congregacion, con objeto de remover en lo sucesivo toda causa de desorden y establecer el metodo y disciplina debidos, y HABIENDO CONSULTADO TAMBIEN A LOS ANCIANOS, acordó y decretó debian prescribirse ciertas reglas o estatutos que hubiesen de ser observados inviolablemente en adelante, a los cuales habran de sujetarse todos aquello a quienes pertenezca. Las reglas son pues las siguientes:

I

El Vicario Apostólico, constutuido por el Sumo Pontífice, es el Superior Eclesiastico de todos los Catolicos residents en Gibraltar, a quien deberan someterse por tanto en las cosas espirituales. El cuidará a los feligreses como su Cura Párroco, y nombrará un Teniente Cura para que le asista en el desempeño de su Ministerio Pas ral.

II

Se mand a todo los Curas de almas por precepto Divino el conocer sus ovejas, ofrecer por ellas el Sacrificio, apacentarlas con la predicacion de la Divina Pala bra, administracion de Sacramentos y egemplo de buenas obras; tener paternal cuidado de los pobres y demas personas desvalidas, y cumplir con las demas obligaciones de su Ministerio. Así pues deberan el Vicario Apostólico y su Vice-Parroco observar escrupulosamente todo esto, y administrar con el mayor esmero todos los auxilios espirituales a los fieles que estubieren bajo su cargo.

III

Igualmente estará obligado el Vicario Apostolico a celebrar Misa por el Pueblo todos los Domingos y Festividades del año, y explicar el Evangelio del dai en Idioma Español: y, en caso de estorbárselo algun impedimento legítimo, bastará lo haga por él su Tenients o, en defecto de este, algun otro Sacerdote idoneo. Mas el Vicario no se considerará precisado a predicar en la Cuaresma, y sí a nombrar cada año otro Sacerdote a proposito para el caso, CON CONSENTIMIENTO DE LOS ANCIANOS.

IV

El Vicario Apostólico deberá ademas celebrar Misa solemne en la Iglesia Parroquial todos los Domingos y dias de Fiesta, precediendo, segun costumbre, la hora canónica de tercia, y luego despues de medio dia las Visperas, a la hora conveniente; y ademas las Preces correspondientes a las Ferias del año por las Almas del Purgatorio consecuente a práctica; todo sin emolumento especial alguno.

V

El Vicario Apostolico, su Teniente, y los demas Eclesiásticos de la Iglesia que no tubieren otra ocupacion, enseñara y explicaran los rudimentos de la doctrina a los párbulos y otras personas ignorantes todos los dias festivos del año, y en la Cuaresma ménos la Semana Santa.

VI

Asímismo deberan asistir solícitamente a los enfermos y prestar todo auxilio Eclasiatico gratis, como igualmente acompañar a los difuntos hasta la Puerta de la Cuidad, desde donde alternativemente regresará el uno, siguiendo el otro con el cadáver hasta el Cementerio para hacerle allí las exequias segun el rito de las Iglesia.

VII

Seran tambien de la obligacion del Vicario Apostolico y de su Vice-Parroco todas las demas funciones Eclesiásticas de Triduos, Novenas Bautismos, Matrimonios, Entierros, Aniverarios de difuntos, y celebrar gratis todo cuanto perteneciere a la administracion de Sacramentos, exceptuando las Misas que no fueren obligatorias. Las gratificaciones voluntarias que se dieren a los Sacerdotes por su Sagrado Ministerio, seran ppara ellos; y por ultimo las fees de Bautismo, de Casamiento, y de Muerto; las de estado libre, y otras que ocurrieren, pertenecerán al Vicario Apostólico, sin que pueda Ilevar por ellas mas de un duro a cada una.

VIII

No pudiéndose cumplir todo lo dicho si el Pastor abondanáre sus ovejas, se ordena al Vicario Apostolico observe el precepto de residencia prescrito en el S.Concilio de Trento en la Sesion 6, Cap.1, y Ses.13, Cap.1 "de Reformatione", bajo las penas Canonicas, sin que le sea licito ausentarse de su Vicariato por mas de ocho dias; y si tubiese causa justa y urgente para ello, deberá constituir en calidad de Teniente Vicario algun Sacerdote idóneo que haga sus veces, para que en el interim no carezcan los fieles de pasto espiritual.

IX

Tambien es necesario no le falte al Vicario Apostolico el subsidio temporal para su Cóngrua Sustentacion. Habiendo pues prometido los Ancianos, como consta, tanto

211

en su nombre como en el del Pueblo Catolico, asignar al Vicario Apostólico un estipendio diario de tres pesos fuertes pagaderos cada trimestre, y tambien la Casa construida para dicho Vicario el ano de 1804, debara ser la primera obligacion de los mismos el cumplirlo con exactitud.

X

SERA DERECHO DE LOS ANCIANOS ELEGIR UN TESORARO, Y UN RECAUDADOR PARA QUE EXIJA DILIGENTEMENTE LOS DINEROS PROVENIENTES DE OBLACIONES PIADOSAS DE LOS FIELES O DE LA IGLESIA, Y LO QUE SE HUBIERE DE RECIBIR POR LOS ACTOS Y DERECHOS DE PARROQUIA, SIEMPRE CON ARREGLO A LOS ARANCE-LES APROBADOS TODO LO QUE SE PONDRA EN PODER DEL TESOR-ERO. DE ESTE ERARIO SE PAGARAN TODAS LAS ASIGNACIONES TANTO DEL VICARIO APOSTOLICO COMO DE LOS DEMAS EMPLEADOS DE LA IGLESIA, CON ARREGLO A LA TASACION PREFIJADA ANTES DEL ANO DE 1810; Y EL SOBRANTE SE INVERTIRA EN EL CULTO Y REPAROS DE LA IGLESIA, Y TAMBIEN EN AUXILIO DE LOS ENFERMOS DEL HOSPI-TAL Y DE LOS POBRES, RESERVANDO SIEMPRE ALGUNA CANTIDAD EN DEPOSITO PARA CUALQUIERA NECESIDAD URGENTE.

La Sacrada Congregacion confia que en lo venidero seran puntualmente observada estas reglas espedidas para el bien de la Religion, paz y discipline; y si alguno osare temerariamente violarlas, deberá ser denunciado a la Sagrada Congregacion, para que se le imponga el condigno castigo.

Dado en Roma, en el Palacio de la S. Congregacion de Propaganda Fide, el dia 17 de Mayo de 1817.

(L.S)   L. Card. Litta, Prefecto.
                                                   C.M. PEDICINI, Secretario.

page 46
[4] .... **provide him with a house.** .... After the Great Siege the Vicar came to live in one or other of the rooms in the clergy house. The Vicar's House at George's Lane was destroyed during that war. Father Zino was given one of the rooms by the Church-Hospital in Cannon Lane exactly where he was before Father Dominguez transferred him into most humble quarters.

page 46
[5] **Table of fees.** .... Obtained from the Annals of the Irish Christian Brothers.

page 47
[6] **life of the people.** .... Gibraltar Catholic Archives, Junta Files, Vol. 3, p.31.

His Excellency
Sir Alexander Woodford
Governor

Catholic Church of St. Mary the Crowned
Gibraltar 6th February 1837

Sir,

Impelled by a deep sense of duty and serious responsibility as the depository of a sacred trust I beg leave to submit to Your Excellency some considerations on the subject of subsisting regulations with regard to marriages of Catholics in this Garrison.

During the period of 22 years that I have held the office of Vicar General Apostolic of this Catholic Church I have ever been so anxious to render in my own person the utmost deference and respect to the dispositions of the Government and to promote its views by every means in my power. And I am confident that so far from considering the liberty I am now taking, as a departure from such my uniform practice, Your Excellency might justly charge me with a dereliction of duty were I not to call attention to evils which for a considerable time have passed under my cognizance and whose continued growth I have every day occasion to lament.

It is superfluous to remind Your Excellency of the regulation by which I am prohibited from celebrating marriages between my Parishioners without the express sanction of the Governor of this Town and that in cases of both or one of the parties being foreigners even though long domiciled here, such sanction is very frequently refused in consequence as I have always understood of the positive orders of the Government at home.

Before adverting to the palpably demoralizing consequences of such an arrangement I do not think it irrelevant to state that a most important part of the exercises of our religion consists in the due administration of the Sacraments whereof Matrimony according to the Doctrine of the Catholic Church formed one and that there are certain periodical observances of our faith which though most essential cannot yet be participated in by persons who are living in a condition directly contrary to the Divine Commandment. It follows that the prohibition of marriages is to no small extent an infringement on the free exercises of the Catholic Religion guaranteed to Gibraltar by solemn engagements which it is but justice to say have ever been in other respects fulfilled with such scrupulous exactitude as was to be expected from the exalted character of the Government by which they were contracted.

There are however other considerations which I am confident will awake the attention of His Majesty's Governors to the urgent necessity of a considerable modification if not total abrogation of the system alluded to.

It is not my intention at present to specify the particular cases of individual hardship which in the exercise of my ministerial functions I have frequently witnessed. My sole object being to point generally to disorders emanating from releasing such as have gone gone astray by causing them to make the reparation which the Church enjoins but also leads to the perversion of those who, originally cherishing virtuous intentions, are by that regulation forced into a most sinful and demoralizing course. Thus inducing among a numerous class of the population a state of prostitution and general corruption involving in some instances as a necessary consequence the crime of infanticide and other perhaps equally heinous.

If as I have been given to understand the object of the system here deprecated is to prevent as much as possible the increase of the native population I need only submit to your Excellency that such a result is in no wise attained by it since its real effect is to substitute for the issue of lawful wedlock a very numerous class of children of suspicious origin repudiated and disgraced without natural protectors, abandoned to the contamination of profligacy and vice, and but too surely destined to become a bane to the society in which they live – but who on the other hand had they not been debarred from that moral position to which by divine Law and social right they are entitled would in every probability have become honest and useful members of the community – numerous instances could I point out where parties having gone so far as to cause the publication of banns in Church have been prevented from executing their intentions by the withholding of the marriage licences in consequence of which they have subsequently become the parents of illegitimate offspring – and Your Excellency may form some idea of the extent of the evil from the past that during the last few years the number of avowedly illegitimate children baptized in my Church generally exceed 40 annually – to which number must be added many more cases where the degrading circumstances attending the birth are studiously and effectually concealed.

Confiding in the Benevolence and enlightened judgement for which Your Excellency is so eminently distinguished I doubt not but Your Excellency will fully concur with me in the necessity of bringing this momentous subject under the immediate consideration of His Majesty's Government with a view to remedy evils whose existence need be merely looked at in order to ensure to them the most solicitous attention.

Although I do not doubt that so desirable a result must very speedily be attained I trust that in the meanwhile Your Excellency will see fit to grant marriage licences for the parties mentioned in the accompanying note – it being by some of them most urgently demanded.

I pray God to preserve Your Excellency many years and have the honour to remain

J.B. Zino Vicar General

page 47
[7]**Military regulations.** . . . Sacred Congregation of Propaganda Fide Archives, Litt. Scrit. Vol.2.
The Junta repeatedly applied for two English speaking priests to be sent and attend to the many English speaking families, Catholic soldiers and the prisoners. After much insistence a Father William Macdonald was sent to meet the needs of the prisoners. There were 1400 Catholic Servicemen at the time

page 47
[8]**Judge of the Supreme Court.** . . . History of the Courts of Gibraltar (1704–1951) by the Hon. Chief Justice Sir Roger Bacon.

page 48
[9]**Rule, Dr. W. Memoirs of a mission to Gibraltar and Spain,** London, 1854.

page 48
[10]**Catholic Schools on the lines of Mr. Rule.** . . . The Junta in their anxiety to get the School for Catholic Poor Children off the ground decided among themselves the rules the school would follow under the Patronage of the Governor:

REGLAMENTOS
PARA LAS
ESCUELAS CATOLICAS DE GIBRALTAR,
Establecidas en 1.º de Enero de 1836,
POR EL REVERENDISIMO Sa. VICARO GENERAL APOSTO-LICO
Y JUNTA DE ANCIANOS DE LA IGLESIA CATOLICA DE GIBRALTAR,
BAJO LOS AUSPICIOS DEL
EXOMO. SEÑOR TENIENTE GOBERNADOR SIR ALEJANDRO WOODFORD,
PATRONO PROTECTOR DE DICHAS ESCUELAS,

Para la instrucion gratuita de la juventud Católica de Gibraltar en los sanos principios de la moral, y para hacer mas esteusivo entre ella el conocimiento del Idioma Inglés.

El Establecimiento consta de tres Escuelas óSecciones separadas.

En la primera se admiten niños que no hayan recibido instruccion alguna, con objeto de prepararlos á ser trasladados á la segunda, segun sus respectivas capacidades.

En la segunda se les enseñará á Leer, Escribir, la Aritmética, Gramática, Geografia, &c.

Y en la tercera, la instruccion gratuita comprenderá el Leer, Escribir, la Aritmética, Teneduría de Libros, Gramática, Geografía, uso de Globos y Geometría; en adicion á lo cual, se establecerán Clases para enseñar el Latin y algunos idiomas modernos, con otros estudios útiles, ecsigiéndose un tanto moderado por cada ramo.

En todas las Escuelas se cuidará con esmero sean instruidos los niños en los preceptos de la religion.

Los Directores del Establecimiento son el Reverendísimo Señor Vicario General Apostólico, y los Ancianos de la Iglesia Católica anualmente elegidos por el pueblo Católico.

Las admisiones de alumnos en dichas Escuelas quedan á cargo de los Directores, prévia la recomendacion de los contribuyentes á los fondos de la Iglesia.

Los contribuyentes anuales de $32 ó mas tendrán derecho de recomendar para su admision en la terccra escuela un alumno por cada trcinta y dos pesos fuertes que suscribiesen, teniendo igual derecho, así como los que lo fueren de sumas menores, para hacerlo á la primera y segunda Escuela.

Se formará una lista de todos los niños recomendados, de la cual seran llenadas por los Directores las vacantes que resulten en las Escuelas; quedando á discrecion de los mismos dar la preferencia á los candidatos que por su mayor edad, mas pobreza, falta de Padres ú otras circunstancias peculiares, les parezcan tener mas derecho á ser admitidos.

Ningun niño que tenga menos de seis aúos de edad podrá ser admitido.

Las horas de Escuela son desde las nueve de la mañana hasta las tres de la tarde, en los dias de enseñanza; y en los Domingos y Fiestas de precepto, desde las nueve de la mañana hasta el medio dia, en cuyas horas asistirán los niños á los Divinos Oficios, vestidos con el trage designado por los Directores.

En los Sábados podrán los Maestros despedir á los niños á la hora que les parezca, segun el comportamiento de estos durante la semana.

Ningun niño podrá faltar á la Escuela sin prévio permiso, á no ser por enfermedad, en cuyo caso deberá avisarse inmediatamente á los Maestros.

Se ecsige de los padres cuiden muy particularmente del asco de sus hijos, y que se presenten con decencia.

No se permitirá en las Escuelas el uso de otros libros que los aprobados por los Directores.

Los Directores se reunirán en las Escuelas todos los Miércoles por la mañana para despachar los asuntos que ocurrieren en ellas, y con el objeto de recibir de los Maestros un parte semanal del estado del Establecimiento; y los niños que aparecieren haberse ausentado frecuentemente sin permiso, faltado á los reglamentos ó al respeto debido á sus preceptores, ó que se hubieren manifestado del todo incorregibles, serán por último espulsados por los Directores.

Al fin de cada año, habrá Ecsámenes Públicos y se distribuirán premios á los que mas se hubiesen distinguido.

Si algun niño de intento destruyere, ó notablemente maltratare, los libros ú otros objetos pertenecientes á las Escuelas, sus padres deberán resarcir el daño.

Cuando un Alumno, habiendo concluido su educacion, dejáre la Escuela, tendrá derecho (si su conducta en dicha Escuela hubiese sido recomendable) á que los Directores le den el correspondiente Certificado; pudiendo además contar con todo el aucsilio que puedan prestarle para proporcionarle trabajo.

CHAPTER TWO

page 50
[1]**The Christian Brothers.**. . . The information compiled in this chapter has been drawn from records in the Annals of the Christian Brothers (proper to those times), from the Junta Files, Vol. 3, pp.20–41, and a few letters in the Archives of Propaganda Fide Litt. Scrit., Vol. 5. For the benefit of history students those letters written by the Junta are transcribed here in full.

page 53
[2]**GIB. ARCHIVES JUNTA FILES VOL. 3**

To Bro. O'Flaherty.
23 August 1836.

Sir,

We the undersigned president and members of the Elders of the Catholic Church beg to acknowledge the receipt of your two letters addressed to the Secretary under date 16th ult. and 18th inst. We had hoped that the explanation already verbally given on the subject both as regards to the contents of your first communication and the cause of its not being earlier noticed would have proved satisfactory but as you see reasons for pressing for a written answer we have no objection to meet your wishes on this as we are fully disposed to do on every occasion.

No time was lost in taking into consideration your application regarding the establishment of summer vacations but under all circumstances and considering particularly that the school itself yet in its infancy required for the present at least exertions and sacrifices which however susceptible of being hereafter dispensed were for the present absolutely necessary that the printed regulations so very recently promulgated and extensively distributed made no provision for vacations of this class and that a large portion of the scholars were only just now and by means of the school itself rescued from the habits of idleness into which any very early intermission of their attendance might produce a relapse likely to prove prejudicial to them and through them to the interest of the establishment itself; we came to the conclusion that the request reasonable as it seemed in itself had better to deferred till a season when its adoption was likely to be without those difficulties which now stand in the way – Little doubting that these considerations would induce you to postpone your application till a more convenient opportunity it was at the same time our unanimous opinion that the communication should be verbal in consequence of which it was settled that any of its members to whom a convenient opportunity might present itself should convey to you the sentiments and wishes of the Elders – We certainly have cause to regret that some one particular was not charged with the duty as from an omission in this respect the task was not performed with the promptitude we proposed to ourselves and your letter was exposed to an apparent neglect very far from our wishes.

Such Sir as has already been verbally stated is the view which we take of the subject and such the cause for your not having received an immediate reply – You will easily percieve that any seeming want of courtesy towards you was quite unpremeditated and unintentional and that it did not proceed from any dissatisfaction at the mode in which you have discharged the duties of your offices. . . .

The Junta.
page 53
[3]To Mr. Edw. P. O'Flaherty.
14th September 1836.

Sir,

We hasten to reply to the letter dated the 12th and received on the 13th inst. which you have been pleased to address to the undersigned President of the Board of Elders of the Catholic Church of this place.

From your use of the plural number we are led to infer that this communication is meant to be considered as proceeding from Mr. Anthony as well as yourself though it is not distinctly stated to be and we shall be happy to find that we in this particular at least have mistaken its purport.

We cannot but regret that you should have been induced to come to the determination of abandoning a charge which was the sole object of your coming to Gibraltar and which we understood to be so peculiarly in accordance with your religious pursuits.

We shall not fail to take with all the expedition which is practicable measures for providing successors from England and upon their arrival we shall consider you at liberty to pursue the course on which you appear to have decided.

You have not thought proper to explain and we are ourselves quite at a loss to conjecture the motives which have influenced this proceeding – one paragraph in your letter indeed states your "regret that circumstances should exist to counteract your efforts and thus oblige you to abandon an object for the love of which your order has made such sacrifices and for which you willingly risked all that could be dear to you in this life". In perfect ignorance of what you allude to we feel ourselves warranted in calling on you for an explanation of your meaning and for a statement of those "circumstances" which have led you to a conclusion opposed to such weighty considerations – this explanation we ask in the purest spirit of good will and in the anxious hope that it may yet be the means of your retaining your present charge – we have and we are sure you can have but one object in view – the well being and advancement in knowledge of good of those numerous youths who mainly depend on the Catholic School for their attainment. Towards this object all of us in common with the congregation at large have afforded pecuniary aid according to our means and some of us at least have bestowed considerable personal attention. We stand fully acquitted to ourselves of having intentionally done anything to counteract any efforts of yours or to diminish in any way the utility of the establishment committed to your direction but if inadvertently we may have given you any just cause of complaint we shall be most happy to offer you every proper satisfaction and atonement.

We have thought it necessary to be thus frank and explicit seeing that the subject is one of the most grave importance and it would be matter of very painful reflection to think that an establishment so loudly called for, so highly beneficial even in its infancy and likely to prove in future so conducive to the interests of religion should receive a dangerous if not fatal shock from considerations of a private or personal nature.

The Junta.

To Mr. Edw. P. O'Flaherty.
19th September 1836.

Sir,

We have to acknowledge receipt of your letter of the 17th instant. From its address and still more from its contents we have considered it as addressed to the lay members of the Board of Elders by whom only this answer will be signed for we should be loath to believe that you could be capable of writing in such a style to an Ecclesiastic holding the office of Vicar General in this place.

As to your determination of returning to England by the Malta packet or at any period before the arrival of your successors we have only to protest and most solemnly against such a proceeding and leave with you the whole responsibility of adopting it.

Your arrival here in November last was sooner than we had anticipated and as you well know before our plans for establishing the School were matured. No time was however lost on our part. A subscription was instantly set on foot and appeal made to the Catholic public was most liberally answered. A house was provided and fitted up and under all the difficulties necessarily attendant on the formation of a wholly novel establishment the school was opened in February of the present year.

With regard to yourself and Mr. Anthony it was always our wish to do everything to meet your views and promote your comfort. That our well meant efforts were unsuccessful we are but too sorry to perceive wherein we have failed we are still at a loss to conjecture. We may have erred – we may possibly have come to wrong conclusions but we repeat most emphatically that intentionally we have not given offence. Seeing a resolution taken on your part which from its nature must rest on very serious motives and which from its inevitable consequences must tend to deprive upwards of 280 children of the religious education they are now receiving, we have asked for explanations we have courted complaint with the avowed and sincere purpose of offering satisfaction for any involuntary offence we may have given and all we receive in return is a general and undefined allegation of ill treatment of which we do not feel conscious and the particular nature or instance of which you decline to specify. The only occurrence of which anything like a distinct allusion is made is what took place in July last. On that occasion at least we gave abundant proof of our desire to act a conciliatory part, a verbal explanation and apology was offered and the very moment you stated that you further required a written one it was given without hestitation and in terms which your own calmer reflection will convince you ought to be and must have been satisfactory. In this spirit we are anxious to proceed and in our earnest anxiety to preserve from ruin an establishment so highly conducive to the religious instruction of the rising generation – there are few sacrifices that we are not prepared to make. Let it be permitted us to hope that in a corresponding spirit you will no longer hesitate to afford us the opportunity of redressing past grievances if any there be to redress and of establishing our future relations on that footing of harmony and good will which we ardently desire should prevail at all time.

Junta less the V.G.

To Mr. Edward P. O'Flaherty   19th September 1836

Sir,

Immediately on receipt of your letter of the 12th instant in which greatly to my surprise you indicated your intention and that of Mr. Anthony to return to England I deemed it my bounden duty to assemble the Elders of the Catholic Church who in union with myself have spared no exertions nor sacrifices to fulfil the wishes of the Holy Congregation for establishing a school of religious instruction of which you are now the principal Master – It was to have been hoped that our letter of the 14th would have suggested considerations amply sufficient to have at least prevented your immediate departure but your reply of the 17th shows but too clearly what are your ideas and how egregiously we were mistaken – Taking all this into consideration and without entering into fruitless discussions I will simply observe that I cannot divine the motives which prevent your remaining – With concern I add that your unforseen and sudden departure is likely to ruin for ever a pious and charitable establishment kept on foot with such labour, whose principal object is catholic religious instructions and which once destroyed cannot easily if it can ever be replaced – Impelled, therefore by religious feeling and your only actual superior and competently authorized by the Holy Congregation de Propaganda Fide to which you are subject I request and order that you defer your departure till a communication shall have been made to that Reverend body and their pleasures shall have been signified – In the meantime and with a view to avoid mistakes for the future I beg to call upon you for a detailed statement of your reasons for not wishing to continue further in your undertaking as I wish you to understand that I shall not fail to lay before the Holy Congregation a full and impartial statement of all that has occurred and of all that may result from your premature departure if notwithstanding my orders to that contrary you shall persist in such a determination.

I remain,
John Baptist Zino
Vicar General

Page 54

⁺To Mr. Edward P. O'Flaherty   19th September 1836

Sir,

I have acknowledge the receipt of your letter of the 20th inst. – With reference of that part of it in which you signify that it would be more agreeable to you to give a verbal answer to the letter addressed to you by the lay members of the Board of Elders of which I am the President – I have convened those Gentlemen and have their authority to say that on this occasion as on all others they are most desirous of accommodating themselves to your wishes and that in consequence a meeting of the Board of Elders presided by me will be held on Saturday the 24th Inst. at 6 o'clock in the afternoon at which the Elders will be happy to see you as well as Mr. Anthony, and as you request it The Rev. Fr. Meehan – For the greater convenience of the discussion the Elders conceive and I concur with them in opinion that you should furnish in writing and in however condensed a form the subjects in which it is your intention to treaty.

John Baptist Zino

To the Very Reverend Vicar General.

Very Re. Sir,

Your note of yesterday I received. With respect to the wish expressed for a written statement of the subjects to be discussed, I beg to say that I do not wish to bring any subject for discussion, but merely to attend for the purpose of giving verbal answer to the letters which lately I received both from you and the Elders. As the hour appointed is one in which Rev. Mr. Meehan (Chaplain to the Military Forces) will be employed, perhaps it could be changed to some other time.

P. O'Flaherty.
22nd September 1836.

To Mr. Edward P. O'Flaherty.
Gibraltar 22 September 1836.

Sir,

I beg to acknowledge the receipt of your note of this day's date – I regret that it will be now impossible to alter the time fixed according to your invitation for the meeting of the Elders.

These Gentlemen have already consented to attend at the meeting called by your own desire and it could scarcely be expected that their avocations which are both numerous and important should yield to those of Mr. Meehan whose presence was solely requested by yourself.

John Baptist Zino.

page 54

⁵**Brother Edmund Rice, the Founder wrote to Bro. O'Flaherty:** (quote from Annals of C.B.)

"Whatever is the case, the Sacred Congregation could never bear to look on and see fall to the ground a work so happily begun, to forward which the

Congregation spared neither care nor expense, and which is known to be not only useful but necessary, and not more to the civil than to the spiritual welfare of that portion of the Christian people. Such are the observations which it becomes my duty to make on the matters in dispute. My prayer is that God may be pleased graciously to give a happy termination to all."

Having consulted Dr. Murray, Archbishop of Dublin, the Founder wrote once again:

"As regards the summer vacations, we are determined you must get that. You have a straightforward course to go by, and the Cardinal Prefect tells us that we are at liberty to represent all difficulties to Propaganda. What need you trouble yourselves if you cannot instruct the children as you would like. Do the best you can under the circumstances. One great good in this affair is that the Junta are so anxious for your remaining, and I trust that God will draw good out of the whole business. When we told Doctor Murray the little good you could yet do from not knowing the language, he immediately said, that you broke the Methodist school, and was not that doing much good."

To Mr. Edward P. O'Flaherty   Gibraltar 26th Sept 1836

Sir,

By directions of the Elders of the Catholic Church I beg to transmit for your perusal a copy of the proposed minutes of what took place at the Meeting of the 24th Instant both while you were present and after you had retired.

The object of their being thus is so clearly explained in the Document itself as to leave me only to add that it would be desirable to have your answer at your very earliest convenience.

Anthony Terry

Page 54
[6]Mr. Edward P. O'Flaherty   Gibraltar 15th October 1836

Sir,

We have to acknowledge your letter of the 13th inst. and it has been a source of peculiar gratification to the new members of the board of Elders introduced by the last annual election to find that they have to treat the subject of the Catholic School in a footing so much more satisfactory than that on which it was latterly presented to their predecessors – We beg to assure you that the same anxious wish as ever prevails amongst us to promote the interests of the School to meet the wishes and attend to the suggestions of the Superiors of your respected and valuable Order and to consult on all occasions your own comfort and convenience.

Previous to replying specifically to the points particularly alluded to in your letter we have to observe that owing to the unqualified terms in which you previously declared your determination to relinquish the management of the Schools and the impossibility which you stated to exist of our obtaining the services of any member of your order we were driven to the necessity of endeavouring to procure assistance in other quarters. There has not yet been time to receive any answer nor have we the means of knowing what steps our

221

friends may have taken. Subject to this we proceed to notice the topics touched on in your letter –

As a preliminary remark and one which it is essential to bear constantly in mind we would observe that English tuition is one of the leading objects of the school and one of greater importance than would seem at first sight to belong to it. It has been the bait and the successful bait held out by the Methodists to attract Catholic children to their schools and the advantages attached to it have unfortunately been sufficient to induce many parents to purchase them at the sacrifice of every other consideration. The Methodist Missionaries have been fully alive to the power of this inducement and have contrived in a comparatively short time to mature a system by which they teach constantly in English. Working as we necessarily do by human means (assisted we presume to hope by the Divine Aid to so holy an undertaking) it is necessary that we should resort to the same means to reclaim as have been used to seduce the unwary. This indefatigable zeal of our opponents it is well known and was forcibly dwelt on at the late meeting of the Elders by the Revd M. Meehan who is well qualified to bear testimony on that subject. At the same time we are by no means blind to the difficulties which beset you in imparting religious instruction growing out of your want of acquaintance with the parish language but we look upon them as surmountable difficulties and even on the all important subject of religious instruction we consider that present slowness of progress however disheartening to your zeal and however lamented by us all is an evil light in comparison to the probability we might almost say the certainty of the scholars being attracted elsewhere and so estranged from their faith. Without being at this moment prepared to propose any definite place to diminish the obstacles attacking this part of your undertaking we will content ourselves with assuring you that this subject shall have our best attention and that no consideration of expenses or of personal exertion on our part shall be permitted to interfere with this adoption of expedients likely to consider towards facilitating the great work in hand.

As to vacations we beg to observe that with every desire to do in this respect what may be agreeable to you we cannot lose sight of consideration which we are persuaded will have the same weight with you that they have with us. The other schools in the Garrison are allowed but very few and very short vacations and this practice is particularly agreeable to the Parents who are thus relieved from the care of their children. Without therefore considering the abstract conveniences of your proposal in this respect we deem it be of importance that for the present at least our school should hold out all the inducements offered by rival establishments. In this view we are of opinion that from the Tuesday in Holy Week to the Wednesday in Easter Week and from the 21st December to the 2nd January would suffice for the Easter and Christmas vacations. As to the Summer vacation we should much desire to dispense with it altogether and the more so as the numerous holidays of obligation during the year unavoidably occasion intermissions of study not occurring in the other schools. We would not however be considered as speaking definitively on this point and in the approach of the next warm season we shall be quite prepared to adopt any plan for your relaxation which may be compaitble with the well being of the school.

While on this subject and by way of illustrating our position we would observe that the present plans of allowing the whole of Saturday as a holiday in which the Elders acquiesced in deferences to your wishes has been already the cause of much discontent and the ground of invidious comparisons with other schools where a similar indulgence is not granted so that it may even be necessary to resort once again to the old system.

We fully acquiesce in the principle that no interference should be allowed in the internal discipline of the School tending to lessen the authority of the master in charge of it. On the contrary, we always have used and will always continue to use our best endeavours to support, uphold and enforce that authority in the eyes both of the scholars and their Parents knowing as we do that it is the very foundation of all good discipline.

We are not insensible to the advantage likely to accrue from the services of another brother of your order but with our present limited resources we do not feel ourselves in a position to incur the additional expense which such an arrangement would necessarily occasion.

Should your superiors decide upon replacing either yourself or Mr. Anthony (we presume you allude particularly to Mr. Anthony whose helath we are sorry to learn suffers from the Climate) we would willingly bear one half of the expense and would do more if our means were equal to our good wills.

In conclusion we cannot but express our great satisfaction at the prospect now open of a cordial co-operation in the great and good undertaking in which we are embarked and we beg to repeat our assurances that no efforts of ours shall be wanting to contribute to the attainment of the object we all have in view. In all we have had occasion to do we have been activated solely by a sense of duty and no feeling of ill will or personal resentment had ever been entertained towards any one.

The Junta

To Mr. E.P. O'Flaherty   Gibraltar 16th October 1836

My Dear Sir,

With the view to diminish your labour I have been requested by my Colleagues the Elders of the Catholic Church to transmit to you a copy of our answer of yesterday's to your letter of the 13th Inst. which I have done with the greatest pleasure and now enclose the same that you may please to forward it with your letter to the Superiors of your respected order by this present packet.

A. Terry (Secretary)

Dublin, 28th June 1837

My Very Dear Brother Patrick,

I have received both your letters, which are of a very disagreeable nature, particularly that in regard to the manner in which the children conduct themselves; for if they are not under your control what good can be got out of them. So you must tell those gentlemen that they are not to interfere with you, nor with the children. The account of the little improvement they have made in the way of piety, etc., is most discouraging, and upon the whole I very much fear for the success of the Mission altogether. Besides what I desired you to inform the Elders of, you can tell them also that you are to have the usual vacation in some part of July or August, and should they refuse, or not be content with this, write to me immediately, and in the meantime take the vacation yourselves, and do not go to school for them. You will know the time in July or Agusut that will answer best for you to have it. Whatever answer the Elders give you about the vacation, etc., write to me. However, have courage, the good seed will grow up in the children's hearts later on.

The heat is so intense here in Dublin now that I am hardly able to write a line. The weather here is, I suppose, as warm as you have in Gibraltar.

You will be rejoiced to hear that Dr. Foran has been appointed Bishop of Waterford. The ornaments for his consecration are being made up here and will not be done for near a month to come.

I hope these lines will let you all have your vacation without further trouble. If they do not I shall write to the Secretary of Propaganda.

Yours most affectionately,
Edmund I. Rice.

July 10th 1837

Very Reverend Sir,

I have received a communication last packet from our Superiors directing us to take our usual vacation either in July or August. This communication leaves us no latitude. It places us under obedience as to the taking of vacation. I would, therefore, feel obliged by knowing your will on this subject with the least possible delay, as we shall write by the next packet.

My Superiors also direct me to say that no one can be allowed to interfere between the children, their parents, and ourselves, except yourself; and that all communications from parents respecting their children be made to and settled by you or us.

I remain, Very Rev. Sir,
Respectfully yours,
E.P. O'Flaherty

Gibraltar, 10th July 1837

Dear Sir,

I have received your favour of this morning, informing me that you have been directed by your Superiors to take a vacation of one month in July or August, and in reply I hasten to state to you that since our last correspondence on the same subject, no change whatever has taken place in the opinion which was then expressed to you by the Elders and myself, viz., that the allowing such a vacation would produce the most serious prejudice to our schools; that by suffering so many children (many of whom have so recently been reclaimed) to remain without instruction for one whole month, we should be giving a great advantage to the Methodist Mission and other rival establishments, where no such vacation is allowed, and that in short, such a step would be equivalent to shutting up the schools altogether.

We shall therefore, find ourselves under the disagreeable necessity of objecting most positively to the proposed vacation.

I remain, ever sincerely yours,
John B. Zino, Vicar Apostolic.

To Mr. P. O'Flaherty   12th August 1837

Sir,

Understanding from the very Revd. Vicar General that you have applied to him for some articles appertaining to you, which you state are in the store room of the Catholic School. On behalf of the Elders I beg leave to inform you that the keys of the Store are in my possession and that I shall be happy to attend there at any time you may please to appoint for delivering you the articles in question.

I beg you will be so good as to inform me when it will be convenient to you to furnish your account of the books and other articles belonging to the school which have been disposed of by you. And also what dispositions you wish to take for delivering up before your departure the household furniture which was provided by the Elders of the Church for your use.

A. Terry (Secretary)

Very Rev. Sir,

Notwithstanding the formal declaration of the Elders lately made of their breaking off all communication with me, of their giving up the furniture of the house to the care of Rev. Fr. Meehan, and of their unjustly locking up part of our property in the school, two of the same Body addressed a letter to me today. What the subject of that letter is I deem it now needless to make known, neither is it of importance to me to do so. With yourself, and with yourself only, I am to treat matters respecting my Mission here. I have many times sought an interview with you on this subject, but as yet without effect. Should you be disengaged on to-morrow I shall feel great pleasure in waiting on you, and hope to be able to close our affairs with mutual satisfaction.

I remain yours,
Vewry Rev. Sir,
E.P. O'Flaherty.

Dublin, August 1837

My dear Father John,

Absence from home prevented me from writing sooner to you on the unexpected removal of our Brothers from Gibraltar, and of the circumstances connected with it. You are aware that when we undertook to send Brothers to Gibraltar it was with the understanding that they were to be immediately under the fostering care and protection of the Holy See and the Vicar-Apostolic of that place.

With this understanding we felt confident that our Brothers would receive the treatment due to Religious persons, and that success would attend our humble efforts in the instructing of the much neglected youth of Gibraltar.

How far we were deceived in supporting ourselves thus connected with the Holy See or its Vicar appears clearly from the fact of a body of laymen called Elders taking upon themselves to dismiss our Brothers from the schools, without even consulting the Holy See, or – as would appear from the dismissing document – without the consent of the Vicar Apostolic; and this they did because these Religious obeyed me, their Superior, in taking a few days' relaxation at a time when even the common feelings of humanity, as well as the common custom of Europe would demand it for them, and when there could be no evil whatever attending it. That you may be able to judge more accurately of what took place, I shall give a more detailed account of it.

Being informed about the latter part of June that the health of these Brothers was declining, and that most likely they would not be able to attend school much longer, I directed them to tell the Elders in my name, that they should take their vacation. They did so, but received a refusal of getting any vacation. This refusal they communicated to me, adding that they would, if health permitted, attend school till they should hear from me again; but in the interim one of them in particular being confined for days to his bed from the effects of the heat, and relaxation being absolutely necessary for him, they dismissed the children, telling them they should return in fifteen days.

They also informed the Vicar Apostolic of what they did, and said they would recommence school sooner should health permit them to do so. Eight days after they received a letter, signed by the Elders but not by the Vicar, stating that the schools were theirs – that because the Brothers dismissed the children under their care, without the leave of the Elders, they found themselves under the painful duty of informing them that they (Elders) would not admit them to superintend their schools any longer, and that they had written to England for other masters.

The Elders, accordingly, locked up the store-room of the school, got a person to take charge of the young children pro-tempore, and had the vacancy published in the public print. The Brothers being placed under these circumstances, and not having means of supporting themselves in Gibraltar till the Holy See and their Superiors could be made acquainted with their situation, availed themselves of a fortunate opportunity which they met of returning home. Another thing worthy of notice is, that the children of whom the Brothers had the charge, and to whom only they gave vacation, were those of the most respectable persons in town, none of whom expressed themselves dissatisfied with it, as it was no more than what they were accustomed to take themselves in other schools. Therefore, there could be no danger whatever of these children going to Methodist or Protestant schools. They never went to such places, nor would they go to them even if the Catholic school was not established.

Neither could the poor school be injured by it, as that portion of the establishment was never influenced or directed by the other, being under different rules and taught by civilians. And here also I wish to remark that the poor children, whose education the Holy See had principally in view when sending the Brothers out, and who only could be injured by Protestants schools, were taken from under the jurisdiction of the Brothers, contrary to their wishes, and placed under two schoolmasters of the town.

From this short account of our Brothers' dismissal by the Elders you can form an idea of our feelings at the treatment which we have received for our successful exertions in rescuing from proselytising schools the poor children of Gibraltar, and forming an establishment therein where the rich received an education suitable to their situation in life, and the poor by that means supplied with all things necessary for a religious and literary education. The schools at the Brothers' departure were filled with boys, and in high estimation with the parents and friends.

Edmund Rice

CHAPTER THREE

page 61
[1]**He was to be relieved.** . . . S.C. Propaganda Fide Archives, Litt. Scrit., Vol. 2.

page 61
[2]**There was a split.** . . . S.C. Propaganda Fide Archives, Litt. Scrit., Vol. 2.

page 63
[3]**A well known man.** . . . Gibraltar Cathedral Archives, Junta Files, Vol. 3, p.71.
The following letter showing how the Junta disclaimed any part in the incident in the church sparked the tension between the Bishop and the Elders.

May it please Your Excellency,

We the undersigned Elders of the Catholic Church of Gibraltar beg to express to Your Excellency our deep regard at the occurrence in the Catholic Church of Thursday last when the funeral service already commenced over the body of an individual who previous to his death had made his confession received the holy communion and extreme unction and had otherwise complied with all the rites of the Church was suddenly suspended and Christian burial ultimately refused to the remains of the deceased on the alleged ground of his having been a Freemason.

We felt it due to ourselves and to the community at large by whom we are elected to communicate to Your Excellency and to request that Your Excellency will be pleased to make known to Her Majesty's Government our Solemn disclaimer of all participation in this proceeding which is reprobated not only by us but generally by the Catholic Community of the Garrison.

The Elders
Gib. 29th August 1840

page 64
[4]**He started questioning their authority.** . . . Gibraltar Cathedral Archives, Junta Files, Vol. 3, p.31.

page 65
[5]**Negocios Eclesiasticos**: Bishop Hughes, Cadiz. 1841.

page 66
[6]**. . . . the Elders insisted that he had no right.** . . . Gibraltar Cathedral Archives, Junta Files Vol. 3. Fol.77.

Gibraltar 15th October 1840

Right Reverend Sir,

Your letter under date of the 29th September last was delivered at my house on Tuesday 6th inst. at about mid-day without any explanation of the great interval between its date and the time of its delivery.

I lost no time in submitting it to the notice of the Elders of the Catholic Church of this place who have authorized me to transmit the following reply:

The Junta of Elders on this as on all other occasions hope to maintain the tone of moderation and courtesy which befits the cause they advocate, the position they occupy, and the respect due to the rank and office of the chief of the ecclesiastical authorities of Gibraltar. Not even the absence of those decencies to which in their corporate capacity at least they are entitled will induce them to adopt a style offensive in itself and but little suited to the serious subject treated of. Still less will they descend to misrepresent or even to colour events which may have occurred, and in pursuing their course they feel that they shall best consult their own duty and best meet the wishes of the public whom they represent.

You are pleased Sir to state that prevented until lately by causes set forth in your letter from attending to matters of minor importance it is only now that your attention has been directed to the Elders, whom you describe as a meeting of servant laymen of your flock calling themselves the Junta de Ancianos of the Catholic Church of Gibraltar.

The Junta consider it advisable to recapitulate a few facts fortunately of recorded and unquestionable authority as best qualified to explain what, from its outset, was your conduct in respect of the Junta, and what was theirs with reference to the attempt lately made to call in question their title, and to usurp the prerogatives of the people entrusted to their charge.

At a meeting of the Junta held on the 26th June 1839, a letter from you dated Rome the 3rd June was produced and read addressed to the then General, the Clergy, and the Junta de Ancianos of this Church, announcing your nomination as Vicar Apostolic of Gibraltar, a proceeding indicating on the face of it, not only a knowledge acquired at Rome itself of the existence of such a body but of their holding such a position as entitled them to be joined with their Vicar and Clergy in receiving intelligence of such importance as that of the appointment of a new head of this church.

On the 15th July following it was determined by the Junta to effect certain repairs and alterations in the house destined by the Junta for your residence to facilitate which they consented to defray the rent to be paid by the former Vicar for a house to which he was about to remove on quitting the one belonging to the Junta. It is well known to you that repairs and alterations were made, that you are now enjoying the fruits of them and that they occasioned a debt now weighing heavily on the pecuniary resources of the church.

On the 9th November 1839, the Junta received a representation signed by upwards of 600 Catholic Inhabitants of Gibraltar protesting strongly against the removal of the former Vicar and calling on the Junta not to recognize your appointment. However much the Elders as individuals sympathized in the fate of their former Pastor they knew well the limits of the authority possessed by the Junta. In a moment of great public excitement and exposed to very severe and painful animadversions they maintained inviolate their principles and returned an answer TO THE EFFECT THAT IN A MATTER BY ITS NATURE OF ECCLESIASTICAL JURISDICTION they had no power to interfere.

On the 2nd January of the present year you Sir arrived in Gibraltar. On the following day the former Vicar the Clergy and the Elders waited on you to present their respects. Your subsequent installation in the church took place in the presence and with the assistance of such of the Elders as were pleased to attend, and you yourself after receiving the complimente of the clergy most particularly and emphatically enquired for the Junta of Elders who in consequence presented themselves and met with a reception corresponding to the rank they held and which but little augsted the treatment they have since experienced.

Your subsequent proceedings and more particularly the abrupt dismissal of the whole of the clergy much and generally esteemed excited in the public mind a degree of alarm and apprehension in which the Junta could not but participate. Of the impolicy and imprudence of this measure (without reference to its justice to your repeated disclaimer of your intention to do anything of the kind) the Junta never for a moment doubted but they felt that these nets however deplorable and however mischievous might be considered as coming within the scope of your spiritual functions and they therefore contented themselves with making a respectful verbal remonstrance which was unhappily altogether fruitless. The retirement of the old Vicar and your dismissal of the Rev. Mr. De Maria after 33 years service called on the Junta to exercise their undoubted and unquestioning right of so dealing with the revenues of the church as to provide at once for the decent subsistence of those gentlemen and (as far as after that provision was made means existed) for the pay of yourself and the other clergy attached to the church. This important subject occupied the Junta in long and careful deliberation. With a delicacy fully appreciated at the time and which the Junta lament has long since ceased you expressed your determination of not being present at a discussion on which your own emoluments were to be considered and properly enough left the consideration of a subject concerning pecuniary matters to those who from their peculiar functions were more especially fit to entertain the question. After a long and mature consideration the Junta came to a decision which under all circumstances seemed to them best adapted to meet the justice of the case. They fixed your own salary at an amount somewhat less than your predecessor and greatly less than they would have willingly allowed under a more prosperous state of finances. But the fact is that they did fix and settle the allowance to everybody both ecclesiastical and lay in the service of the church and the fact equally is that you, Sir, at the very next meeting of the Junta at which you presided did cheerfully and unhesitatingly acquiesce in all that had been done and signed the Minute in which the decision of the Junta was recorded in their book of proceedings. After this you not only continued to attend all the meetings of the Junta and to sign the Minutes of such meetings but you continued in conformity with ancient and unvaried practice to put over to the Treasurer all the monies collected for Parochial dues and by the Treasurer from the monies so collected were paid those who had claims on the church. So things continued till the end of August last, when an event occurred so discreditable in itself, and so fraught with consequences likely to prove detrimental to the best interests of true religion to the peace and harmony of the congregation and to the Military subordination of the Garrison that the Junta found themselves called on to express their sentiments on the occasion. A meeting was accordingly convened to which you were duly invited but at which most strange to say you did not think proper to attend returning a verbal and only a verbal answer that you were unwell though the contrary was known to everyone. Deprived thus of all the opportunity of hearing what in the shape of explanation you might have had to offer the Junta had no recourse but to proceed upon the unquestioned facts of the case and in so doing they gave another proof of the moderation which has always marked their conduct. They spoke only of the transaction as it occurred, they named nobody and contented themselves with disclaiming all participation in a proceeding with which no well thinking person would willingly have been identified. The Junta forbear from further remark on this event which they only now notice for the purpose of observing that from this moment commenced the line of conduct which you have since thought proper to pursue and for the consequences of which you solely are responsible. Without a word of notice of your intention you have thought proper to retain in your own hands funds to the possession of which you have not even the shadow of title and have presumed even to remove from their place in the church the tables of fees established by the Junta and in virtue of which alone you are entitled to collect one farthing from the public. On this subject the Junta forbear to enlarge as it will form matter of consideration for the Court to which you have compelled them to resort for the vindication of those rights of the public which have been so flagrantly usurped and from which they are sure they will not fail to receive ample justice.

The Junta feel it incumbent on them to notice that part of your letter in which you allude to your request to examine the documents preserved in the archives.

The Junta are unwilling to impute to you wilful perversion of a very plain case but they are at a loss to imagine how any misunderstanding could have arisen on which is so perfectly intelligible. The documents in question are the property of the Junta and by the Junta are and always have been kept in the Archives under the custody of the Secretary a person of their own choice and confidence responsible to them, and himself according to the regulations of the Junta without power to allow a single paper to be removed. You ask to have these documents transferred to your custody for the avowed purpose of questioning the right of the Body to whom they belong and whose title you dispute. A positive refusal under such circumstances might have been well justified, but you were informed the papers were open to your inspection and, that the Secretary would attend and exhibit them to you at such hours as might best suit your own convenience. No reserve was made or intended to be made; no restriction was even hinted at any more than it was contemplated save that the documents were not to be removed from the archives the opening of which necessarily implied the presence of its keeper the Secretary.

Such, Sir, is the plain truth in this particular and the Junta have seen with feelings of deep regret that in your letter you should have descended to a misrepresentation of the case so extraordinary and so wholly at variance with the fact. As to the documents being kept in the bedroom of the Organist the Junta have only to observe that that appropriation of the apartment is of your own unsanctioned making and would if the Junta were disposed to multiply complaints form one item of a series of unauthorized interference with property legitimately under their control.

The Junta content themselves with observing that at the time they came to the determination, the Chamber was not in the occupation of anybody save of the Junta for the custody of its records and the difficulty to which you allude is one of your own making. As to the assertion of your being permitted to read only such papers as I would allow you to see and as long as it would be convenient to me to attend, the Junta content themselves with referring to the written communications on the subject which your own candour and better thoughts will convince you do not warrant such an imputation.

The Junta beg to be clearly understood as seeking nothing but the recovery of funds over which at all times and even under your own government of the church they have exercised control. As to the alms given by the faithful besides the parochial dues and the donations collected in manner heretofore accustomed and consigned to the depositories in the custody of the Junta, the intentions of the donors would of course be the guide for their application, but it would require a clear and special declaration of such intention to exempt them from the rule governing generally all receipts of the church and to consign them to any paid by a fixed salary and therefore without title to receive more.

The Junta about to discuss judicially their rights do not choose to notice the many unbeseeming and unworthy annoyances to which it has been studiously designed to subject them both individually and collectively; they can only deplore that asserted zeal for religion should have been made the pretext for the proceedings so little indicative of the politeness and good education to which in your letter you have been pleasing to refer.

Such Sir, is the answer which in my own name and in that of the Junta I have to return to your before mentioned letter.

I have the honour. . . .
Emilio Gonzalez de Estrada.
(Sec. to the Junta)

page 67
[7]**Privy Council.** . . . Government Secretariat Archives, Privy Council: Hughes v Porral.

page 68
[8]**Mother Ball.** . . . H.J. Coleridge S.J. The Life of Mother Frances Mary Teresa Ball. (Dublin 1881) p.236.

page 68
[9]**three Loreto nuns.** . . . Prop. Fide Litt. Scrit. Vol. 4.
The group of four nuns was led by Mother Mary A. Hickey. She was always called upon to accompany the Superior General, Mother Ball, in the visitation of houses of her order. Whenever there was a Convent in distress or difficulty, she was made its protecting and resting Angel. The Houses in Kilherney and Killarney were opened and founded by her. She died in Gibraltar on 15 December 1862.

CHAPTER FOUR

page 70
[1]**three-fourths of the children.** . . . Gibraltar Cathedral Archives, Olla Podrida, p.5.

page 70
[2]**concience clause.** . . . Gibraltar Cathedral Archives, pp.11–23.

page 70
[3]**Archdeacon Sleeman:** Rev. Dawson was his successor. Gibraltar Cathedral Archives, Olla Podrida, p.16.

Dear Sirs,

I beg to acknowledge your letter received this morning and to return its enclosure. I have nothing to add to the assertion which was made at my request, in the Chronicle of the 15th inst. neither can I furnish you with the date of the "satisfactory change" to which you allude.

I have simply to assure you, that I found the Conscience Clause in operation in our Church of England School upon my arrival here.

You will, I am sure, acquit me of any discourtesy when I say, that I must decline further correspondence on this subject.

B.S. Dawson.

page 71
[4]**it died a natural death.** . . . S.C. Propaganda Fide, Litt. Scritt. Vol. 2.

page 74
[5]**the Jesuits decided not.** . . . S.C. Propaganda Fide, Vol. 4, p.153.

page 75
[6]**Mgr. Scandella also worked hard.** . . . Gibraltar Cathedral Archives, Olla Podrida p.24 on Report of the Aliens Question.

page 76
[7]**letter to the Secretary of State.** . . . Gibraltar Cathedral Archives, Olla Podrida p.30 of BLUE BOOK in the Gibraltar Garrison Library.

page 77
[8]**extradiction for crime smuggling.** . . . Gibraltar Cathedral Archives, Olla Podrida. "Return to Judgement".

The spirit and meaning of the Bishop's reasoning run to this effect:
a) The proposed Scheme, if enforced, will be the ruin of Gibraltar.
b) Gibraltar does not merit the infliction of such a measure. According to the Minister's expressed admission, its trade its perfectly legitimate. Its traders are not smugglers.
c) The smugglers are Spaniards.
d) If the Minister will act, pray him to act against them, not against Gibraltarian traders.
e) In such case extradition would be far more preferable, far less injurious to local trade and far better calculated to curb the evil complained of, than the threatened Scheme.
f) England, surely, will not crush legitimate trade. Such a sweeping measure cannot come without compensation.

page 79
[9]**Even Mr. Ryland.** . . . Gibraltar Cathedral Archives, Olla Podrida. Correspondence on Customs Bill p. 2.

My dear Bishop,—I beg to acknowledge the receipt of copy of your letter to Lord Carnarvon with reference to Gibraltar, which I have perused with much interest.

I am quite of opinion that your interference in behalf of the inhabitants of Gibraltar has been calculated to promote their interests, and I hope that the arguments you have made use of will not be without weight upon Lord Carnarvon's mind.

In view of the great distress which the operation of the proposed Ordinance would be likely to produce amongst the poorer classes in Gibraltar, I think that it was quite within your duty, as a Christian Bishop, to urge upon the Colonial Office the strong claims which that population has upon their favorable consideration, and I am quite convinced that nothing you have said is likely to weaken our efforts in Parliament against the proposed measure.

You may rely upon my best endeavours to promote the object you have so much at heart and I have no doubt we shall get influential assistance both in the House and out of it.

I do not think that you can do more by remaining in this country to promote the object of your visit. — Believe me, your's very faithfully,

(Signed) PETER RYLANDS.

The Right Reverend Bishop of Gibraltar.

page 80

[10]. . . . **in their support**. . . . Gibraltar Cathedral Archives, Scandella Letters. Whatever Bishop Scandella wrote in favour of the Brothers was recognized by the Orders' Superior who wrote to him with the following information:

My dear Lord,

You may see by the attached leaf, that Cardinal Simeoni has the interests of Gibraltar deeply at heart, and that the phraseology in which he couches his letter, manifests coincidence in the views you have placed before him. I quite understand the delicacy you felt in importuning him too much, and I believe you were right. Still an occasion may arise wherein a friendly remonstrance may not wear such an aspect.

We principally rely upon the guarantees given us by Rome. First. We considered our Brief unimpeachable, and in virtue of which, we gave all that we possessed, youth, health, strength, talents etc and now to say, that after 60 or 70 years peaceable enjoyment of same, under the fostering and paternal protection of the Holy See, that it can be tampered with, mutilated and explained away, is more than we ever thought possible.

It is this shock that has shaken our Institute to its very foundation, and with anxiety we await to see what Rome in its wisdom will say to such an occurrence. Second. Its rescripts, granting particular privileges which consolidated more and more the work once begun and which has produced those results mentioned in the last line of Cardinal Simeoni's letter, and which we hope to be able to perpetuate and increase. All we have to do is to leave ourselves in the hands of God, but I know, that perfect confidence among our members will only be restored, by the Sacred Congregation taking us under its protection, and not leaving our Institute to experience such shocks for the future. For if to day a National, Provincial or Diocesan Synod can question, change and alter our Brief, tomorrow or in the future, similar rights can be put forward, and thus instability and uncertainty must be the result.

P.D. McDonnell

233

My Very Dear Br. Director

The following letter from the Prefect of Propaganda, came to hand on yesterday.

A principal cause of delaying the settlement of our case in Rome, has been the dilatoriness of some of the Bishops in replying to the statements in our Remonstrance, copies of which had been forwarded to them by Propaganda.

J.A.H.

SIGNORE

Monsignor Scandella, Vicar-Apostolic of Gibraltar, has just informed me of the deplorable condition of the Schools of that diocese, owing to the want of good teachers; and at the same time he has urged me to exert my influence, that your Society may kindly send him four other subjects.

Knowing how great a necessity exists in Gibraltar for opening Catholic Schools, in order to prevent the youth, especially of poor families, from frequenting the schools of Protestants, with evident danger of perversion; and on the other hand, conscious of the unfitness of the secular masters, I cannot but warmly recommend to your Society the request of the aforesaid Bishop, that it may endeavour to second his desires. Thus it shall perfect the work already commenced, by means of the Subjects sent to labour there, and efficaciously cooperate in the salvation of many souls.

In this hope, I pray the Lord, that He may long conserve Your Society and give it His benediction.

Rome, from the Propaganda, 3rd May, 1878.

From Yours
Most Affectionately,
GIOVANNI CARD. SIMEONI, Preft.

CHAPTER FIVE

page 83
[1] .... **Father Fernando Moreno.** .... Gibraltar Cathedral Archives, Olla Podrida. "Vindication" by Mgr. Thomas McAuliffe.
A mission priest who studied in Rome at Propaganda Fide and was sent to assist in Gibraltar. He worked on the Rock for as long as Bishop Scandella was Vicar Apostolic of that place.

page 83
[2] .... **Father Stephanopolis.** .... S.C. Propaganda Fide, Litt. Scrit., Vol. 5.
The document referred to was written and sent by Mgr. McAuliffe. In it he details how strange it was for Stephanopolis to have become so violently opposed to Canilla since the latter was in Gibraltar his only companion and enjoyed his company.

page 84
[3] **El Calpense.** A daily newspaper published in the Spanish language owned by a local family. On 6 April it published the rumour going round that Fr. Canilla had been appointed Vicar Apostolic of Gibraltar and predicts that the Holy Father's choice would lead many people away from the church.

"Esta mañana ha circulado la noticia de que S.S. Leon XIII ha decretado el nombramiento del presbitero Don Gonzalo Canilla para Vicario Apostolico de Gibraltar.

Si se confirmase y es un hecho puede tenerse una idea de lo mas que han podido las influencias del Clero de nuestra Iglesia y sus maquinaciones puestas en juego, que la voluntad del pueblo cuya protesta ha sido casi general en contra del referido nombramiento.

Hasta ahora, por nuestra parte, hemos creido y seguiremos en la misma opinion de que el advenimiento del Sr. Canilla a la silla de nuestro Vicariato no puede ser beneficioso a los intereses de los catolicos, ya bastante lastimados desde hace mucho tiempo.

No podremos apreciar cual sea el grado de consideracion que el Papa haya merecido las protestas asi del pueblo como del mismo presbitero electo, mas lo que se deja ver muy claro es el mal efecto que la noticia ha de producirr en los habitantes de esta feligresia y que indudablemente es un precedente nada lisongero por verse contraida la peticion de los fieles.

No es nuestro animo sembrar al nuevo Vicario el camino de espinas, como algunos han pretendido y quisieramos equivocarnos al hacer hoy conjeturas; pero la determinacion de S.S. alejara a muchos de la Iglesia y enfriara el animo de todos los fieles que tanto contribuyen al mantenimiento del culto y de la instruccion de los ninos en esta Ciudad.

page 85
[4] .... **took the memorial**. . . . Gibraltar Cathedral Archives, Olla Podrida. "Correspondence related to the Appointment of The Right Rev. Dr. Canilla".

page 92
[6]   Sir,

Gibraltar, August 17, 1881

I am credibly informed that it is the intention of Messrs. Louis F. Imossi, Juan Gareze, Candido Savignon, Emilio Castro, Nicholas Femenias, Avelino Gaggero, Adolfo Conti, Jaime Bado, and Felice Benvenuto, individuals named at Mr. Imossi's meeting at the theatre on Friday last, as a junta or board for the administration of our churches here, with powers to add to their number, to present themselves within to-morrow at St. Mary's for the purpose of demanding and taking possession of said church, and of the archives belonging thereto. Under these exceptional and emergent circumstances, besides appealing directly to the acting police magistrate, I feel it my duty to lay the matter of such proposed outrage at once, through you, before his Excellency.

I am requesting his worship "to post a sufficient number of police officers within the sacred edifice and the archive office belonging thereto, as well as in the yard and other precincts thereof, with a view to the preservation of the peace and the protection of the said church and of the clergy attached thereto in the possession thereof, which they have peacefully enjoyed for an uninterrupted series of years with the full sanction of the Government," and with which none but Government, who left it for Catholic uses in 1784, can in any way claim any right of interference.

I beg most respectfully to solicit through you that His Excellency be pleased to add his own prompt and decisive support for our full and enduring protection.

I have, &c.

(Signed) + GONZALO CANILLA,

Vicar Apostolic.

To Major-General R.S. Baynes,
Colonial Secretary,
&c.   &c.
Gibraltar

page 95

6   No. 1

ACTING-GOVERNOR MAJOR-GENERAL ANDERSON to the RIGHT HON.
THE EARL OF KIMBERLEY. (Received September 29, 1881.)

MY LORD,   Gibraltar, September 21, 1881.

I have the honour to forward for your Lordship's consideration a memorial,
signed by certain inhabitants of Gibraltar, as the representatives of the majority
of the Roman Catholic community of this city respecting the recent appointment
of the Reverend Dr. Canilla as Vicar Apostolic of Gibraltar, and in which they
solicit the intercession of Her Majesty's Government with the Holy See in order
that the appointment may be revoked and cancelled.

I have, &c.

(Signed) D. ANDERSON,

Major-General, Acting-Governor.

The Right Hon. the Earl of Kimberley,
&c.   &c.   &c.

Enclosure 1 in No. 1.

To the Right Honourable the Earl of Kimberley, &c., Her Majesty's Principal
Secretary of State for the Colonies.

The humble Memorial of Lewis F. Imossi, John Garese, Candido Savinon,
Emilio Castro, Nicholas Femenias, Avelino Gaggero, Adolfo Conti, James
Bado, and Felice Benvenuto, all of Gibraltar, inhabitants.

SHEWETH,

1. That your memorialists who are the representatives of the majority of the Roman
Catholic community of Gibraltar so appointed at a public meeting held on the twelfth
ultimo, desire to approach your Lordship with the greatest respect, and to lay before
your Lordship the following facts.

2. The late Roman Catholic Vicar Apostolic of Gibraltar the Right Reverend John
Baptist Scandella Bishop of Antinoe died in Gibraltar on the twenty-seventh day of
July one thousand eight hundred and eighty, and thereupon it became necessary to
appoint a successor to that office as the Spiritual Head of the Roman Catholic
Churches and community of this city.

3. The said late Vicar Apostolic of Gibraltar was the second Vicar Apostolic of
Gibraltar, the late Right Reverend Thomas Hughes Bishop of Heliopolis having been
the first occupant of that dignity.

4. It is conceded, and admitted to be the fact, that in such cases, Roman Catholic

communities have the right both by canon and secular law, to recommend a successor to their deceased head, and this is a right conferred by the Council of Trent, and has been acknowledged, in the case now laid before your Lordship, by His Eminence Cardinal Manning, and other high dignitaries of the Church of Rome.

5. That a written application, signed by the most influential of the Roman Catholic community of this city, was made to the Vatican for the nomination as the Vicar Apostolic of Gibraltar, in the stead of the late Right Reverend Vicar Apostolic, of a priest of English or Irish nationality, having sufficient rank, capacity, and experience to conduct the spiritual affairs of this Roman Catholic community, and in particular of an age carefully to weigh and consider difficulties of an onerous and peculiar character under which this community, as regards their Church, had been long labouring.

6. Amongst the Roman Catholic clergymen in Gibraltar at this period was a gentleman named Gonzalo Canilla, a native of Gibraltar, but shortly ordained, who had never taken any active part in the affairs of the Church, of youth, and necessarily of inexperience, and one to whom no weight whatever was, or is, attached by this community, either for capacity, influence, or position, in consequence also of matters personal to said gentleman, and with which your Memorialists and this community, were acquainted; the community had reason to be otherwise dissatisfied with the said Reverend Gonzalo Canilla.

7. Notwithstanding the aforesaid ineligibility of the said Reverend Gonzalo Canilla, and well-known opposition to him on the part of this community, the rest of the Roman Catholic clergymen of Gibraltar, with the exception of two, decided, at a private meeting, to recommend the said Reverend Gonzalo Canilla to the Holy See for the high dignity and office of Vicar Apostolic of Gibraltar, and such recommendation was accordingly privately made, and, in consequence of the Holy See being misled as to the feeling of this community (as regards the said Reverend Gonzalo Canilla, such recommendation was attended to, and the said Reverend Gonzalo Canilla raised to the Bishopric as Bishop of Lystra in "partibus infidelium," and nominated Vicar Apostolic of Gibraltar, without this community being in any way consulted or considered.

8. That in view of the foregoing nomination the Roman Catholic community of this city held a largely attended meeting in the Theatre Royal and protested against the above-mentioned appointment, when it was unanimously agreed that supplications should be directed to His Holiness the Pope, and to his Eminence Cardinal Simeoni, prefect of the Propaganda, setting forth their strenuous objection to this appointment, and their reasons for such objection, and praying that such appointment might be annulled, and your memorialists have also reason to believe, from statements made by the Right Reverend the Bishop of Lystra himself, that he was most desirous that the renunciation, which he stated he had tendered to the Holy See, might be accepted, but no reply of any kind has been received by your memorialists, or by the Roman Catholic community generally in this city, from Rome in answer to their aforesaid numerous, and respectful solicitations, nor has the alleged renunciation of the said Reverend Bishop of Lystra been noticed in anyway.

9. That the Roman Catholic community of this city wrote to their Eminences Cardinals Manning and Howard, praying them to use their powerful influence with the Vatican to prevent the direful consequences to religion that would ensue from the appointment of the said Bishop of Lystra as Vicar Apostolic of Gibraltar, but this application, having been unattended to, another numerously attended meeting was held to protest against the aforesaid appointment, and this meeting was succeeded by

237

several others, all convened with the same object, and in each and all of these meetings this Roman Catholic community steadily and unanimously decided to reject the said nomination of this vicariate.

10. That your memorialists, and the Roman Catholic community of Gibraltar, have very strong reasons for believing that the disregard which has been paid by the Vatican to all their humble and respectful entreaties, and supplications has been caused by information given to Rome by the clergy, and partisans of the Bishop of Lystra, to the effect that the opposition made to his appointment as Vicar Apostolic of Gibraltar, is made by only a few of this Roman Catholic community, and those of doubtful orthodoxy, whereas, as your Lordship will observe, such opposition has proceeded from the immense majority of such community, including in such majority, the most devoted and sincerest, as well as influential, of the Roman Catholic inhabitants of Gibraltar.

11. That your memorialists view with the greatest sorrow this apparent indifference on the part of the Holy See to their respectful and humble remonstrances, and are greatly concerned to acquaint your Lordship with the excited and disturbed condition of their constituents, in this city, and their fear lest any action should be taken by or on behalf of the said Bishop of Lystra, which should precipitate a public disturbance, of which manifest signs are appearing, and your memorialists are the more concerned to observe this, lest any share or action in this question should be taken by the Roman Catholic troops in the Fortress, which might be fraught with disastrous consequences.

12. That with the object of anticipating, if possible, any overt act on the part of the said Right Reverend Bishop of Lystra which might cause a public disturbance, and entail more lamentable results than at present exist, your memorialists caused a protest to be served upon the said Right Reverend Bishop of Lystra, of which your memorialists crave leave to annex a copy, for your Lordship's consideration, but of which no notice has been taken by him.

13. That your memoralists assure your Lordship of the utter impossibility of the Right Reverend Bishop of Lystra being accepted by this Roman Catholic community as their Spiritual Head and Vicar Apostolic, and that his continuance in Gibraltar, with this assumption, will only lead to further troubles, and possibly grave disturbances, and your memorialists in their earnest desire for peace and tranquillity, and certain assurance that Her Majesty's Government will aid their endeavours, humbly pray that your Lordship will be pleased to lend a favourable ear to this their memorial, and afford to them your powerful assistance to bring about a happy and peaceful solution of this distressing state of affairs in their Church and community.

14. That your memorialists beg to represent that when the Bishop of Lystra forwarded he was supported by the rest of this community and by the priests, the nuns, and sisters of charity, assertions which it will be at once seen are totally at variance with his letter of the 14th February published in the local papers of that date, and of which your memorialists crave permission to annex a copy.

15. That your memorialists are informed and believe that the said Bishop of Lystra, in his interview with your Lordship, did not state that his nomination was opposed by this community at all, much less than that such opposition had the support of an immense majority of this Roman Catholic community, notwithstanding that the said Bishop of Lystra was fully aware of the fact, not only by reason of public meetings held before he left Gibraltar for England, to protest against his appointment, but also by reason of telegrams and letters addressed to his Eminence Cardinal Manning to the same effect during his stay in England, and of which the said Bishop of Lystra had full cognisance.

16. That your memorialists are advised and believe that Her Majesty's Government in aid of this community, Her Majesty's most loyal subjects will cause intercession to be made on their behalf, to the Holy See, in such form as to the Government may see fit, for the withdrawal of the aforesaid appointment, which is so obnoxious to this community, and which has been, and, it is feared, will be, the cause of great and unhappy dissensions and differences.

Wherefore your memorialists humbly and respectfully trust that your Lordship will be pleased to take this their memorial into your favourable consideration, and also humbly and respectfully pray that your Lordship will cause such directions to be given either to Her Majesty's Ambassador Extraordinary and Plenipotentiary at the Court of Italy, or in such other manner as to your Lordship may see fit, as will procure the favourable consideration by the Holy See of their fervent supplications that the aforesaid nomination of the Right Reverend the Bishop of Lystra as Vicar Apostolic of Gibraltar, may be revoked and cancelled.

And your memorialists (as in duty bound) will ever pray, &c. &c.

	(Signed)	Lewis F. Imossi.
	"	John Garese.
	"	Candido Savinon.
	"	Emilio Castro.
	"	Nicholas Femenias.
	"	Avelino Gaggero.
	"	Adolfo Conti.
	"	James Bado.
	"	Felice Benvenuto.

Gibraltar, 8th September 1881.

page 95
[7]**Fr. Weld.** . . . He is no stranger to the reader since he was the priest who proposed to Bishop Scandella that the Jesuits should take over St. Bernard's School. The Jesuits were not attracted by the confused situation in Gibraltar and withdrew their offer. They furthermore discovered that Spanish children would have the freedom to attend that school. New sanitary laws were being pressed so that outsiders who could possibly endanger the health of local children were stopped.

page 96
[8]**Our Lady of Europe.** . . . Ibid., Olla Podrida, Correspondence, enclosure 1 in 6. The Gibraltar Chronicle:

"Yesterday at noon, the Right Rev. Gonzalo Canilla, Bishop of Lystra, and Vicar Apostolic of Gibraltar, was duly installed as such in the Chapel of Our Lady of Europe. The function which was carried out with the imposing solemnity of the Catholic ritual, was witnessed by several members of the clergy and religious. Gabriel Femenias (Pro-Secretary). 28th November 1881."

page 101
⁹**letter to the Secretary of State.** . . . Correspondence: enclosures 9 in 9.

The Right Reverend Dr. GONZALO CANILLA to the Right Hon. the EARL OF KIMBERLEY.

MY LORD,   Gibraltar, January 6, 1882.

An imperative duty obliges me most respectfully to lay before your Lordship an exact statement of the recent disgraceful scenes which have occurred in Gibraltar, and the action of our local government in the matter.

As your Lordship is aware, His Holiness Pope Leo XIII. was pleased to appoint me Vicar Apostolic of Gibraltar eight months after the demise of my illustrious predecessor Mgr. Scandella.

I made known to His Excellency the Governor my appointment on the 16th May last, and apprised him of my proximate departure for England. After my consecration, I had the honour of an interview with your Lordship, in which I signified to you the opposition which a portion of this population raised against my appointment. Your Lordship was then pleased to assure me that I could rely on the sympathy and support of your Lordship's Department.

On the day before my arrival in Gibraltar, my secretary made known to the local authorities that I was expected on the following day, and claimed the protection of the police on my behalf. I reached this Colony on the 11th August last, and proceeded to the principal church to perform my duties as Vicar Apostolic. A number of people had taken possession of the court leading into the church, creating a great disturbance by shouting and brawling in the sacred precincts, so that I was forced to withdraw to prevent a greater conflict. There were some policemen in the church, and in spite of them several of the clergy were insulted, and one of them was even assaulted whilst standing at the altar. No action was taken by the local authorities to punish the offenders.

On the following night an opposition meeting, anonymously convened, was publicly held in the Theatre Royal, and they appointed a would-be church body for the administration of our churches here. On the 17th it was currently reported that on the following day they would march to the church to demand and take possession of the same, and of the archives belonging to it. I informed His Excellency the Governor and the police magistrate of the projected outrage, and asked for protection. I beg to transcribe copies of the correspondence on the subject.

THE RIGHT HON. THE EARL OF KIMBERLEY TO GOVERNOR LORD NAPIER OF MAGDALA, G.C.B., G.C.S.I.

MY LORD,   Downing Street, January 19, 1882.

I have the honour to acknowledge the receipt of your Lordship's despatches of the 17th and the 22nd ultimo,* relative to the hostility of the Roman Catholic community of Gibraltar to the new Vicar Apostolic, and to the forcible ejectment of Monseigneur Weld from the presbytery adjoining the Church of St. Mary the Crowned.

2. I regret to learn that the disorderly conduct of the mob, culminating in violence and insult to a distinguished clergyman, who was on a visit to Gibraltar,

has thus been permitted to proceed to lengths altogether intolerable, especially in a fortress in which the Government has ample means of at once suppressing any disorder.

The neglect of the police to arrest the ringleaders at the time of the attack on the presbytery appears most unsatisfactory.

3. I desire that measures may be at once taken for enforcing order and obedience to law, and for enabling the Vicar Apostolic, and any other duly constituted ecclesiastical authorities, to have full and free access without molestation of any kind to the cathedral and presbytery and those other buildings which have been used by them or their predecessors.

4. After measures have been taken to effectually prevent any further disturbance of the peace, I shall be prepared to consider what should be the future arrangement for the jurisdiction over the buildings hitherto used by the Roman Catholic Communion.

5. It would be desirable that public notice should be given warning all persons that any attempt at renewing these disorders will be summarily repressed.

I have, &c.
(Signed(KIMBERLEY
Lord Napier of Magdala.

page 110
[10] . . . . **secular burials to Rome.** . . . S.C. Propaganda Fide, Litt. Scrit., Vol. 5.

page 110
[11]**Mgr. MacAuliffe.** . . . S.C. Propaganda Fide, Litt. Scrit., Vol. 5.
As a student of the Urban College of Propaganda Fide he felt obliged to report whatever he saw would interest the authorities in Rome. His writings are numerous. While Chaplain to the Forces on the Rock he did not hesitate to assist the bishops as secretary. He did this without payment. He was already suffering from diabetes when the crisis vis-à-vis Dr. Canilla was at its worst. He was made the scapegoat of the unsuccessful attempts made by the opposition to oust the Bishop. Every effort was used to force him out of the City.

page 115
[12]**Newsletter.** This was a weekly publication produced in the Spanish language in the Cathedral. Eventually these "Boletines" were gathered and bound in hard covers. Kept in the Cathedral Archives they show the Bishop's eagerness to see social reform in Gibraltar.

PART III – THE DIOCESE OF GIBRALTAR

pages 117–142
The information presented in the following chapter has been based on report given to the author by the following persons who were witnesses of such occurrences:

The Right Reverend Monsignor Carmel Grech.
Father Francis Azzopardi.
Father Isidoro Montegriffo.
Father Hector Carter.
Mr. Ernest Stagnetto.
Mrs. Cecilia Hankey.
Mrs. Ana Galliano (Bonnel).

The superficial treatment of the Second World War and the evacuation is due to the author's reliance on his memory and because someone else is presently about to produce a book on the Evacuation.

INDEX